BIRTHPLACE
OF
ADDICTION

BIRTHPLACE
OF
ADDICTION

BY
DAVID C. FOSS
AND
CRYSTAL J. EACK

XULON ELITE

Xulon Press Elite
2301 Lucien Way #415
Maitland, FL 32751
407.339.4217
www.xulonpress.com

© 2018 by David C. Foss and Crystal J. Eack

All rights reserved solely by the author. The author guarantees all contents are original and do not infringe upon the legal rights of any other person or work. No part of this book may be reproduced in any form without the permission of the author. The views expressed in this book are not necessarily those of the publisher.

Unless otherwise indicated, Scripture quotations taken from the New American Standard Bible (NASB). Copyright © 1960, 1962, 1963, 1968, 1971, 1972, 1973, 1975, 1977, 1995 by The Lockman Foundation. Used by permission. All rights reserved.

Printed in the United States of America.

ISBN-13: 9781545633946

DEDICATION

To my Mom, Dad, my Step-Dad Thad, Grandmas, Grandpas, brothers Jeff, Dan, Joe and Ken, my dear cousin Elizabeth, other Family, my best friend, Loren, and Peggy, the Mother of my beautiful daughter Chelsey, and my talented son David. You have believed in me, supported, guided and loved me most or all of my life. I love and cherish all of you!

To my Hope by the Sea family, Frank, John, Netta, Pong, other staff, my housemates and clients who gave me hope again, helped me retrieve my life and self-respect and guided me back to Jesus. My debt to all of you is larger than I could ever hope to repay.

I also cannot forget my many friends at North Shore Church especially, Cherylee, Nicole, Cameo, Pastor Ross, Bill, Cindy, Martha, Mark and so many more who prayed for me, befriended, inspired and helped me on my path to sobriety. Celebrate Recovery!

Thank you, one and all! **To God be the glory!**

FOREWORD

David's book gives an accurate perspective of what *The Work* is. His written experiences are an honest recall of what we had done together during his stay in treatment. He put himself in a very vulnerable position to share his *Work* in this book. It is not always easy, but it shows David's dedication to his readers which makes the message so much stronger.

The idea behind creating an Alternative Track was to give people struggling with addiction an extra tool they could add to whatever they were already doing. Writing is that tool, and it takes effort and hard work. It is the reason my groups are called *The Work*, because that is what it takes. David understood and embraced it.

The effort to change is not only while in treatment. There, we only start the process. The real *Work* happens when you leave treatment, and you face the reality of your life. Writing is not a new concept. We know the practice of keeping a journal has proven to be very helpful and beneficial, and those people who do it feel better.

I am including David's letter because I feel it is the best foreword for his book. It tells how he felt months after being in treatment and how grateful he was. It reads as follows:

Friday, September 15, 2017
Dear Frank,

It's David Foss. I want to touch base with you to express my gratitude for your help. When I arrived in your class at Hope by the Sea, I was scared and broken. When I left, I could stand on my own; and I could see a life of happiness ahead of me. The tools you gave to me have changed my life profoundly. The writing tool is the most powerful, helpful thing I have ever embraced in my life.

I completed a book this week entitled *Birthplace of Addiction* based on the ninety-two days I spent in California. I am hoping you will do me the honor of reading it and giving me some feedback. I haven't shown the completed work to anyone outside of my immediate family. I believe it is an accurate account of the Alternative Track from a client's point of view. I hope you agree. I am going to publish it soon, but I don't want to without your opinion of *The Work*.

Hope by the Sea saved me in indescribable ways, and I feel God shines His light on the place and the staff who bring it to life. My book is the fulfillment of one of my future projections; and you and *The Work* were a paramount component of it. Future projections are still the favorite writing I do each week.

I am hoping upon reading my book, you will consider writing a foreword for it. Nobody is more qualified than you to do this. ... Sincerely, David Foss

I feel David's book will inspire people who are in the same condition he was when he came to Hope by The Sea. I believe they will see with effort and dedication they, too, can achieve what David did. His message is a message of hope -- there is a way to happiness if you are willing to make the effort.

So, David, thank you for your book and for the opportunity to be part of it.

With Love,
Frank Buffa.
Bio-Psycho-Genealogist
Hope by the Sea
Instructor, Alternative Track

INTRODUCTION

Dear Readers:

In researching the notion of writing a book based on my life experiences with childhood trauma and addiction, it became apparent early in the process there weren't many. Scores of books have been written about addiction, dozens on childhood trauma too; but very few are about both. The ones I found tended to be written by clinical professionals, accomplished academics and experts in the medical and mental health fields. I, of course, am not one of them.

My book is written from my personal experience living with PTSD, depression, anxiety, and substance addiction brought on by traumas in my early childhood suffered at the hands of my teacher in second and third grade. In less than three weeks of being at Hope by the Sea, I had ideas on how a book could help many others who may have had similar and other types of childhood or adult traumas.

Writing from the client's perspective of a ninety-day, co-occurring, dual diagnosis multi-track treatment and recovery facility has been my privilege. For most people finding themselves at in-patient treatment centers, their lives have become no more than an intolerable, hopeless existence. I was one of them.

I wrote this book not to politicize or even criticize, although a little of both seeps through because I am so passionate about it. My greatest wish is to get people talking about drug addiction: on TV and radio programs, in churches and schools, by clinician circles and medical professionals and by teenagers and their families at their kitchen tables. **David C. Foss**

My son, David C. Foss, was unable to finish writing the Introduction to this book because he passed to his eternal heavenly home on October 15, 2017. His earthly death was caused by a massive heart attack of natural causes. He had completed the bulk of his first manuscript for this book a few weeks earlier.

He worked for about ten months to write his narrative as he had lived it. I personally know how much this book meant to him. He hand wrote most of it, while I typed and edited it for him. This is his true story of how he finally remembered Mrs. F's dark, dingy closet that had given him haunting nightmares for most of his life.

The traumatic experiences suffered in her classroom and closet were blocked from his memory near the age of ten. Even though the book is a true account, David changed the names of most of the people in his book to protect their privacy. Family names, of course, have not been changed.

David loved learning and school up until the time Mrs. F. was his teacher for two successive years. His love of school ended in her classroom. No matter what anyone said or did during second and third grade, and thereafter, David hated going to school. For the first time, I now know the awful, total truth of why he hated it so much.

My son was a complex man who possessed an exceptional intellect, a true compassion for others and a great sense of humor, and his story needs to be told. One of David's treatment assignments was to make a list of ways he was different from other people. I think what he said will give you a little more insight into who my son, David, was. He listed the following: (Mom added last three to his list)

- I am my mother's son.
- I often prefer puppies to people.
- I was a caregiver for my dying Dad.
- I am a helpful brother.
- I am a tender person.
- I am a gentle man.
- I am a mischievous joker.
- I cook breakfast for supper.
- I like chick flicks.
- I am a band wagon sports fan.
- I am my father's son.
- My life is unique.
- My kids are unique.
- My life is different.
- I put Cheez-whiz on my peanut butter and jelly sandwiches.
- I like ranch dressing on pizza.
- I think women are better sales people than men.
- I am not done living.
- I want to be of service to my fellow man.
- I have a superior work ethic and seldom miss work.
- I am a loving father.
- I earned a G.E.D.
- I completed Executive training at Harvard Business School.
- I am a Business Development Strategist.
- I helped build a twenty-million-dollar company.

David wanted his book to reach people who have been hurt from all types of trauma. For many years, he was a functioning alcoholic, and he abused drugs from time to time. Of course, David would be the first to say alcohol was one of the worst drugs of all. He wrote his book for those who suffer from alcohol and drug addiction. He wanted them to see hope for a better life free of addicting substances is attainable, if you seek it and work for it.

For anyone looking for help for an addicted loved one, we recommend getting treatment for him or her at a *dual diagnosis* treatment and recovery center. Hope by the Sea is such a treatment center. Many, if not most, alcoholics and drug addicts have underlying mental health issues, and they need to be clients at *dual diagnosis* treatment centers to leave addiction behind them.

Whoever you are, you can find the love and healing David did at Hope by the Sea. Wonderful care is given to every client. I saw it for myself at Family Weekend when I attended classes and met some of the staff, a few of the clients and their families. It is a very warm and welcoming environment.

At the time of his death, my son and another Christian friend were exploring plans to design and build safe and sober living places for those who have completed treatment and have no safe place to go when they leave. These safe and sober homes would provide a supervised sober living environment where the recovering resident could learn life skills such as: interviewing, resume writing, budgeting, money management and cooking skills, as needed. For a reasonable room and board fee, this living arrangement would be available to them for up to a year after leaving treatment. Residents could stay there while obtaining skills through classes offered at local college and technical schools or by working for a reputable employer in the area. They would be responsible for chores at the house and would be expected to wash their own laundry and to keep their rooms clean and tidy. He believed this kind of environment was vital to the success of any former addict. David came home to safe and sober living in our home, but unfortunately, for many recovering addicts, these safe places do not exist. I would love to see my son's dream become a reality.

May God bless each one of you as you read my son's story. As part of his treatment assignment in the Alternative Track called *The Work*, he writes many letters not physically sent to the addressee. His book begins with one such letter which is written to his teacher, Mrs. F. David wanted you to experience the raw emotion taking place at the time he wrote his letters and read them aloud in class. Therefore, these letters are for the most part unedited. His letters and journal entries are all set apart with indented margins from the rest of the book. I hope you will enjoy the book as you accompany my son on his journey to sobriety.

Sincerely, Crystal J. Eack, Mom of David C. Foss

CHAPTER 1

The journey to my Birthplace of Addiction began in early September 1980, as I boarded the school bus with my brothers to start second grade in the classroom of Mrs. F for half of the day. I had another teacher for the rest of the day. I was seven years old. The following letter is written from me to Mrs. F thirty-six years later at my treatment center Instructor's request:

October 6, 2016

Dear Mrs. F,

For thirty-five years I have lived my life believing you were little more than a bad teacher. You yelled a lot, not just at me, but everyone else too. I do not know what caused the truth to surface now. Was it losing almost everything at the end of 2013? Was it losing even more the past two years? I may never know the answer to those questions. What I do know for certain is on a school day when I was seven years old, you began hurting me; and this did not end for two long, awful years. I don't know how a person entrusted to teach, care and safeguard children could act as you did. You hit me with a chalkboard eraser at first; then with a *Highlights* children's magazine; next your bare hand that felt like the driest possible skin. I can still remember how it felt, and it is likely why to this day so many years later I am mindful of my hands being clean and soft. Next, you hit me with a yardstick. In 1980, yardsticks were solid sticks with little give in them. I can remember you striking my hands and other areas not easily bruised or noticeable to others. I remember these things now because of the nightmares I suffer when I try to sleep at night. I'd as soon go without sleep than to be visited by the likes of you in my dreams. You told me over and over in private and in open class how I was no good and an awful child who would always be no good. If only I could have ignored you and not let you alter my life. I do not know why I did not tell Mom and Dad. They knew I was not the child I was in first grade. Every time they asked about school, I shut down and refused to talk to them. Mom said sometimes tears would run down my cheeks. I do not remember these conversations, but I have no reason to doubt they happened.

It was in third grade you began to frequently put me in the dark cabinet closet during noon recess. This year the class was no longer split between second and third grade teachers as it was in second grade. I was in third grade now, and the only teacher I had was you.

I had no idea why you put me in the closet. One day you opened the door and grabbed me by the neck and squeezed so hard I could barely breathe. Then, I felt a shock that made me scream in pain, except no sound came out. It seemed like the pain lasted forever, and during my whole life, its intensity has been unmatched. This happened at least three or four times a week for the rest of the year. You would always tell me how awful a little boy I was, and I deserved this punishment. You shocked me through my clothes and genital area using a device no bigger than a clothes iron. I think it was a modified cattle prong, but I'm not sure. It was always covered in a damp rag of some kind.

I have never been the same as everyone else again. I became awkward and anti-social. I believed I was no good. I shut down and pulled away when people yelled, and I still do. I hate being touched; and when people are behind me or where I can't see them, I am very nervous and uneasy. I have never had a healthy relationship and really do not know what it means to feel love. I believe I am kind to people, and I am a gentle person. I am at the same time always worried about what others think of me; especially those I care for like girl friends or my ex-wife.

> *I have cried oceans of tears the past seven months. I am scared to go to sleep because it's like being in your dingy closet waiting for Hell to unleash.*

How could you be so cruel and wicked to me? You are a sick, evil, twisted witch put on this earth by the devil himself. I have cried oceans of tears the past seven months. I am scared to go to sleep because it's like being in your dingy closet waiting for Hell to unleash.

Mrs. F, I hope your death is a slow, painful one befitting your evil deeds. I believe others were hurt by you as well. You deserve no pity or compassion. I truly, truly hate you.

Through the years, I have received validation in the workplace for top performance of my assigned tasks by all my employers. It was the same type of recognition you robbed me of in the classroom. Yes, despite you, I have received praise and accolades in my professional life, and albeit socially awkward, in my personal life too. In my overachieving professional life, I found success and a degree of satisfaction. I never could understand why addiction was such a powerful presence in my life for so long. Time and again it has robbed me of status, livelihood, relationships, friends and even family. I have had seven months to think about my life with your influence somewhat known to me. I believe a great deal of my make-up as a person was altered irrevocably by your wicked, evil acts. I am left with nothing and no one in my life now. My credibility is shot. My family, girlfriend, ex-wife and kids don't speak to me; and a host of mental health and addiction illnesses and afflictions still plague me.

I have suffered several losses of loved ones through death without processing my grief, and I have no clue how to fix it. Eventually the music stops, and you cannot find a chair. I feel I'm drowning or suffocating often while I am wide awake. I feel a hopelessness so dark and cold I can't stand it, and you are the miserable bitch who is to blame for me being me. I am to blame for what I have become, and my behaviors and actions are for me to atone. What a rotten deal it is that you got to live free of consequences!

David

CHAPTER 2

"David, at recess time, how long were you in the closet?" Frank asked.

I said, "I don't know precisely, I think about thirty minutes."

He continued, "That is why your PTSD is so severe, David, you would be in the closet, terrified, 'Is she coming, or isn't she'?"

"Yes, I can remember times when she never came back except to let me out."

"David, I know it was difficult writing this and sharing it with me in private. There is a lot of work to be done here, and it will require you to write no less than seven letters."

"Whatever it takes to quiet the nightmares is what I am willing to do," I said.

"Releasing this should become our top priority. I would like you to write a letter a day, and we will make time to allow you to read them aloud," Frank directed.

"I'll do it," is all I could say. Even though reading it now and writing it in the first place has taken a toll emotionally, I knew I had to do it.

"Let's go get some lunch, and I will see you tomorrow morning. You did great; The Work is going to be difficult for a while. Write the same thing you already wrote if need be, just write and don't overthink this," Frank emphasized.

"So, keep writing to her from me now?" I asked again.

"Yes. Just like the first one and be as detailed as you possibly can. I know it is hard, David."

"Okay," and I went downstairs to get some lunch.

Lunch at the Center is served from noon until one o'clock, and I find it to be a good meal.

CHAPTER 3

Hope by the Sea is a residential dual diagnosis, co-occurring treatment center in southern California specializing in mental health illnesses as well as substance addiction. I came to Hope by the Sea on the first day of October 2016, to enroll in the Alternative Track offered here; Frank is the head of this course of treatment. The unique non-twelve-step program focuses on cognitive behavior and psycho therapies centered around traumas and abuse disorders. Since remembering what happened to me as a child, my life has been out of control. The constant nightmares allow very little sleep or rest of any kind for me.

San Juan Capistrano, California, where Hope by the Sea is located is a beautiful place on the Pacific Ocean between San Diego and Los Angeles. The mountains, ocean and ideal climate make this part of the U.S.A. sought after and extremely expensive to call home. The gentle breezes, low humidity, and year-round mild temperatures are quite different from Minnesota where I have made my home for most of my life.

During the lunch hour, I enjoy walking across the road to the city park. About 100 yards down the parkway is an equine-assisted therapy center complete with a corral of horses. Since my first week at the Treatment Center, I have relished this part of the day; and, particularly on the day I read the above letter to Frank. Reading the letter out loud was terribly difficult for me. I could not hold back my tears, and the flurry of emotion was overwhelming. Now, he wants me to do it again tomorrow with a fresh letter. Holding feelings inside, deep inside, is how I have always lived. The fear of being hurt and the feelings of worthlessness I have held my entire life are coming out, and it terrifies me to the core.

> *Going back thirty-five years and beyond is difficult by itself, and I struggle with putting feelings to those memories. Since discovering these memories of childhood, I find myself analyzing my life.*

I learned my first day in the Alternative Track it is different. It is something that makes sense to me; it is why I came to California for treatment. I decided to put my trust in this program while I was feeding apples to the horses at lunchtime. As I will discover over the next ninety days, the time for recovery work has only begun for me.

Afternoons at Hope by the Sea consist of group therapy and one-on-one time with a Therapist or Case Manager. My mind is occupied with the letter I need to write for tomorrow, and I can think of little else. Going back thirty-five years and beyond is difficult by itself, and I struggle with putting feelings to those memories. Since discovering these memories of childhood, I find myself analyzing my life. It is scary how everything in my life seems to have roots to those awful times in the room of Mrs. F.

I must now go back to Minnesota to Glenville, a town and time I have spent most of my life trying to avoid and ignore. Prior to January of 2016, I had no recollection of the events I am writing about; yet now, I can trace things back there with ease. I have always believed to a certain degree I am not a good person. I have always had low self-worth, a lack of healthy relationships and an inability to express anything. I simply found it easier to jam my feelings deep down inside of me and ignore things completely. I find my mind racing in a pool of what ifs, and it's all depressing. It is as if the life I should have had was stolen from me but has forever transformed me. Who am I? is something I ask myself more and more these days. The coming weeks will be difficult as I go back to Glenville, back to elementary school, back to the classroom of Mrs. F and back to the scary, dark closet.

The house where I stay with six other men and a couple House Managers is nestled in the hills of Laguna five miles from the treatment center. The house is impressive and a nice place to call home for a few months. Most nights the Center has evening treatment components of meditation for the Alternative Track clients, and attendance at a twelve-step meeting in the community for the Christian and Traditional Track clients. We got back to the house from this outing around eight o'clock, and I still am needing to write a letter I have committed to do for my morning class.

I anticipated the second letter would be hard to write, and it is. I find myself tearing up and overcome with emotions. I walk outside by the pool to bring myself back into focus a little bit before resuming my writing. Knowing so much of my writing is going to be talking about this part of my life is very depressing for me and makes me want to isolate myself from my housemates and other people at the Treatment Center. It could be said isolation has become so much a part of my make-up, doing anything else would be like learning to walk with one leg. I go back to my letter, finish writing at eleven o'clock and attempt to sleep. Most of my nights these past months, like this night, are not restful, because the nightmares have become a regular interruption to my sleep. Writing about them in my journal and living them in these letters I guess is a perfect storm.

CHAPTER 4

Tom is my roommate. He goes to bed early, wakes up at four o'clock in the morning and reads his Bible for three hours every day. Tom was one of the first people to talk to me when I arrived. I met him at church, and I remember this glow radiating from him, and a sincerity you don't see in folks very often. I saw him every day my first week in the Detox House. He approached me, said hello and asked when I was coming to the Horse Shoe House.

I believe Tom to be a devout Christian not because of his words or because he reads the Bible, but rather because of how he lives. He says things like "being of service to others," and when Tom says, "What can I do to help?" you know full well he means it. He is ready to roll up his sleeves and dig in. He reminds me of my Dad because of his faith and kindness, and the genuine care he gives to so many at both the House and the Center. I get up at six o'clock every morning, and I wave to Tom as I make my way to the kitchen where coffee is waiting – thanks to Tom.

The sun rises above the mountains and light explodes across the valley. Sitting by the pool smoking cigarettes and drinking coffee with my housemates is becoming one of my favorite parts of the day. We leave for the Center at seven-thirty o'clock sharp, so time is short with shower, meds, and breakfast all needing to be done timely, making the view and conversation precious.

Hope by the Sea has houses all around the valley where up to fifty men reside. About the same number of women are housed and treated at different buildings in the same general area. Class begins at eight o'clock and the Alternative Track meets upstairs. The Christian and Traditional Tracks meet downstairs. The building has a small kitchen, reception area and several offices for Therapists and Case Managers.

CHAPTER 5

The serious attitudes of the people in the Alternative Track are prominent, and they are one of the first things I observe. Frank expects and demands nothing less. We write, we share our writings, and we begin to create new neural pathways in our brains. This process will be discussed throughout the book as we move through the ninety-two days I am a client at Hope by the Sea.

When people write in the Alternative Track, the topics often focus on dark, awful things. Because of this, we do daily gratitude work. If all we do is uncover and focus on the negative, it will be impossible to work through all the toxic feelings we have been harboring in some cases for a lifetime. Baring our souls and most intimate secrets in this group setting of men creates a certain bond most of us have never experienced even with family. I am opening my journal, and many of the letters I wrote, to allow you, the reader, a better understanding of the challenges and afflictions keeping so many in hopelessness.

Journal Entry: Gratitude

October 7, 2016

- I am grateful and thankful for a safe place to work on me -- free from outside distractions that detour me from recovery.
- I am grateful and thankful for my mom who believes in me still and loves me unconditionally despite my past missteps in life.
- I am grateful and thankful for the capacity to learn new things like Frank's creative writing tool. I do not fully understand it, but I have begun to benefit by writing about things I likely never would have disclosed to anyone.
- A quality I admire about myself is I am slow to anger. In a place like this, things do not always go as planned. Some things may not live up to my expectations or be contrary to what I have been told. Being patient in these situations, gives me the ability to learn and appreciate new opportunities. Being angry or frustrated would likely result in missing events, possibly the best of all.

CHAPTER 6

The first hour of Frank's class each morning is devoted to either gratitude work or another form of expressive writing we share with the group one at a time. The next one to two hours is devoted to letters if there are any to share; otherwise, we explore different forms of writing. Today, I will share my second letter to Mrs. F which I composed last night. Sharing this with my group of eight people gives me a lot of anxiety; more than yesterday when Frank was my only audience.

Letter to Mrs. F – #2

October 7, 2016

Dear Mrs. F,

I spent a lot of time at my Grandma and Grandpa's house when I was in second and third grades and before that too. My Mom and Dad were loving parents in every measurable sense. When I look back at it now, it is easy to see why I went to their house so often. Grandma and Grandpa never asked about school. They knew I was different from second grade going forward. They didn't know, nor did anyone else, of the horror taking place at school. I found solace at their house.

I became detached as a person after you started hitting me and constantly telling me I was an awful child and deserved to be repeatedly punished. At conferences, you told my parents I was a child who was not smart and had severe learning disabilities. My parents were skeptical as anyone would be who had a child with advanced placement test scores in kindergarten and first grade.

It was in third grade, the second year I had you for a teacher, when I think you broke me into a million pieces -- never again to be David. You hit me and verbally abused and chastised me on an almost daily basis all the while telling me what a terrible person I was.

My mother tried to get the school to have me placed in another teacher's class, but it wasn't to be. Therefore, in third grade I have you again, all day long this time, and I am sent to special education for a couple of hours each day. I complete my week's worth of work in a few hours at a near perfect level. However, you maintained you were correct in your assessment of me. Because you were a tenured teacher, no one can cross you or they will have to contend with the entirely too powerful teacher's union. My Mom kept pushing the principal to do something, anything to show you were inaccurate in your claims about me.

I don't understand any of this at eight years old. All I know is I get smacked around a lot, and it isn't even Halloween yet of my third-grade year.

Around this same time, my parents told me I was going to spend two or three days with a different teacher, and it was important I do my best work for her. I remember there being a lot of oral tests, puzzles, math problems, reading comprehension, and many more exercises.

> *I believed I was a horrible person undeserving of any goodness, absolutely none. I spent all my school years feeling the same way; and even now, at age forty-three, I feel worthless most of the time.*

The testing took two days. I found out years later I had taken an extensive IQ test. My score was 145. After those test days, things changed for the worse for me in your class. Were you mad because I proved you wrong? Is that why you began putting me into the closet? Is that why you began choking me? Is that why you began shocking me with that prong? I was still in your class, and it was not likely anyone would fire you with all your tenure.

I have been able to recall this Hell for about eight months now, and I am forced to conclude that you derived a sick pleasure in torturing me as you did. During recess, when you wouldn't let me play because I was such a bad, awful boy, I would be in the dark closet fearing I was going to die any day from you either breaking my neck from the choking, or from the intense pain of the electricity. Some days you would leave me in the closet and let me out after recess without further harm. I honestly don't know what was worse--the misery of the act, or the anticipation of it.

You did this to me until the end of the school year up to four times a week. I believed I was a horrible person undeserving of any goodness, absolutely none. I spent all my school years feeling the same way; and even now, at age forty-three, I feel worthless most of the time. Except for my Mom and step Dad, everyone else from my brothers to my kids believe my entire life is nothing more than self-centered choices leading to engagement in damaging behaviors.

I've thought about trying to find out if you are dead or alive, but I don't think I want to know the answer. I hope you are miserable, and karma has visited you and made you hurt, you awful monster.

David

Very nice. How was it?" Frank asked.
"It definitely brought a lot of memories back, mostly bad memories that produced a lot of emotion," I answered.
He continued, "That's good, exactly what needs to be happening to get to a spot where you can release the hatred and other emotions. Let's keep writing. This time make it more of a 'I hate you letter' to bring those feelings of anger and hatred to the surface."
"I wasn't doing that already?" I asked.
Frank said, "Focus less on storytelling and talk about feelings. Have the conversations while paying attention to the feelings that were produced."
"All right, I got an idea what you mean," I said.
"If it was happening to your son in second or third grade, what would you do about it? How would you react if it was your son in the closet and you found out about it? Do you see what I am looking for in the next letter?"
Not knowing what to say, I went with "I believe I do. I'll get to work on it over the weekend."
Frank is a man of few words; yet, as I am finding a little more every day, they are spot on. It didn't take me long at all to realize he is one of the smartest people I have ever met. Some see him as arrogant or pompous, but I see him for what he is, and that is competent.
Reading the letter in the presence of my peers is difficult because powerfully charged emotions are flooding over me when I am reading, writing or even talking about what happened to me. The more I write, the more I remember the awful truth, and that is my brain's way of telling me I am broken. The writing is showing me reality is worse than the nightmare. How can that be? It terrifies me to think about what may come into focus with the next letter. The feelings of shame I feel are strong as I try to see through the eyes of me so long ago.
The looks on the faces of my peers in the Alternative Track are those of empathy and connection. The topics of their letters are as serious and troubling as mine, creating a sense of trust and unity among us. As my first week at Hope is winding down,

Birthplace of Addiction

I realize I am meant to be here dealing with problems that have had power over me my whole life.

Hope by the Sea is a dual diagnosis treatment center. In addition to offering solutions for substance addiction, they have a staff of psychologists who treat mental health disorders. I have known for some time my addiction was a symptom of something else. My PTSD, Depression and Anxiety diagnoses confirmed what I have felt for a long time. Being treated for these mental conditions and addiction in the same facility by a team of clinicians was a major consideration for coming here.

Nancy is the Therapist assigned to me and our first one-on-one is today. I have been looking forward to this and hope she can help me with my issues. Her office has a book shelf with baskets of toys in them- many, many, toys. This seems a little out of place in a men's adult facility, but I am sure the reason for them will be revealed in time.

> *I have known for some time my addiction was a symptom of something else. My PTSD, Depression and Anxiety diagnoses confirmed what I have felt for a long time. Being treated for these mental conditions and addiction in the same facility by a team of clinicians was a major consideration for coming here.*

Nancy introduced herself, "My name is Nancy, and I am a licensed Therapist. Anything we discuss is confidential with the following exceptions: If it comes to my attention that you wish to inflict harm on yourself, the elderly or a child, I am obligated to inform the appropriate people or authorities."

"David, how are you doing today?" she asked.

"I am doing okay. I am still getting adjusted to this place and getting to know folks," I replied.

"Okay, well today I would like to review your treatment plan and gain some insight from you on what your goals and expectations are for our sessions going forward."

"Sounds fine to me. I am eager to get going with this." I encouraged.

She continued, "Tell me about your family and home life."

"I have two kids; I am divorced; and I have not been in communication with my kids since August. Tension has been considerable between my children and me in the months leading up to arriving here," I explained.

"Do you have a relationship with your ex-wife?" he inquired.

"Not a good one," I said with a smirk.

"You are very insightful and aware, David, almost everybody I ask that says, 'No'! However, you recognize that yes, you have one, but it is not good," she said.

"It consists pretty much of sending necessary text messages regarding the kids."

"How old are the kids and where are they now?"

"David is sixteen and Chelsey is twenty-one. David is with his mother, and I don't know where Chelsey is. They both lived with me through early August of this year," I said.

"How do you feel about the situation with your children right now?" She continued.

"I am really not sure. Everything is a bit numb where feelings are concerned. I think the amount of anger, frustration, and hurt on both sides contributes to making things worse. I hope with the passage of time a relationship with them will be possible," I replied.

"We will leave the topic for now and possibly get into it in the coming weeks if you want to. For now, we will move forward. What are some of the goals you have for our therapy sessions?" she asked.

"I would like to get to the root of the PTSD and silence the nightmares that terrorize my dreams when I try to sleep. That is my top priority. Beyond that, I would like to find some peace in my life and learn to love and forgive myself."

"What can you tell me about what happened and how long the nightmares have been happening?" She queried.

"Until February of 2016, the memory of being tortured and locked in a closet on and off for two years by my second and third grade teacher, Mrs. F, was frozen in my mind. I was a client at a dual diagnosis treatment center in February of this year. At the time, I thought I had addressed this, but the nightmares started again, only much more vivid and terrifying. I am afraid to sleep, and it is affecting every part of my life. These are the reasons I did methamphetamine to stay awake and to be safe from the terror of the nightmares."

She asked, "Would you say these nightmares are what caused you to relapse after being in treatment earlier this year?"

"I would say it had a great deal to do with it. I take responsibility for it, and I do not blame anything or anyone but me for my circumstances today."

"David, I believe based on what you have told me, the treatment center prior to this place essentially cut you open and did not put you back together in a way that completely dealt with everything. That is why the nightmares came back so strong and powerfully. Does that make sense?" Nancy asked.

"So far, yes." I said.

She continued, "Because I do not want that to happen again to you, I do not want to cut you wide open and begin work we may not be able to finish. How long are you here for?"

"I am here for no less than ninety days."

"We see each other once a week so about twelve sessions. We should focus on present life and how you will live going forward. Those would be my top concerns as your Therapist. When you get home, you will want to continue intensive therapy to adequately settle the past. Before we close for today, is there anything else we need to address today?"

I said, "If possible, I would prefer to meet after eleven o'clock, so I don't miss the Track specific stuff in the morning."

She replied, "No problem. I will make a note of that. Have a good weekend."

CHAPTER 7

Something about the meeting with Nancy is not setting right with me. Could this be an issue not handled correctly at the treatment center back in Minnesota? When I reflect on it, I am reasonably sure those folks did a decent job. Being a dual diagnosis treatment center was brand new to them. The Minnesota treatment center is a twenty-eight-day facility like most treatment centers in the country. One could take a position that twenty-eight days is not adequate treatment time when a client is diagnosed with significant mental health disorders. As I consider this, I realize it is only a part of what is bothering me about my therapy session.

One would think devoting ninety days of their life to a clinical setting for personal growth and wellbeing would be the optimal condition for in-depth therapy. As Nancy put it, to *cut one open* in this safe environment would be the ideal setting for it to take place. I can't see how a therapy that does not address my past, along with now and going forward, is going to help me at all. This is contrary to the work I have started in the Alternative Track where digging deep is the purpose. To do the therapies suggested by Nancy would defeat my purpose of being here all together. Doing this kind of work at home, I feel would fall short of the expectations I have for this program. After further weekend reflection, I plan to discuss this with my Case Manager on Monday.

It is seven grown men who storm Target in search of Pictionary supplies. The amount of laughter heard throughout the store is infectious, and it is the most I have laughed all year.

Life at the Horse Shoe House has a remarkable therapeutic vibe to it. Everyone here comes from a very different walk of life. Most of us even live in different states. At some point in our not so distant past, we all discovered our lives were in some way out of control. This observation means different things to some of us no doubt. Yet, our situations are remarkably similar. Many of us are here for ninety days to work on our lives. Many of us desire a stronger spiritual life and renewed contact with God. I don't say this as a religious statement, but rather a strengthening one. No matter what your beliefs happen to be, most will agree spiritual health is part of any successful formula for a complete life.

At the Horse Shoe House, we always seem to be going somewhere on the weekend. Anthony must have his monsters, someone else needs to stop at Target or the grocery store, really any number of places, nothing surprises me. So, when at nine-thirty o'clock on a Sunday night we got an idea to play Pictionary, it did not surprise me to load in the van and head for Target on a true mission. It is seven grown men who storm Target in search of Pictionary supplies. The amount of laughter heard throughout the store is infectious, and it is the most I have laughed all year. We stay up half the night playing the game, and it is truly fun! Looking back at it now, I think the act of getting the game was more fun than the game itself. I don't know if Hope by the Sea designed the housing with the idea of therapy taking place, but it does in a big way!

CHAPTER 8

Monday morning is the same in a treatment center as it is every place else. Not enough sleep and not enough weekend is the general attitude in the van this day. Despite lack of sleep, I look forward to a busy day at the Center, where I will talk with my Case Manager about my therapy session and find a resolution together. Reading my letter will also be a relief; it is the one I found the most difficult to write thus far.

Frank's classes are all entitled *The Work* and on Monday and Wednesday we are with him three hours instead of two. After doing the gratitude work and sharing in hour one; we take a break. Then, Frank asks us to write a break-up letter to our addiction. A good-bye letter will be assigned later. We have twenty minutes to write before sharing it with the group.

Break-up with Alcohol and Drugs   Letter 1

October 10, 2016

Dear Alcohol and Drugs,

A long history we have, no doubt about that. I have never been very social in my personal life, so I jumped in with both feet at an early age and immediately loved some of your qualities. Among my favorites are the warm sensation in my chest as I take my first gulps; the way you numb my thoughts, and give me liquid courage; all of which, makes me a legend in my own mind.

Unfortunately for me and you, there are dozens of reasons why you are an insidious demon that has no care or consideration whatsoever for me. Over time your allure has worn thin and all that remains are your addictive qualities. My use of you has gotten more destructive and has cost me dearly. Losing countless friends, relationships, and money, as well as incurring legal troubles, have taken a near fatal toll on me. My physical, mental, and spiritual systems are pretty much all on life support, and you know what -- enough is enough!

It is time we break-up and move on with life. You, of course, will thrive as ever without me. Your cunningness grips millions, and your hunger for more souls is endless.

I find myself in mourning almost daily after your absence. I am weak, vulnerable to relapse. I live my days now in a place far, far from home and usual surroundings. My selfish actions and obsessive behaviors have left a wake of destruction that continues to grow.

> *It is time we break-up and move on with life. You, of course, will thrive as ever without me. Your cunningness grips millions, and your hunger for more souls is endless.*

This place is arming me with a resolve that has been absent for years. I have been given tools that in time will enable me to live a life free from you. These words are not just words that sound good; I am ready for the work that will make this reality.

David Foss

"Very nice. How was it?" Frank is very consistent when asking about writing. He recognizes the difficulty we have in writing about our lives, and the courage that is necessary in sharing with the group.

I said, "It felt strange at first writing from this perspective, but it got easier as it began to take shape."

Frank instructed, "I want all of you to see you received a perceived benefit of some sort during your use. It is important to get in touch with those feelings if you ever want to understand what it was that caused you to use in the first place. Addiction is a part of a bigger thing, a much bigger thing. Addiction is not the problem; and until you accept this and find what is, you will not be successful. That is why we write. Now, I want you to reverse it and write to yourself from your addiction and share it with the group."

> *Addiction is a part of a bigger thing, a much bigger thing. Addiction is not the problem; and until you accept this and find what is, you will not be successful.*

That is a lot different! I have never heard the problem is not alcohol and drugs. Everyone from my family, friends, employers, even clinicians in the treatment world have always said substances are at the heart of the matter. I am not certain of this, yet I am aware of the limited results I have experienced in the short time I have been here, so I will follow Frank's direction.

"Okay, I will start working on it tonight."

Nine people are in the room this morning when we share our writings, but when Frank gives us direction, it feels like a one-on-one session. I also learn from the writing and direction given to others. This class is a high-quality learning experience for me. I am fully engaged, and I feel I am healing a little each day.

The Alternative Track is simple in terms of work. It requires us to write a considerable amount outside our daily classes to get to the level Frank demands of us. Therefore, when Frank asks who has letters to share and only one or two hands from nine people go up, we can expect Frank will notice. I took comfort I had done the work asked of me and had the third letter to Mrs. F ready to be read today.

CHAPTER 9

Letter to Mrs. F - No. 3

October 10, 2016

Dear Mrs. F,

The more I write to you the more I realize the hold you have on me, and that is unacceptable. Thinking about the horrific things you did to me, an eight-year old child who loved learning, loved school and socialized well. Everything changed for me in second grade. For me, that is where my innocence died forever.

The man helping me deal with everything you did to me suggested I write you a *go to Hell* letter. He said to bring feelings of rage as if it were my son, David, you had hurt, just like you had hurt me. I was taught not to use profanity in expression as it tends to diminish and lower one's self. Having said that, I will trust Frank and plow forward.

> *Everything changed for me in second grade. For me, that is where my innocence died forever.*

You would get a visit from me if you put my son in a dingy cabinet, choked him so his screams could be heard by no one when you electrocuted him in his genitals and other areas for what seemed like an eternity to him. Gone is the frightened, forever scarred, seven and eight-year old boy. Instead, you have an enraged Father ready to hand down retribution.

A throat punch would get your attention and now nobody can hear you as your breath is gone. A strange sensation is coming into focus as I smash your knee cap with a sledgehammer. This renders you helpless and immobile as I once was in the closet so long ago. How do you like it, you evil bitch? How do you like being the helpless subject of rage? Another throat punch muffles any response you want to give.

I see terror in your eyes. Gone is your gaze that haunts me every day and every night in my nightmares. Gone is your smugness when you proclaimed so many years ago I was awful and deserving of punishment. Where is your resolve? Where is your teachers' union now?

By your hair I drag your sorry ass to the dingy closet you love so much. I see the space is made for an eight-year old child rather than a full- grown bitch. I smash the other knee and with all my strength, force you into the space. Now the time has come to end your poor excuse of a life once and for all. With a wooden match and some diesel fuel the space ignites, and I leave to reflect on things. It almost immediately occurs to me that you got off easy.

Death is too good for a beastly predator like you! You robbed me of my humanity. I went through childhood scared of my own shadow, incapable of accepting love or anything good. You instilled in my core how awful a person I was when it was you Mrs. F who was the fundamental definition of evil.

For two long years, you tortured me for being David. The light in my eyes has never again shined as it did at the age of seven. To say I hate you is a surface look. Deep down where nobody can touch, lives a great many fears I cannot explain. I am afraid and time-warped back to 1980. Every time people yell at me, it chills me to my core.

You stole my self-worth. Praise is wasted on me. I simply do not believe I am worthy of goodness. I do not feel as others feel. Those teachings of my youth were primarily instilled by your evil hand. How does God allow the likes of you to roam free to inflict these horrors upon me? You evil, evil bitch, I would not pee on you if you were on fire.

I have trouble writing this. I am not a violent man. I tend to be kind and gentle to others. I was so scared and ashamed I couldn't tell a soul because then they would know what an awful little boy I was.

I have hurt a lot of people; some from my addiction to alcohol; but so many more from my cold nature. I often fake my feelings in relationships, scared to let people in, not really knowing what feelings are, let alone how to express them. I also am afraid if people find what lies beneath, they will reject me and hurt me more than I have hurt myself. You have caused such turmoil in my life that it is impossible for me to know the life I have lost in my shattered childhood and adolescence. I do not understand why for thirty-five years my mind capped the memories and preserved them only to haunt me for the past eight months.

I feel so lost right now. As I put pen to paper, I feel my soul aching, dying and rotting my core. I don't want you in my head or heart, I want you squashed like the parasitic dung bag you are.

I know you hurt others; you must have. In eighth grade I had a private tutor who I met with three days a week at a church across from the elementary school. The powers that be at the Glenville School determined I was too disruptive to go to normal school. I ate lunch at the elementary school. One day walking in with my teacher to have lunch, I saw you in the same room where I had been your prey six years earlier. I froze, and an electric charge went through me and made me double over; you just starred with your dead lights looking down into my very soul. You knew I was still the scared child I was the last time you saw me. You smirked and turned away. I did not know then what you had done to me. My real memories of second and third grades were buried by then, and I just thought you were a bad teacher who was mean, not the evil predator that you are and were.

> *I feel so lost right now. As I put pen to paper, I feel my soul aching, dying and rotting my core. I don't want you in my head or heart, I want you squashed like the parasitic dung bag you are.*

David Foss

"Okay, that was very good. How was it?"
"It was very difficult for me to write. I felt a lot of guilt and shame writing in that way. I came very close to drinking over it on Saturday afternoon. Had it not been for one of my housemates, I am certain I would have."

I was going to tell one of the House Managers I needed to go to Wal-Mart where I would purchase a couple of pints, conceal them, and go back to the house and drink it all. I encountered my roommate, Tom, in the kitchen before going to the House

Manager, and he wanted my help with a personal problem. After talking with him for about a half hour, I realized alcohol was not the answer for what I was experiencing.

Frank said, "When feelings come out of the writing, they are not good or bad, right or wrong. They are just feelings. Normally you would seek to numb these feelings like you have done with drugs or alcohol. Even though the alcohol and drugs are out of your system, the feelings and problems remain. You are now learning to process these things in your life, for the first time maybe, without alcohol and drugs. It is why I say addiction is only a symptom of something else. If it were the primary problem, you would be cured because it is out of your system. No?"

"So, how do I process the feelings I had after the writing Saturday?" I asked.

"You are in effect creating new neural paths in your brain. Your old way would be to drink. By not drinking, you create new paths, and they take some time to become strong. It is not unlike learning to ride a bike or speaking a second language. In the beginning it is not natural, but over time with repetition, it gets easier and easier," Frank explained.

I asked, "Are the daily gratitude work and journal check-ins a form of this also?"

Journal check-ins are like a diary entry or prayer journal. It is an outlet in which to put thoughts on paper. I am finding it to be helpful in going through my recovery process.

Frank said, "When we write letters we often focus on the negative because it is essential to deal with the negative before any positive can be looked at. The gratitude injects the positive. When you don't want to do this writing, it is a strong indication you need to write."

"Okay, I'll keep at it," I replied.

"Good job. Now let's write from you at eight years old to yourself now in 2016. Focus on the feelings now in your life. What's home like? Parents? Brothers? And anything before the age of seven. Don't overthink, just write."

"I will get started on that tonight."

CHAPTER 10

My Case Manager is Kim, and she is a licensed Counselor. I meet with her every week. I have been looking forward to discussing my treatment plan and Therapist with her. The meeting was on the first floor in her private office, and as it turns out, it has a small sofa that is quite comfortable.

"Hello, David. How have things been going for you so far?" Kim inquired.

I said, "I am adjusting to things fairly well. I have a lot of emotions and charged feelings from all the writing in the Alternative Track."

"So far, is it what you expected when you first arrived?" she asked.

I said, "This place is nice and the house I stay in is incredible. The men I live with have helped me get settled and feel at home. I can't say enough about the Horse Shoe House, the managers, and the housemates. It is as if we have all known one another for years. The rapport and trust level we enjoy makes it very conducive for healing, and we have a lot of fun as well. When you live, cry, laugh and heal together, a level of closeness like no other is the result."

Kim said, "We will be meeting no less than once a week and as your Case Manager, it is my job to see you are getting the care and attention you require. We will also work together to work through the substance portion of your treatment plan, and we will be reviewing it right now. Is there anything you would like to discuss before we get started?"

I said, "I would like to discuss my Therapist and my first session I had with her."

"No problem. We can talk about that as soon as we go over your treatment plan," she said.

I agreed, and she handed me a copy of the treatment plan. Kim is a no-nonsense kind of person who tells it like it is in a direct, blunt fashion. I'm not quite sure what to think about her, so for now, I will just roll with the punches.

The treatment plan is based in part on the assessment given to me both on the phone and in person before and after my arrival at Hope. My diagnoses my plan is built around are:

1. Post-Traumatic Stress Disorder (PTSD)
2. Major Depressive Disorder

3. Generalized Anxiety Disorder
4. Alcohol Use Disorder Severe
5. Methamphetamine Use Disorder Mild
6. Insomnia Disorder

Kim said, "The mental health disorders will be worked on with your Therapist, and the alcohol and methamphetamine will be done with me. The Alternative Track you chose means we will work through your *Smart Recovery* book together."

Smart Recovery, a recovery program, has meetings and offers support for those having a desire to be abstinent from drugs and alcohol. It is science and cognitive behavior rooted, and it does not use twelve-step processes featured in Alcoholic Anonymous and Celebrate Recovery programs. *Smart Recovery*'s cognitive behavior methodologies are good companions for the Alternative program. I find it to be refreshing and empowering.

I said, "That sounds good to me, and I have already read a fair amount of it and completed exercises in the first four chapters." I quipped.

Kim said, "How have cravings been since you arrived here?"

"I almost went to buy a bottle over the weekend. It wasn't so much a craving as it was a numbing thing," I replied.

I went on to explain, "The writing I was working on over the weekend was difficult and emotional. The feelings of depression, guilt, shame and anxiety have always been the trigger ingredients for me to drink or do some drugs. I was beginning to scheme as to how I was going to accomplish the procurement of them to numb the pain inside of me as I have done for decades. If I had not run into one of my housemates and begun talking to him about a personal problem he was having, I likely would have relapsed."

> *"I want you to write a letter about what it means to love David for our next meeting,"* Kim requested. *"I don't have the first clue what it means, or even what you think it means,"* I said.

"When you used, was it generally to deal with some type of emotional issue?" Kim inquired.

"It often was, especially these last few years when loss was extremely high in my life. I've been overwhelmed with death, divorce, broken relationships, livelihood and financial issues. I never realized what I was doing from a clinical standpoint; it was just what I did to feel normal," I said.

Kim said, "That is a large number of issues. I think it would be hard for anyone."

I said, "I suppose it is."

I continued, "The truth is I am in a pit of despair, and I don't know if there is a way out. I came to treatment because I believed I should try. I didn't come because I believed there would be light at the end of the tunnel for me. I have felt this way so long it has become my normal. I do want to get better. If I do get better, what kind of life can there be when almost all I care about is either gone, ripped, or lost forever?"

Kim said, "It sounds like you need to learn to love yourself, David."

I said, "Those words are true; however, executing them is another matter entirely."

"I want you to write a letter about what it means to love David for our next meeting," Kim requested.

"I don't have the first clue what it means, or even what you think it means," I said.

"It doesn't matter what I think it means, only what you think it does. Write what you think, you may surprise yourself," She answered.

I said, "Can we talk about my meeting with my Therapist, now?"

"Sure, as long as you understand the assignment."

"I do," I assured her.

I began telling Kim exactly what Nancy said about cutting me open, and her assessment of not doing it here for fear of not being able to finish what we start. She said I should do this kind of thing on my own with a Therapist after leaving here. I continued by telling her I felt if a ninety-day stay at an in-patient treatment facility was not the ideal time for such therapy to occur, then there is none. I also expressed meeting only once a week, given my diagnoses, was unacceptable to me.

She said, "I don't like the term *cut open,* and I will talk to the Clinical Director, Mel, at our clinical meeting tonight."

I said, "It is also contrary to what I am working on in the Alternative Track. We dig in deep in our writing every day. It is difficult work, and it takes a lot out of me every day. I continue to work hard because I experience value from *The Work* almost immediately. So, anything that does not work in concert with the Alternative curriculum seems like a waste of resources. Is that how I should look at my treatment process to ensure I receive the most bang for my buck?" I stated my case and then, inquired.

She said, "Yes, that is how you should look at this experience. I have all of this written down, and I will talk with you tomorrow and let you know what resolution we reach."

I wanted to add the work in the Alternative program has been eighty-five percent of my treatment thus far but thought better of it. I said, "Okay, I look forward to hearing from you."

The meeting had gone quite well. I expected pushback on Kim's part, but I got none. Perhaps I was over-thinking and worrying about things I can't control. Everyone experiences in varying degrees the necessity to be in control at one time or another. People like me and other victims of trauma and addiction tend to obsess over control. This obsession is unattainable, because almost everything in this life cannot be controlled. What we can do is manage how we react to uncontrollables. People, places, and things are what we seek to control; and when it is not achieved, we react, and often cope in unhealthy ways.

CHAPTER 11

We have a choice the final hour every day at the Center to go to Cross Fit or spend the hour writing in the park across the street. This is becoming my favorite part of the day. I find the picnic table a great place to get a good amount of writing accomplished, except when somebody comes and sits down at my picnic table and starts gum flapping. Gum flapping for those who don't understand, is uninvited conversation, mostly uninvited anyway. Harlan, a Case Manager at Hope by the Sea, is always in the park during the final hour of the day and often finds the picnic table where I am writing. Harlan has been sober for thirty-five years and has worked in the field of recovery since then. The man knows as much about how to stay clean and sober and live a happy, meaningful life as anyone I have ever met.

"How's the battle today?" Harlan inquired.

"Another beautiful, sunny day to be alive," I said, sitting at the table under a shady maple. I noticed his eyes on my open journal and open letter tablet when he finally said, "Don't know which one to write in this afternoon?" He asked with his big ear-to-ear grin he almost always has on his face.

> *I find the picnic table a great place to get a good amount of writing accomplished, except when somebody comes and sits down at my picnic table and starts gum flapping. Gum flapping for those who don't understand, is uninvited conversation, mostly uninvited anyway.*

"I guess I am feeling a little overwhelmed today. I have several letters I could be working on and my journal is a bit lacking lately," I said with a little frustration in my voice.

Harlan is not my Case Manager, and he is not my Therapist. I rarely have had him in a class either. Despite all that, I have had more one-on-one time with this man than any other person at Hope. A man with the life and recovery experience of Harlan one-on-one three or four days a week at the picnic table is worth a lot; plus, he is a great friend to boot.

With a more somber face he asks, "How long did it take you to end up here with me at this table today?"

Not wanting to hear that today I uttered, "What do you mean?"

He said, "I think you know full well what I am asking; so, I'd appreciate you cutting the bull and answering the question!"

"It took a long time, a better part of twenty years, costing me a great many people and things that can never be gotten back or undone!" I said with emotion.

He lowered his voice and reached across the table putting his hand on mine and said, "Don't you think it may take a bit longer than you've been here to put things in a place where you can live again?" Not waiting for an answer, he went on to say, "I have been on your side of the table, son. I know how much hurt and hopelessness you feel right now; and I know, too, how suffocating it is, but this shall pass."

"When will it pass? I am so exhausted! I have nightmares that won't let me rest, and I feel this hole I've dug for myself is caving in around me, and as hard as I try, I am sinking."

"You will have bad days, maybe many bad days as you go through this work you have begun, but trust me when I say, it won't always be like that."

"What do I do today? Right now?" I inquired.

> *"I have been on your side of the table, son. I know how much hurt and hopelessness you feel right now; and I know, too, how suffocating it is, but this shall pass."*

Harlan thought about that for a few moments, then looked at me and said, "Pack up your books there and don't pull them out for 24 hours. Go back to your house, have something good for supper and go to bed early and see what tomorrow looks like."

"Okay, I will. Thanks for the talk."

"You're welcome, and I'll see you tomorrow."

CHAPTER 12

Sometimes the simplest things in life are the most difficult to grasp. I know from experience Harlan's advice is sound; yet, had I not had the conversation in the park, I certainly would have remained stuck. In the van going back to the house I was already beginning to feel more relaxed and looking forward to some down time.

Nick and Stan are the House Managers at the Horse Shoe House and both perform their jobs at a high level. Being in recovery themselves makes them both able to relate to what we go through as clients of Hope by the Sea. Stan is from the area and has just over six months of being clean while Nick is from Massachusetts and has over a year of being clean and sober. Both men are in their 20's and are opposite in every way but being clean. I am reminded of Felix Unger and Oscar Madison when I watch the two carry out their various components of running the house.

Most of the time, gathering around the pool smoking cigarettes and telling stories or discussing the day of treatment are common topics. There are little to no bugs in southern California, so it is normal to have the doors to the house wide open, making the patio an extension of the house. Rain is rare, and temperatures are in the seventies year around with minimal humidity. The outdoors is like another great room complete with an outdoor kitchen, lovely, soft furniture, the pool and the hot tub. Beautiful sunsets complete the picture with a great view of the valley, too.

Wednesday nights consist of a topnotch meal like bacon-wrapped chicken parmesan and all the trimmings prepared by Nick. This being a Tuesday means Stan is working, and there will not be one scrap of food prepared by him. Stan couldn't burn a pot of water correctly let alone serve anything to eat. Clear example of the Oscar and Felix I mentioned before.

After the Tuesday supper that wasn't, it is back in the van to be to the Center by six-thirty o'clock. My roommate, Tom, is telling me about the activity he is going to tonight as part of the Christian Track. He says it's his favorite part of the week. As we are riding to the Center, Tom asked, "So, David, are you going to join us at The Effect tonight?"

I am a Christian myself. I picked the Alternative Track for the kind of work done there. Normally, I would go to meditation I am not fond of doing, because it's hard for me to sit still.

"Why not?" I said grinning ear-to-ear. "I am looking forward to it."

The parking lot at the Treatment Center is a staging area for eleven van loads of men and women to redeploy to different vans destined for the track specific event. What looks like chaos is really a well-oiled machine with everyone accounted for and delivered to their destinations timely and efficiently.

The Effect is a worship center located within a retail strip mall about a mile from the Center. This event, albeit open to the public, seems to be just Hope folks. This event, unlike most, includes the Women's and Men's Centers. This explains the rather pungent cologne smell in the van on the short drive over. It would be remiss of me not to note that the ladies at The Effect added an ambiance that makes the evening more enjoyable.

There is barely enough seating for everyone, and people are placing items on chairs to reserve spots. This, of course, allows more time for the coffee, cookies and fellowship to be enjoyed and without losing a good seat. I can see why Tom likes the event. It feels like we are not in treatment, but rather just a group of sober and clean people gathering together in fellowship.

The music starts at seven-fifteen o'clock. There are five musicians playing guitars, keyboard and drums singing Christian music at a high skill level with amazing vocals. There are no open seats, and most are singing along with the words.

It has been a long time since I have been to a church or religious event. Reading the music lyrics from the monitors I began to reflect on my life. I thought about how I've done little to reflect my Christian upbringing.

Seated toward the back, I watch people praying at an altar in the front; many are being prayed over by others and some are praying alone. No doubt, between the music and the prayers God is present. I feel tears running down my cheeks as I think of all the wasted years I spent in addiction. All of yesterday is gone forever. I don't know any of the music playing, and the lyrics are unfamiliar as well. Still, the tears fall, and the feelings are familiar at first. What happens next is something I know is real; and now, it is happening to me.

> *By the time the song ends, I experience something I don't recall feeling before. It is hope for better days and a happier life for me.*

The musicians are playing Amazing Grace. I know the hymn. I suppose most people do. Tonight, I feel the Holy Spirit working in me as I sing the words to this beautiful hymn. My tears, running down my cheeks, are somehow different. Instead of feeling despair, I feel as if a slice of it is removed. By the time the song ends, I experience something I don't recall feeling before. It is hope for better days and a happier life for me.

Back at the house I shared with Tom what happened. He said, "You know what it was, don't you?"

I said, "Yes, I know precisely what it was. Thanks for telling me about the Effect and encouraging me to check it out."

"You're welcome, sir."

That night sleep didn't come easy to me. I kept thinking about the music at The Effect and the emotions and feelings it stirred in me. My spiritual life has been lacking for as long as I can remember. Going forward I must incorporate God into my life. One thing is certain; tonight, was a great night. I feel more at peace.

CHAPTER 13

Frank was off the past several days, and I'm glad to see him back. It will be good to get back to normal in the Alternative Track. Hope had some folks cover the classes, but there really is no substitute for Frank. No one read any letters in class while Frank was gone because we depend on his guidance and wisdom on the very serious topics we reveal in them.

Tim is a younger man from Florida I have gotten to know well, and he has become a good friend. Given the subject matter and intimacy of our writings, it isn't hard to see how we become close. Tim has been working through childhood trauma involving abuse stemming from his father. He has never mentioned this to anyone; not even his mother knew what was happening to him. I derive courage from his strength in working through his past. It helps me dig into my own past with the work ethic required to face my own trials and tribulations. I have a couple of letters to share, the first is a second one involving alcohol.

I already shared a break-up letter; this is a reversal from alcohol to me.

Letter from Alcohol to Me

October 14, 2016

Dear David,

Well, at least you are consistent, consistently full of crap that is. You gotta be kidding me! You have a better chance of getting struck by lightning than staying clear of my alluring nectar. We go through this every time you hit a crisis in your life like legal troubles or thinking you can make others happy by abandoning me.

I am the one constant in your life that remains forever loyal. I don't understand your failure to realize we will always be together no matter how hard you fight. Sure, you may have to go to jail or prison someday, but I'll be waiting for you like the loyal mistress I am. I can medicate or even numb your pains all together while pushing those who love you aside completely.

I am a jealous slimebucket, and I always get what I want; and if you were not so naive as to think you can live without me, you could be wrapped in my numbness now. The liquid warming your stomach as only I can. A few moments pass, and you feel nothing, no pain, no love, just nothingness.

> *I am a jealous slimebucket, and I always get what I want; and if you were not so naive as to think you can live without me, you could be wrapped in my numbness now.*

The past few years or so you have been letting a flood of sorrow and tears come to the party and my how you cry, cry, cry. This suits me just fine as you just wrap tighter in my blanket of emptiness, and you stay much longer. Your body shakes and nausea are overwhelming when you try to shed me. I bring you to your knees and make you wish you were dead.

You see, you silly, silly, boy, I am your Alpha and Omega and there isn't thing one you can do about it. So, go ahead and do your fancy treatment, and I will see you soon enough. It's more fun any way when you are happy and successful. You have destroyed yourself before, and it will no doubt happen again, and I'll be waiting.

Alcohol

"That was some nice writing. How was it?" Frank said with a smile.

"I have never written from that perspective before. However, my view of alcohol, if alcohol were a person, is -- it is a cunning deceiver."

"Go ahead and write a final goodbye letter and then you will likely be ready to release it by burning the letters and moving on," Frank instructed.

I thought about this and had a moment of clarity as to what the Alternative Track means to me. "So, by releasing this, what does that mean?" I inquired.

"It means you have purged the negative from you through the writing. The way to get to the place where you have come to terms with your feelings and what you feel about moving forward, is one of the ways we create new neuropaths in our brains. Normally, you would drink or use drugs to cope with pain, negative feelings, sadness, grief or even loss. By processing those feelings and life in general, in this case by writing, you are taking away the need to numb your feelings with drugs or alcohol. Make sense?"

"I think I am beginning to understand what you mean," I answered.

Frank said, "Welcome to neuro-plasticity. In the coming weeks, you will understand exactly what I am sharing with all of you."

While some of the other men read some letters, I am busy trying to process the feedback Frank gave and the notion of releasing things. Will I ever get to a place where I will be able to release what causes my nightmares and has had such influence over me these past thirty plus years? Thoughts of it happening, feel like a pipe dream, but I trust and believe Frank is helping me. I understand little of the work being done; yet, I have moments of clarity like a few minutes ago.

CHAPTER 14

The next letter is the fourth one in the Mrs. F series. This one is from myself at age forty-three to my then eight-year-old self.

Letter to My eight-year-old self from me at 43 years old

October 18, 2016

Dear David,

This isn't right or fair to be in this kind of Hell at eight years old. I wish I could tell you your third-grade year would be better, and even if I did, you wouldn't believe it because Mrs. F is your teacher for the second year in a row.

You spent your summer trying to fit somewhere, but you were sad and angry mostly at the other kids and your brothers for picking on you all the time. What I can tell you, is -- you are going to survive and live on for some time to come.

I am with you in the class room, and the closet too. I still feel what you feel thirty-five years later. I cry, I tremble, and I wake up terrified of that monster hurting us. I don't know if you thought about telling Mom and Dad. I can't piece certain things together. Some things I remember as if it were 1980, yet mysteries remain.

I also realize how scared you are from the time you wake up until the time you arrive back home. I know the agony and utter hopelessness you are living now.

I know now why I took the closet doors off in the bedrooms everywhere I have lived. I have always had this fear both physical and emotional going to my core deep within me.

It has taken thirty-five years to remember any of what you are living now. As a grown man, I often weep when I am jolted from sleep having had another nightmare. I know you don't understand the mean, awful hurt that is being inflicted upon you; and being terrified, wondering if today you will lose your life. The fear and anxiety of "Is she gonna hurt me today, or just let me out?" You are convinced you will not live to see Christmas.

David, you are going to live and one day you will be able to process and be rid of this once and for all. You are not a bad boy; you are good, so very good. You deserve goodness in your life.

You feel alone in this world and can't comprehend how this evil can happen to you. Fear of everything and deserving of nothing good is the reality haunting your every waking moment.

> *I know you don't understand the mean, awful hurt that is being inflicted upon you; and being terrified, wondering if today you will lose your life. The fear and anxiety of "Is she gonna hurt me today, or just let me out?"*

In the coming years, you will experience a great many things in life, good and bad. The worst is happening now, but it will continue in the coming months, too. After third grade, the physical pain will cease, but the mental suppression to adapt the wreckage of what your life has become, will happen. I wish I could tell you your childhood and adolescence would be a happy time, full of learning and experiences that will enrich your life for the better. However, the truth is, your path will be full of adversity and trial. Your ability to adapt is your greatest asset. Thinking on your feet and the ability to teach yourself will serve as a foundation of competence that will unfold later in life.

The courage and perseverance you show now is amazing. The kindness you show others is inspiring.

At some point that I do not remember, you will protect yourself by freezing this awful torture, so you don't remember any of it. I believe this will be a completely accepted break by you, and thereby the evil memories lost forever.

I will work hard for both our sakes to address our past and even though I don't know how exactly it will happen, I have come to believe it will. I have full confidence in the process Frank is teaching me. I believe it will happen as I follow his instructions. One day this may be a closed chapter of the past and will no longer affect you today or tomorrow."

David

"Okay, how was it?"
"This one was a lot more difficult for me; it was hard going back there."
Frank said, "You are doing a better job of expressing the feelings behind the actions rather than just telling a story. That's why the emotions are coming to the surface more."
"When I finished writing it, I was down in the dumps for the rest of the night. I couldn't stop thinking about things and didn't sleep much last night. Is this what I can expect as I move through this?"
"When dealings with feelings and the subconscious, we have little control over them. Remember feelings aren't good or bad, right or wrong. They are just feelings. What else are you working on?" He queried.
I said, "I do gratitude work each night, or sometimes in the afternoon. I list three things for which I'm grateful and thankful and why. I write down one thing about myself I admire and why, and then, I list ten positive occurrences in the last twenty-four hours. I also do a daily check-in of fifteen to twenty minutes of writing where I talk about the day's negatives and positives. That's about it." I concluded.
He said, "That's good. Try to end the day writing about the ten positives before bed. It is important to write about the positives in life, especially when you feel low and bad. We spend a lot of energy bringing out the negative; but not at the expense of the positives going on in your life right now. This gratitude work creates new neural pathways that get stronger the more you use them."
I said, "I'll adjust my writing schedule."
Frank said, "Okay, nice work. Keep writing to the teacher." "All right. I'll get started today."
I haven't been able to stop thinking about Frank's feedback on the letters I shared today. Being a man of few words, he had a lot to say today or perhaps, I was just listening more. Normally, when people talk about science and the brain I lose interest fast. Today, and some of the things he said on other days, have given me a clearer understanding of what Frank's program is and why it works.

For as long as I can remember, most of my life I suppose, I have silenced my feelings and emotions. Because of the suppression, I don't identify with other people's feelings and emotions. Now in my forty-fourth year, I am not only beginning to learn, but also understand how to process them so I can be free to live again. This work is helping me. It's showing me feelings aren't right or wrong, and they are not good or bad. *They are only feelings we all have.*

In the past, I often used alcohol or drugs to numb my feelings or ignore them all together. Anxiety would surface, and I would drink to lessen or eliminate it. When I experienced loss or grief, I would drink and not process the feelings, or allow myself to grieve. Such actions and behaviors became second nature to me to the point of being my normal.

I kept wondering why I am who I am? Why was I depressed? How did I get such low self-esteem? Not until recently, when I remembered the truth of my early school years, did I find the answers to these questions that have dominated my thoughts for so long. Do all my answers reside in the awful school classroom with the nasty teacher, Mrs. F? If yes is the answer, then what shall I do going forward?

> *The journal work makes me realize almost everything I have ever experienced, in so many ways, goes back to the time in Mrs. F's classroom when my innocence was taken from me.*

The more letters I write bringing the traumatic details into focus, the more overwhelming the flood of emotion becomes. The journal work makes me realize almost everything I have ever experienced, in so many ways, goes back to the time in Mrs. F's classroom when my innocence was taken from me. I lost the ability to trust another person. I have never had a healthy relationship. Expressing and receiving love is lost on me.

For the last eight months, I have become aware of some of what happened to me all those years ago. The nightmares I still experience, and the writing that makes things clearer, have brought me to a place where I believe help is possible.

CHAPTER 15

The work done in the Alternative Track exercises my mind. I have discovered how much easier it is to write the negatives about myself. For instance, when asked to write about past guilt and shame, I have options I could write about for days. When asked to write a positive memory of the past, focusing on the feelings surrounding it, it is difficult.

POSITIVE MEMORY

October 18, 2016

Every year about now, the smell of crop dust is in the air in Minnesota. This was my favorite time of year growing up because I spent a lot of time in the field with my Grandpa.

Driving the tractor was my favorite activity in the world. I have memories as young as three or four years old of driving on my Grandpa's lap in his Allis Chalmers 185 tractor. Sometimes I would ride along in the John Deere 105 combine. It was my escape from my older brothers, other kids, teachers and school.

Grandpa always made me feel special, and he was happy to see me; and I could feel safe to be me. My dog, Goldie, was usually with us running up and down the rows beside the tractor.

On the tractor or combine I had no fear, no sadness, no anger. I felt only happiness and joy in this safest of places. I couldn't wait for school to be over, as I would be thinking of what field I would find Grandpa in. Sometimes I would see him on the bus coming home or on my way to school. Just the sight of the tractor and wagons in route to the elevator, full of grain, often brought happiness out of darkness for me.

I wished I didn't have to go to school at all. I learn more farming than from awful Mrs. F. Grandpa always made me feel special, and he was happy to see me; and I could feel safe to be me. My dog, Goldie, was usually with us running up and down the rows beside the tractor.

Going to town to dump the grain was great fun. We would get some pop out of the old-fashioned pop machine and occasionally, some candy.

The only unhappy part was when Mom would come to the field and make me come home because it was a school night. I didn't know at the time Mom knew this was my happy place and my safe place. In my mind, it was one of the only truly safe places for me. Nobody picked on me, hit me or told me I was no good. I felt important at harvest time at a very young age, when I was allowed to move wagons around the field for Grandpa to keep the combine moving efficiently.

I would have given anything to remain in the field forever and not go to school. I do believe serenity lived in those rows of corn. For me, each time I was out there, I received peace, sanity and joy.

Frank said, "Very nice. How was it?"
"Once I could decide on something, it went well. I like farm talk." I answered.
"Identifying positives is as important as working through the negatives. We spend most of our time focusing on the negative, and that is why you must do the gratitude work on your own time as we don't have enough time in class most days. When you feel low or like you don't want to do it, that's when you must do it, or you will almost certainly return to using eventually," Frank stated.

I have noticed some of the men in the Alternative Track don't write outside of class, and it shows in their overall attitudes as well. Frank tells it like it is and doesn't waste his time on those who refuse to allot the time and work to complete *The Work* he assigns. The work ethic required to harness the potential of the tools Frank is giving us is heavy. For me, *The Work* is literally life or death, it's just that simple. I probably have another addiction run in me; another chance of recovering is what I do not have.

The Alternative Track does require you to write outside of class, a great amount to say the least. The Christian and Traditional Tracks have little to no work apart from class work. Since what we do in the Alternative Track is write and share, it doesn't make sense for anyone who won't write and share to be in Alternative Track. Therefore, people don't always remain in this track and move over to the Christian or Traditional Tracks.

The Women's Center has seventy percent enrollment in Alternative Track; the men have thirty percent enrollment in the Alternative Track. Women are generally more inclined to express feelings and are more prone to write about them. Many of the women are victims of trauma, violence and sexual assaults. The Alternative Track helps both men and women when you do *The Work*. The highest recovery success rates are in the Alternative Track. Based on how I feel since my arrival, and the daily progress I am making, I believe I made the right decision when I chose the Alternative Track.

Hope by the Sea has a medical doctor, a psychiatrist and two physician assistants that work with everyone at the Center based upon the individual needs of the clients. Evaluations, physicals, lab work and medication management are some of the services available to us.

Like many of the clients here, I had not been to a doctor for a very long time, and it showed in the various examinations and assessments. I have been prescribed various medications for high blood pressure over the years, but nothing more than daily tablets. It is normal for people in active addiction to neglect physical health and avoid seeing doctors or therapists.

> *The highest recovery success rates are in the Alternative Track. Based on how I feel since my arrival, and the daily progress I am making, I believe I made the right decision when I chose the Alternative Track.*

I have been grateful these past weeks for the professional care given to me in all aspects of treatment. I now take over twenty pills throughout the day for high blood pressure, PTSD, depression and anxiety. I feel good and the levels of medication are adjusted as needed each week by the professionals here at the Center.

People often try to avoid medications in the healing of themselves. This makes no sense to me. If a doctor, upon examination, prescribes medication as part of our recovery, then not taking it, is simply addict behavior. By that I mean, *addicts* often fall into various levels of denial in early recovery. It amounts to making excuses or second guessing the professionals who are trying to help them.

Any reputable treatment facility will have procedures in place for the administration and security of their clients' medications.

When I arrived at Hope by the Sea, I put my life in their capable hands. The most important component was to develop a trust with all staff at every level of care. I believe the lack of honesty with yourself and those who are trying to help you, results in a great many failures in treatment today. Hope by the Sea, based on my observations in the first weeks here, embraces the above model of treatment. It is the combination of medicine and various therapies working together that will achieve the desired outcome.

My history with drugs and alcohol covers nearly thirty years of my life. I have used opioids, benzodiazepines and amphetamines i.e., Oxycodone, Vicodin, Xanax, Valium and Adderall. Thousands in the United States die every year overdosing on these prescription medications. There are dozens of medications in each of these categories that are prescribed every day for disorders like: anxiety, chronic pain and ADHD.

Birthplace of Addiction

All the medications listed above and hundreds more are used by millions of Americans every year. Most people taking these medicines never become addicted to them or use them as not prescribed.

Nevertheless, people like me and thousands of others take them in an abusive way, often acquiring them illegally to satisfy an addiction. In my case, I combined these dangerous medications with alcohol on many occasions. This reckless behavior often leads to lengthy blackouts and near brushes with death.

There was a time not so long ago when my medical doctor prescribed Xanax, Oxycodone, and Adderall for my use all at the same time. I abused these drugs like any drug I have taken. When the label on the bottle read *may cause drowsiness or dizziness, alcohol may intensify this effect*, it was like giving me a directive to maximize getting drunk or high. At the time, viewing prescription meds any other way did not make sense to me.

Heavy drinking while taking these powerful pills is a formula for death. Why I am alive today remains unanswered, except to say God must have a plan for me. This reckless addictive behavior can cause black-outs for days and days with no memory of it. When people tried to tell me what I did during this time, it still did not restore the events to my mind. I could have hurt or killed people while driving and not even remember it. When I consider the reality of this addictive behavior, it humbles me and makes me grateful for my life today.

Active addiction made me cunning and self-serving in my quest to fulfill my next drunk or high. I was a successful executive in 2013, and I went to my medical doctor and convincingly discussed the necessary symptoms to obtain what I wanted. My doctor is not to blame. The responsibility falls to me the moment I was not truthful with him.

When I consider the reality of this addictive behavior, it humbles me and makes me grateful for my life today.

It is this rampant abuse of prescription drugs that gives many families and individual addicts pause when the professionals at places like Hope by the Sea prescribe numerous prescription medications. This often becomes a source of tension for everyone involved in the treatment and aftercare process. I am not referring to the prescription medicine in the preceding paragraph that contributed to my addictive behaviors. The medications prescribed to me here are by medical professionals who are aware of my addictions. However, it is so important to ask the physician questions about each medication. Questions like: What is this medicine for? and What side effects are there?" Asking questions will engage the addict in their own treatment as well as provide information to loved ones who are concerned about the medications. Where my treatment is concerned, I consider the unasked question, the only bad one.

CHAPTER 16

Kim, my Case Manager, met with me briefly a couple of days after our last meeting. She said I would continue with Nancy as my Therapist and would begin meeting with her twice a week. This is not the outcome I wanted, but I have faith in Hope by the Sea, so I decide to have an open mind about my meeting with Nancy today.

Nancy was pecking away at her computer when I walked in and took a seat next to the door. She is a good-looking woman about five foot five inches tall somewhere in her fifties maybe.

Nancy turned away from her desk, and facing me, she smiled and said, "Hello, David, it is good to see you."

I return the smile, uncross my arms and say, "Nice to see you too."

Reaching for a pad off her desk, she said, "I want to talk about our last session, and what the clinical team had to say about your concerns with the therapy going forward." I nodded in acknowledgment, and she continued. "The clinical team believes you have made a lot of progress these first few weeks; and in my observations of you in group therapies and around the Center, I believe you have more light in your eyes."

Considering her words carefully, after a long pause, I said, "It has been twenty-one days since I arrived, and I have begun to feel there may be hope for me."

She said, "At the time I said I didn't want to cut you open so to speak, because I didn't believe you could handle it. Based on the last week or so, I believe we can become more aggressive and meet more often."

This sounds good to me, and I am happy about meeting more often. So, I said, "Okay!"

Nancy began grabbing the many baskets of small toy figures on the ground. There must be two or three hundred toys from green army men to transformers and dolls. Reaching for a tub of sand, she said, "Okay, what I want you to do is divide the sand with a line down the middle. I want the left side to be an arrangement of you now, and on the other side I want you to create you in the future."

Nancy spoke at a rapid clip, gusting at around 150 words per minute sometimes, and I need some time to take it all in.

This is quite the picture here on the floor. I must say I am a little impressed at the exercise. "So, how many of the toy figures can I have for each side?" I asked.

"No rules. Use as many or few as you like. I'll be quiet now and when you finish, I will tell you what I see, and we'll talk about it."

I get on the floor surrounded by toys and a gray tub half full of sand. I make a line down the middle with my finger and scan all the toys. I decide on a large, monster bird-like figure, and a small boy with a cup on his head for the right now side. On the other side I put a man, boy and girl with a house and car.

"All done," I announce as I look it over from my chair.

Nancy has been watching my every move. She finally said, "There is a lot going on in this small space. You identify as a child now, and this scary image with wings I see flying away at some time in the future, but not yet. The future seems happy and bright with a home and family. What do you see?"

I said, "Well, the boy is me now, and the monster figure with wings is my second and third grade teacher who after thirty-five years still has power over me. I have nightmares, and I fear her. I haven't been able to get past it, and I fear I never will." I wipe the tears from my face and continue, "The other side is the future, and I put me, a house, car and my two kids. We will likely never share the same house, but I do want to have a relationship again one day."

Nancy is making some notes and then looks at me and says, "The future you made for yourself is bright and shows family unity, and I believe you know it is possible; otherwise, the figure you chose for the teacher would not have wings."

A good share of the work in the Alternative Track is understanding the power the subconscious has on our brains. I consider that for a few moments and say, "I agree. I believe my children and I will one day have a happy relationship. What I don't understand is why this teacher from so long ago has this incredible power over me? Working through the trauma these past weeks is doing little to stop the nightmares or the fear still plaguing me," I commented.

Nancy related, "Traumas in our lives are powerful, and they require a lot from us to move past them. I want you to know from the outside looking in, your work is apparent in what I see in you. The power she has will lessen by your writing and other therapies we do here. It will likely never be gone all together. The best outcome is to come to a place where you can accept and live without it defining your tomorrow."

I replied, "This work is proving to be the most difficult of my life so far. I see the necessity, and I am discovering some positive things along the way."

Nancy looks at the clock and says, "We have gone over into your break, so we will stop here and continue in a few days."

"Okay, I will see you then," I say and walk out the door. She told me to close the door because taking the sandbox down in front of me would send messages to my subconscious of both of my worlds collapsing. Not completely understanding this, I step outside to have a cigarette.

Kim likes to meet after lunch, and I am five minutes early. I take a seat on her couch. After the usual pleasantries, she asks if I have completed the assignment due today.

My Case Manager is a tall woman with glasses who is a no-nonsense woman. I came to this conclusion while witnessing some of the younger clients sassing back to her. I had expected her to ask about the paper and looking through my bag I pull out the book where I have written the letter. "Got it right here," I say with a smile.

"Would you mind reading it out loud to me?" She requested.

"Not at all," I said, turning to the first page of the letter.

What Does It Mean to Love David?

October 25, 2016

Love is one of those words that gets thrown around a lot, often with little thought to what it really means. Some end phone calls with *love-ya-bye*; others begin and end with a proclamation of love.

Webster's Dictionary defines love as: A feeling of strong or constant affection for a person. I suppose it is a healthy way to feel about one's self.

If I am ever to love myself, it would be important to live in a way -- I could admire; I could respect; I could be loyal to and even honor. I see these qualities in others but have rarely considered them in myself until recently in my gratitude work. While I find this exercise to be valuable and useful, it has not yet been helpful in raising my core self-esteem.

I have spent a lifetime feeling internal bad will and hatred for myself. Loving me is an endeavor that will no doubt be a pile of work. I didn't become me overnight. I became me through learned behavior and practice. It will be the same way I expect in allowing goodness to be accepted back into my life.

Being a loving person to me is becoming someone capable of receiving and expressing love to another. I have at times in my life demonstrated what it means to love. Transitioning this actionable process inward on me should be quite simple based on the information available. Then why in Heaven's Name is it nearly impossible to envision myself doing this for my betterment?

It has been said by some throughout my life I tend to over complicate seemingly simple to understand things in life. I am **quite** sure this isn't one of those times!

Loving David looks like allowing myself to receive compliments and be accepting of goodness in my life. It means continuing to be kind to others and good to animals because it feels good. It means being open to ideas that may not always make sense. Loving myself is a lesson in patience and will require a measure of loyalty and work ethic so it does not die.

Love isn't always tangible and requires a measure of faith and trust to blossom. Perhaps it means loving others and me as God loves us all. I believe loving David will be a labor of love lasting my whole life through.

That was good, David, how do you feel about it? Kim inquired.

"The feelings in my writing often confuse me. I didn't realize it, but rarely do I question the genuine nature of feelings. Are my feelings real or are they masks to hide my shame? My life has been full of masks I created and wore to protect myself from people becoming aware of all the shame I harbored and hid beneath them. I have kept everyone in my life at arm's length. I was simply petrified of anyone getting close enough to hurt me.

When I reflect on my life with a restored memory, it is easy to see I wore masks for almost every situation life has thrown at me. I now know the reason why I have low self-esteem, and it has given me pause to endlessly stew over my life. This letter about love, has stirred up feelings held deeply inside of me all my life. I know what love is from watching others like my Mom and Dad.

I would project emotions for what I thought others would accept without triggering a lot of follow-up questions. This all seemed normal to me; I don't know another way. When it comes to feelings and emotions, I find myself to be an infant in many ways."

Processing feelings honestly is ridiculously hard for me, so I said, "Okay, I will keep working to better understand my feelings and what to do with them.

Talking through this with Kim is hard for me, and picking up on it she injects, "David, we all wear masks in life at times, some more than others."

I contemplate her input for a minute and think about the relationships I've had. I think of my kids and realize I don't know what feelings are masked and what feelings are real. So, I ask, "What do I do about all this confusing chaos I feel inside of me?"

Kim answered, "It's okay to just realize you are learning to process feelings. I understand what you are going through, and I can tell you from personal experience it gets better."

It gets better? It gets better! I have always lacked patience, but I realize I need to give things a chance to work. My mind gets stuck lately, and often I don't know what to do about it. Processing feelings honestly is ridiculously hard for me, so I said, "Okay, I will keep working to better understand my feelings and what to do with them. I appreciate your feedback."

Kim is a shrewd cat and considers all her words carefully, so when she said, "Do you realize the amazing progress you have made in a very short time?" Not waiting for an answer, she added, "I think you know me well enough to realize I don't pump hot air into anyone's tail pipe. If I say you are doing well, you can bet your last dollar I mean what I say."

"I appreciate the vote of confidence, and I will put forth some effort to acknowledge the positives in my life more than I do right now." I reply with as much sincerity as I can muster at the moment.

Not missing a beat, she said, "Let's change topics for now. As we are out of time, I will see you next week."

With a sigh of relief and wiping away my tears, I said, "Sounds good. I'll see you then."

CHAPTER 17

It is three o'clock in the morning, and I just woke up in a cold sweat crying. I am forty-three years old, and I just had a nightmare as real as the night sky. Before I came to California, I had them almost every time I would try and sleep. Now I take medicine to block my dreams according to the doctors, but I am experiencing no less than two nightmares per week. Generally, I cannot go back to sleep when it happens, so I go out by the pool to think about things.

Mostly, I am depressed in times like this. The memories of the actual nightmare are choppy at best. They fade in minutes of being awake, leaving me physically exhausted, yet unable to rest. The fear of going through life as I am right now, is a horrible picture. Will I ever be happy again? These nightmares are crippling because they take so much out of me.

I often reflect on my life and wonder what has become of me? Looking at my emotional problems and being able to trace the hows and whys brings little solace to me. Successes and things I have achieved in my life, leave me nothing to show but a wake of hurt and despair. I was once a successful businessman rising to the top of my profession only to be self-sabotaged and destroyed.

> *I guess I'll just sit here awhile, breathe the night air and try to count my blessings.*

My life as father to my children is full of regret and guilt. Sitting out on the patio of the Horse Shoe House looking at the lights across the city is peaceful and bright. I wonder will my life be either? Nights like these are difficult for me. Sometimes writing pulls me out of the funk, sometimes not.

I guess I'll just sit here awhile, breathe the night air and try to count my blessings.

CHAPTER 18

There are a couple of new faces in the Alternative Track today; I hope they stick to it and do some work. A lot of folks seem to switch tracks after a couple of days. Frank does not allow people who won't do the work to stay, and he lets everyone know it every day. The passion he has for the Alternative Track, and belief in all of us who work, is inspiring to me.

Frank asked if anyone has work to share, and I want to get my letter to the teacher Mrs. F off my chest.

Letter to Mrs. F. No. 4

October 27, 2016

Dear Mrs. F,

In fourth through ninth grades my life was tumultuous. I was almost always in trouble it seemed. I took no joy in anything having to do with the Glenville school system.

Because the school was small, every teacher already seemed to have me labeled as a problem child, although a few of them took me at face value. I was gloomy and depressed. I wanted attention. I wanted to be noticed. I wanted not to feel worthless.

I longed for understanding and friendship. One thing I get confused about is -- at what point did I bury all this horror, never again to be seen until 2016? As I write in search of answers, I remember some very terrible things.

At two o'clock each day we went to gym as a class. Good weather was outside and bad weather indoors. We often played kickball.

One day I was in the equipment room looking for a soccer ball when you came in abruptly and closed the windowless door. I froze like a sculpture unable to move. What Hell is this, I thought?

My insides were chaotic, and time seemed to stand still. You picked up a rubber bat used for playing softball. Then you grabbed me by my hair and jerked me toward you, and you said in my ear if I made a sound I would never have recess again. You hit my back, legs, and butt for what seemed an eternity. I just stood there and never made a sound as you hit me with the bat until you tired and labored for breath.

I remember seeing marks when I showered, and the water stung something awful. My pajamas and clothes covered the marks, so nobody could see. I also remember being scared to go to sleep because you would terrorize my dreams.

I spend a lot of time these days trying to piece together the why? I realize this is a waste of time, and I will likely never know your motives or intent. I write how evil you are over and over. You are a demonic monster and destroyer of youthful growth.

> *Then you grabbed me by my hair and jerked me toward you, and you said in my ear if I made a sound I would never have recess again. You hit my back, legs, and butt for what seemed an eternity.*

As much as I find you thoroughly and completely disgusting because of your actions and remain scared by the ripple effect you've had in my life, I shouldn't let you live rent free in my heart. After all, it's not like you know the damage you've caused.

How is it that you got the entire faculty to look away as if it were best to ignore the ugliness in their midst?

I resent you the most for what I became after third grade. The boy I became on the other side was a stranger to all who knew me two short years earlier. I couldn't grasp simple things like right and wrong, or, that is was okay to take a stand on things you believe in. I was not able to express feelings of like, love, or affection in general due primarily to my low opinion of myself.

At some point, I blocked all the evil things that happened in those two years, so I didn't understand why I felt or behaved the way I did.

Counselors, teachers, parents, no one could seem to help me, and often said I was holding back. I just lacked the ability to remember all your torturous behaviors toward me. I began to believe I was a cold-hearted, evil and nasty person, as you had reminded me of daily, all those years ago.

I want so badly to turn the page; and eventually, I will be able to. Guidance and hard work is showing me that this too shall pass.

David

Whenever someone was reading a letter, Frank was always listening. He often rubs his forehead with thumb and index finger meeting just over the bridge of his nose. At any given time, there are as many as forty clients in the Alternative Track between the Men's and Women's Centers. Frank's ability to recollect something from a letter or exercise many weeks back with perfect clarity is astounding to me because he takes no notes as we read, just listens intently.

After a thirty second or so pause, Frank looked up and said, "How many have we written to the teacher now?"

As I thumbed through my book I said, "This makes six or seven if we include the letters to my younger self."

Frank said, "Have you written a reversal to the letter you wrote to yourself at eight years old yet?" He was doing the forehead thing again and continued, "I want you to focus on how you felt in the closet and in general at the age of eight or nine. Be as specific as possible, and we will need to get into home life. Something must have been going on that you didn't tell anyone."

I thought about what my home life was like and asked, "Do you want me to do letters to Mom and Dad?" I asked for clarification.

Frank said, "You will need to write to parents and grandparents too; but now we need to keep our focus on the teacher and feelings you have about that."

Everything here seems to boil down to feelings. I am learning I know very little about such things. Identifying, processing, expressing are all so foreign to me. "I will have the reversal done for tomorrow," I told him.

"Okay, nice job," he said.

Sometimes I feel like I am making a lot of progress and have a good understanding of where I need to go. Other times, I feel like a kid in kindergarten learning how to feel for the first time.

CHAPTER 19

After lunch, I am coming back from feeding the horse, Topper, an apple and decide on the table with the most shade. I might have been writing for fifteen minutes or so when Harlan took up the other side of the picnic table with his big smile. It always made me smile too. He handed his sign-in sheet to me, and said, "How are you doing' today?"

I am working on letters and not getting very far with them. Trying to recall things from thirty-five years ago is difficult. Trying to associate and identify feelings is frustrating. Looking up, I answered, "You know the drill, living the dream one nightmare at a time."

Harlan has been telling me for several days I need to be less serious and to find a way to have some fun. Harlan began working in the treatment business when he got sober more than thirty years ago, and he knows his stuff. He asked me, "What are you writing about today?"

> *"How much do you think a kite costs?" I give a who-the-heck knows look, and Harlan continued, "We have that ball field down there, and it is perfect for kites. Everyone likes a kite."*

I told him about the letter I read in class today and about the reversal I am writing for tomorrow's class. I said, "I get really emotional when I try to be my eight-year-old self and write to me now about what I felt then. It's just so damn hard."

One thing about Harlan, he always knows what and what not to say in these serious, emotionally charged moments. In this instance, he said, "How much do you think a kite costs?" I give a who-the-heck knows look, and Harlan continued, "We have that ball field down there, and it is perfect for kites. Everyone likes a kite."

I am thinking about the logistics of flying a kite, and how fun it might be on a windy day. Mostly, I am happy to be out of my head if only for a moment or two. "Something tells me they didn't teach this kite business in counselor school, huh?"

He began laughing and said, "Nope, and you're getting a bill because insurance won't pay for it either!"

We part ways for the day, and I am in a much better place. Getting out of myself each day is proving to be an essential part of healing. It is hard for me to do. I have always been a type-A workaholic. The idea of investing in self is like learning to ride a bike backwards – it isn't natural.

CHAPTER 20

Writing from the perspective of being eight years old and talking about myself today is not an easy thing. Facing what turns out to be my biggest fear makes my tear ducts work overtime. I can't help but wonder if these memories and nightmares will ever leave me.

It was after midnight when I went to bed after completing the letter I am going to read today. At three o'clock, I was jolted awake by the evil of my dreams, and it was as if I were back in her dark, smelly closet. I felt the electricity. My heart was racing. I was sweating and crying like a child. After last night, it is difficult to see the wisdom of reliving all of this.

In Frank's class this morning, listening to another client read his letter is helpful to me. My brothers and sisters in the Alternative Track have become as close and dear to me as anyone I have ever known including my own brothers. We all come from different walks of life and have varying interests. However, what it boils down to is, we are all learning the same life tools together in hopes of living free of addiction and having a chance at happiness someday.

> *At three o'clock, I was jolted awake by the evil of my dreams, and it was as if I were back in her dark, smelly closet. I felt the electricity. My heart was racing. I was sweating and crying like a child.*

Pulling my notebook out, I said, "I will read my letter now." This letter is a reversal to my current self from my eight-year-old self.

Letter from myself at eight years to me at forty-three years.

October 28, 2017

Dear David,

"It is dark. I am shaking. I don't know why I keep getting scared at every sound, wondering if Mrs. F is coming to hurt me again. I sit in this closet for what seems forever, but it's just recess I think.

I don't understand why you wrote to me or how you know all this stuff, so I guess you must be from later. I hate school so much. I don't want to come here; I want to stay with Grandpa in the field or even be with Grandma. They never ask me about school and just let me be me. It's very safe there.

Mom and Dad are good parents who love me. I just hate and can't stand talking about school. I am afraid things could get worse. After all, she is my teacher again this year. She hits me more, yells constantly, shaking me, telling me to keep still and straighten up.

Why does she put me in the closet and shock me with that thing over and over? It looks like the cattle shocker at our uncle's house up the road. This one does not have the long tube on it. This is about the size of an iron or hand mixer with something sticking out about the size of a shoe. It has a wet cloth over it kind of like the stuff Mom wraps around a cut after I wipe out on my bike.

> *She hits me more, yells constantly, shaking me, telling me to keep still and straighten up.*

Life is not like first grade any longer. Things were a lot of fun then, and I was learning stuff. I don't ever want to learn anything again if it doesn't involve farming with Grandpa. He didn't go to school, and he's smart as can be. I shouldn't have to go either.

I can't take the pain the shocking thing does to me. Then, there is the way she hits me with things or uses those dry scratchy hands to hurt me. She is constantly yelling I am nothing but an awful boy and I'm just no good or ever will be.

It is hard for me to think I do not deserve all of this for something I have done. All I do at home is play with my farm tractor toys, ride my bike, swim, go to Sunday School and to Grandpa's house. I keep my tractors in the living room and use all the carpets in the house as fields to disk, plow, plant or harvest.

I don't know what to say to you about any of this. My brothers pick on me because I am so weird; and I don't have friends for the same reason. I don't fit in anywhere. Kids at church are like my brothers who are mean because I am not like them.

Dad works nights, and I don't see him much except on weekends. We go to church, and if I'm lucky we go to Grandpa and Grandma's house afterward.

Grandpa lets me mow the lawn every week, and I love it. It takes three hours, and he has a cool lawn tractor.

I also spend a lot of time with our dogs: Goldie, Skippy and Teenie. They like me and protect me from stuff too. Once in a while I sneak Goldie into my room, and she keeps me safe. She jumps in my bed when I have nightmares, and I pet her.

Anyway, everything lasts forever at school and all morning I wonder if I am going to the closet at recess. I try to purposely get the attention of the principal, so I can be in his office instead of the classroom. He sometimes spanks me, depending upon what I do. It is nothing by comparison to being punished by Mrs. F. He has me stand in the corner until the buses arrive to take us home. This is hard to write. I hate talking about this. It makes me sad. I am all alone."

David

"One of the harder letters to read out loud in class?" When Frank asked how it was, I didn't answer for a minute. "Troublesome, I slept very little last night, terrible nightmares, were so realistic."

Frank said, "You're beginning to release the darkness that has lived in you so long. You have begun to feel and recognize the feelings you need to release."

I admit I don't comprehend what he is talking about all the time. I have had to put all my faith and trust in him and this process to an enormous degree. I explain the best I can the horror I feel, "The memories coming back to me when I am writing are vivid and powerful. They completely overwhelm me most of the time. I want it to stop. I don't want to be afraid anymore."

> "The memories coming back to me when I am writing are vivid and powerful. They completely overwhelm me most of the time. I want it to stop. I don't want to be afraid anymore."

He said, "Remember, we deal with the negative, so we can create positives in our lives. The negative is why you drank and did drugs because you were trying to numb and dull your pain. Addiction is a symptom of a bigger thing; it is not your problem." He said with firm conviction, then continued, "Keep writing; write about home life before and during this time. You're doing a good job. Keep writing and focusing on the feelings as you are experiencing them; it's fine if you repeat."

Feelings are so elusive to me, or maybe it is their meaning that I find so difficult to comprehend in this work. "I will begin work on the next letter; should I be writing to parents or brothers?" I asked.

Frank said, "Eventually, yes. Right now, we need to stay on the teacher and that time of your life. I get the difficulty. I can tell you the sooner we get past the teacher, the better for you."

"Okay." I uttered.

It will soon be a month since I arrived at this place, and I have never worked so hard in my whole life. Nothing has ever challenged me to this level. Anyone who says treatment isn't a matter of life and death, either isn't ready to stop, or is still in denial.

Another thing has happened to me in the last month. I no longer believe I cannot be helped. Like many who enter this place, I was completely lost and a broken shell of a human being. Even before leaving the Midwest to come to California, I had little faith I would ever be anything but a failure for the rest of my life. Now, I don't feel a lot better; however, if I continue to put in the work, I may one day be better.

I feel I have been given a gift in uncovering what happened to me so long ago. Okay, maybe gift isn't the word yet. When I look at all the whys and why nots in my life, whether it be good, bad or ugly, it all goes back to the second and third grades when I changed forever.

My whole life I have always had these overwhelming feelings I wasn't good enough. I believed I wasn't a good person. I grew up in a good home, and I could never figure out why I felt the way I did. Why was I not like other people? The older I became the more entrenched these beliefs became inside of me.

Alcohol and drug use were part of my life at an early age. My brothers and people I have known over the years would be able to take them or leave them. As for me, I could never numb what hurt so much. Like my feelings, I never understood why I could not control my use. When the goal and purpose of use is to reach black-out levels of intoxication to achieve numbness, it isn't difficult to understand how addiction takes shape.

It surprised me how many trauma victims suppressed their memories also. They included people who were raped, molested, tortured and those who experienced multiple acts of violence. When this happens, and we try to live our lives with the trauma existing only at a sub-conscience level, our lives become a projection of those deep-seeded feelings of contempt, anger, sadness and self-loathing only to name a few. These memories may or may not ever surface. Each trauma victim is unique in how their mind processes the event. It is like repairing a hole in a dam with duct tape, the hole still seeps some water. Depending on the pressure of the dam, more and more water gets through and sometimes the dam even breaks, flooding your life all at once.

It's hard not to replay life without this terrible trauma and to consider all the outcomes that might have been. Ultimately, it always ends in a pity party of depression. What I try to do is take some comfort in knowing by processing this horrible thing now, it may mean for the first time, it will no longer sabotage my future.

I am starting to believe second and third grade are really the birthplace of all wrongs in my life. I have been looking for the **birthplace of my addiction** for as long as I can remember, and I have discovered it in 2016 in southern California at Hope by the Sea.

I have been looking for the birthplace of my addiction for as long as I can remember, and I have discovered it in 2016 in southern California at Hope by the Sea.

Frank's class is finished, and it is time for lunch.

CHAPTER 21

Topper keeps me a little longer today eating two apples instead of his one only preference. He must know I need more time with him today. He loved the apples and allowed me to pet his soft nose longer than usual. What a treat he is for me! Horses are second only to golden retrievers in my love of animals. Thus, I was a little late getting back to the picnic table.

Harlan showed up per usual and sat down across from me at the picnic table. He must have known I wanted to talk to him about something because he said nothing. Therefore, I started our daily exchange by offering, "Today in Alternative Track some things were uncovered to make me somewhat optimistic. It could be an epiphany of sorts."

I could tell I had his interest because he put his clipboard down and settled in. "Don't act so surprised! After all, you are here to learn, are you not? Hell! Occasionally, something we say as staff actually sticks," he said with a mischievous smile.

> *I could tell I had his interest because he put his clipboard down and settled in. "Don't act so surprised! After all, you are here to learn, are you not?*

I begin to tell him my thoughts about the years going back to second and third grade. I explain it is a focal point in my life. So, I asked, "Do you think those years are my **birthplace of addiction** along with a lot of other defects of character?"

Harlan considered it for a few moments and said, "It could be I suppose, but why is it a profound discovery, or am I not understanding you correctly?"

"You understand correctly," I said, then continued, "The reason I believe it to be so significant is I have wondered often in torment why I am the way I am, and how did I get this way? I am still working it out in my head, yet I see enormous potential in being able to come to peace with my past because now I have the answer to the how, where, and when I got to be the way I am."

The **birthplace of my addiction** was not when I took my first drink or picked up some drugs for the first time which is the common place people believe and embrace as the cause and beginning of addiction. For me it was in second and third grade when my trauma occurred. It was where my personal Hell began, and the mental afflictions I suffer still today lead right back to that place and time. My addictive behaviors came many years later. With my traumatic memories buried deep within me, I was left with an overwhelming belief I was no good. This self-loathing spilled out into every part of me; it was a hard-wired core belief.

Harlan is a firm believer in Alcoholics Anonymous and the twelve steps. He is one of the facilitators of the Traditional Track at Hope by the Sea. He has shown me how he believes the Alternative Track has many similarities to AA. While I agree with the spirit of what he is saying, we agree to disagree on this point while keeping our mutual respect.

Harlan considered what I had said very carefully before he said, "I understand the value you see in your position. Newly discovered information can have a tremendous impact on your individual program. One concern I would have for you would be, having tunnel vision and not seeing other valuable tools and gifts you will likely be exposed to in your time here and when you leave. Have you considered this?"

"Valuable insight," I replied, then continued, "Having only been in my head a few hours, I don't think I have made any firm conclusions other than I know it's pretty exciting. To some degree, this second and third grade business has been in my head in some capacity for about eight months with little positives to take from it. I believe those outlooks might be changing."

> *The birthplace of my addiction was not when I took my first drink or picked up some drugs for the first time which is the common place people believe and embrace as the cause and beginning of addiction.*

"Have you decided how long you are going to be staying with us?" He asked with an empathetic expression.

I said, "I intend to stay ninety days, if not longer. Thirty days has gone by in a blink, and while I have started some good work, it is far from over."

Smiling again, Harlan said, "That's a nice decision I doubt you will ever regret."

"I don't want to have to do this again. I may have another run of booze and drugs in me, I guess only God knows. I don't think I have another recovery in me. That boils down to life or death, and I don't want to die from addiction." These statements are repeated throughout the book because it is true and is worth repeating.

Harlan said, "I don't either son; I don't either."

Most of us who come to Hope by the Sea, or any treatment facility for that matter, expect privacy, confidentiality and anonymity. With my own story, I share as I see fit in this book. I do not tell anyone else's story in a way it could possibly identify them. The people I live with and go to treatment with here are among my closest friends, and some of the finest men I have ever had the privilege of knowing.

My roommate, Tom, is leaving on Monday, and he will be missed by many. He is taking all of us in the House out for a nice dinner tonight. This token of generosity is a demonstration of the kind of man he is.

Had it not been for Tom, it is unlikely I would have God in my life again. His example of what a Godly man is, and his friendship are things for which I am truly grateful.

We went to the Outback on Saturday night with Tom, and we sat around a large table together enjoying each other's company over a great meal. The fellowship was wonderful. We told stories for a couple of hours and left the restaurant with bloated bellies and smiling faces. A night I shall never forget!

> *Had it not been for Tom, it is unlikely I would have God in my life again. His example of what a Godly man is, and his friendship are things for which I am truly grateful.*

CHAPTER 22

In the van on the way to the Center I feel anxious. I haven't been able to stop thinking about my life, or rather what my life might be had I never known Mrs. F. Would I have been married or had children? Would I have become addicted to alcohol and drugs? I know thinking like this is a one-way ticket to nowhere, yet my mind is drawn to these what ifs. I guess I am ultrasensitive to how experiences and decisions have consequences, and they are permanent even if unforeseen. I realize I cannot change what was, only what is and what will be, are in my realm of influence.

On Mondays, we write future projections and share them. It is a letter to ourselves from ourselves some point in the future. I find this exercise to be among my favorites. People look at them as goals and dreams, but I look at them as a glimpse into the subconscious. Positive nourishment is worked through often in this room. Today, I will write to myself from three years into my future.

Future Projection

October 31, 2019

As I look out over the city enjoying fresh fruit and Arabic coffee, I realize today is, in fact, a great day to live.

I never would have believed *Birthplace of Addiction* would become a best seller. A record of the journey to overcome my addictive behaviors has been quite a ride. It has been three years since I was a patient at Hope by the Sea, and my experience there has been the footing of the life I enjoy today.

Raush Limbaugh is interviewing me on his show today, live from his New York Studio, kicking off my book tour that spans forty-seven cities in the next three months. Hope by the Sea was gracious in allowing this leave to pursue my dream of helping people overcome their own addictive behaviors. My work as a Case Manager and Therapist in the same facility and treatment track where I was a client only three years ago is nothing shy of miraculous. I have been humbled and truly blessed by this work.

After the interview, I met my finance for lunch in Manhattan. There, we planned the next few months of travel with a few days here and there for fun, leisure, and relaxation together. I can hardly believe I am getting married again next year.

Life is so incredible this late autumn day in New York. The day winds down at Freedom Tower and the 9-11 Memorial. I have goose bumps; I feel honored and privileged to pay my respects to those who lost their lives here. Freedom is what sums me up now. The chains of addiction are in the past, and I am free. Free to be happy, free to be sad and free to live.

David

"Finally, I can retire!" Frank said with a smile and continued, "Very nice writing. Isn't it amazing how much easier it is to write about tomorrow in a positive way than it is to find positives in your past?"

I said, "I enjoy writing like this and am beginning to understand how relevant the subconscious is in our lives."

"Your future projections should be over the top positive. The subconscious processes everything and doesn't sort information or judge the way the conscious does. What we project as people is a lot more of a snapshot of the subconscious than it is the conscious. It is why we write projections; why we write positive memories; and why our daily gratitude work is so important," Frank opined.

Frank often reminds us of this because it is so important, and because there are some in the Alternative Track who don't do *The Work*. This frustrates him because he knows if *The Work* isn't being done here, it will not be done when we leave; and a return to addictive behavior will ensue.

He continued, "Training your newly created neural paths happen when you leave here and continue to do *The Work* on your own. Now you do *The Work* because I ask you to do it; it is not the same thing. Here I am teaching you to use this life tool and begin some routines and disciplines. It will be up to you to decide if it is important enough to continue."

On break, between classes I asked Frank if this tool we are learning to use has a wider use than what we are doing here. I want to know if in addition to eradicating addiction through new neural paths, could I enrich my life with it for other things?

Then, Frank told me about the work he does with cancer patients and other terminal patients. The gratitude work, future projections, and getting the negatives processed, puts their minds in a position so to speak to work on eradicating their diseases in a way similarly to how we position ourselves with addiction. I need to bring this up again when we have more time to discuss it.

CHAPTER 23

Letters to be read is how the next two hours are allotted on Mondays, and it appears there are many to be shared today. I decide to go first with the seventh letter in the series to Mrs. F.

Letter to Mrs. F- # 7

October 31, 2016

Dear Mrs. F,

I have three older brothers, and they are three, five and six years older than me. Today, I understand brothers razz and pick on one another as a form of expression. I even get nobody outside of the family can pick on us without risking aggravation from all of us. I wish I had known this code when I was in your closet being shocked. You chastised me, hit me and endlessly hurt my feelings to the level that what remained were only hopeless and worthless feelings toward myself.

I wish I had known brotherhood was strong in 1982. Instead, I believed for too many years my brothers were mean and always picked on me. When they excluded me from activities, I thought they were ashamed of me and believed as you believed. I came to believe I was not worthy of any goodness in my life, not ever!

This is all your fault you psycho, sadistic, dirt bag. Because you tortured me for two years, my childhood and adolescence were ripped away from me. You see I didn't know much of anything at the age of eight and nine. I wasn't supposed to.

Making and keeping a friend, accepting praise, looking people in the eye, receiving love, trusting people, a sense of good and bad, even right from wrong were beyond my grasp thanks to you.

For instance, it must be okay to lie, corrupt, inflict physical pain by electric shock, choke and torment mentally to the point breathing becomes a chore. The reality is simple: you committed egregious acts against a child you were charged with teaching and caring for while school was in session. You had absolutely zero consequences for the Hell you unleashed on me; not just for two years, but for the years of ripple effect that is my life.

My perception at age eight and nine was – the problem was me. I am the awful human being who received your justice. All I knew for sure back then was you had power over all things in my life from the first school day in September to the last day in late May. These are the facts of the values I had instilled in me going into fourth grade.

My brothers, my parents and my teachers all had serious doubts if I was ever honest or had the moral character of my family values. My father once told me he couldn't tell either way if I was lying or telling the truth. I was twelve or thirteen, and I believe my Dad had no idea the effect of those words. Words like these had only one place to go, the only one they could go. It was my own perceived values, my sense of right and wrong. He confirmed my misguided view of myself you had given me by your words and actions a few years earlier.

All those years ago you left an ocean of scars and a desert of hopelessness; a misguided boy who built his life with a core belief of being a bad, awful person who deserved nothing good. Somewhere along the line, I don't know when, I blocked you and remembered only a skewed vision of anything resembling the truth.

What an evil witch you are, Mrs. F. It is you who should be in torment and despair, not me.

I have been writing about you for nearly a month thinking about you almost exclusively. I must tell you I think you may have to hire pall bearers at your own funeral because I can't imagine many, if any, would attend otherwise.

I grew up having dogs as best friends, but my grandpa was the one I felt safest around. I have no doubt Mom and Dad loved me, and they wanted me to be happy. I also know how disgusted they were with the school and some of the teachers over the years. It was likely a very difficult spot to be in as parents. In the end, they never stopped fighting for me.

I wish I would have told them what you did to me; if I had, would I be here at this wonderful place of healing? I must have faith there is hope, and it can manifest itself into reality.

I hate what I have become in life; I squandered a great many things, important things and people as well. I don't see me forgiving you; you hurt me so completely and left nothing but Hell for me. I hope Hell is what is in store for you. How many others did you hurt? Was it two or five or ten or seventy? You make me sick. If I had told somebody, maybe you wouldn't have hurt others too.

David

"Good. How was it?" Frank asked.
"It is definitely easier to read than it was writing this. The memories become so vivid of her actions."
"So, work on connecting to your feelings; write more from your eight and nine-year-old self; and try get to what life was like prior to second grade. There must be a reason you didn't tell your folks," Frank concluded.
"It is difficult remembering second grade, yet alone before, but I will begin to try," I said a bit uncertain.
Frank said, "Okay, so you're working on a letter from eight and nine years old to now. Let's also do a letter prior to seven years old, parents, brothers, and other family members. So that's two, then let's do a reverse from the teacher to your current self. Remember on all of them, to focus on the feelings and not as much on the story."
"A reversal from the teacher; all right, I'll start today. This should be interesting to say the least."

CHAPTER 24

Hope by the Sea does many things to ensure the safety of the clients they serve. Despite that, sometimes people relapse. A relapse, put simply, is a return to addictive behavior ending in the return to the use of a drug of choice. Two people relapsed over the weekend -- testing positive for opioids. Urinalysis tests are done twice each week, and on demand if staff feels a need. With this rigid policy, there won't be anyone getting away with relapsing.

Testing positive for drugs is one of the few things for which a client will be kicked out of the program. This is the right action to take. When someone's recovery is in jeopardy, due to the actions of others, swift action is necessary to keep everyone safe. Every case is different at this Center of healing. In this case, the young men came clean and begged to stay. They were sent to detox until they can pass the UA.

At Hope by the Sea, many of the patients are admitted for opioid addictions, many as young as eighteen. According to the Center for Disease Control (CDC) one in four people who receive opioid prescriptions long term for non-cancer pain, struggle with addiction. The CDC also reports over 1000 people are treated every day in emergency departments for the misuse of opioid prescriptions.

What is even more stunning to me, is none of those numbers account for heroin, the most powerful opiate sold illegally on the streets of America. Many heroin addicts in America, and here at this treatment center, began with prescriptions from doctors for opioids like hydrocodone. When the doctor won't refill the prescription, they look on the street for the drug. Finding their drug to be too expensive on the street, many find heroin to be the most affordable and most potent.

I never thought much about one substance being worse than another. I tend to believe alcohol is among the worst and the most insidious of them all. I have known many people personally who have died of opioid overdoses -- some from heroin and some from pills. One was eighteen years old and had his entire life ahead of him.

At Hope, during a process group in the afternoon, the men came clean with the group about their relapses. They are apologetic and seem to be committed to doing better and working their programs. Some of the clients are angry, and they let all of us know it. I understand being upset is justified in this situation. I am not sure how

I would react if this had happened in the Horse Shoe House. I am certain and aware of how close I am to my next use. The process group put this in clear perspective.

The gossip about the relapse was typical I guess. At the Horse Shoe House, we are grateful to have the men we do; and none of us, God willing, will have to experience having temptation under our roof. Not one man at Hope by the Sea hasn't had his share of relapses. Those of us who are here are the lucky ones. Too many never have the chance to come to places like this because they are dead. It is the sad truth about drugs and alcohol.

A couple of years ago, with love and support of family, I once again had put together a string of sober weeks. I had a roof over my head, a good job, and a truck to get me back and forth. New in sobriety again, I was aware of my fragility at this stage of recovery.

A too familiar pattern in my life is the rise of success, often great success and even deeper falls. This time, I was grief stricken with the loss of my businesses, my uncle who was my mentor, my marriage, and another loss. All were ripped away from me in less than two weeks the end of 2013. These feelings of loss and my broken heart, like everything else in my life since 1982, were unresolved and jammed deep within me. I knew no other way to get through such pain. So, in the autumn of 2015, with a job, truck and roof over my head, I was a ticking time bomb waiting to explode.

Life was going well for me, so well I decided to try and connect with the girl who had left me a year before. This would be my broken heart mentioned above. As luck would have it, things were good, and it looked like our love was rekindled. I was so happy we got back together. What happened next was predictable. The relationship soured, and the feelings of sadness and my unworthiness of goodness flooded over me. This is an example of the many feelings I would numb with alcohol or drugs, and it was exactly what I did.

I had not been diagnosed with any mental health disorders then. Likely, because I rarely saw a doctor. It is also worth noting I was still several months from remembering what had happened to me back in second grade.

The longer I used substances, the more it consumed me. Eventually, all the reasons I was attracted to it, didn't work anymore. It ceased to be fun or useful, and turned me into an isolationist to hide my shame. Becoming addicted, for me and many others, was never what we envisioned for our lives.

We are victims of trauma with suppressed memory loss, who often do not even understand why or what is troubling us, we only know it hurts. I fell into this category for thirty-five years. I didn't know what made me different or prone to low self-esteem. At the beginning of my alcohol and drug abuse I felt getting drunk or wasted reduced my pain and gave me a confidence I never had before. Alcohol and drugs became my best friend, a cunning, baffling, and powerful friend for a long, long time. This, of course, is a deception packed full of lies which I now know all too well. Once addicted, the ultimate betrayal and merciless infliction was the all-encompassing suffering, and it was infinite in scope.

Birthplace of Addiction

It wasn't long after the relationship went south that the job followed suit. The next couple of months saw the most alcohol abuse of my life. Alcohol only feeds depression, and the reality of being one of life's problems. The problem was intensified because I had spent a lifetime not processing feelings, believing I was never good enough. My teenage kids and family loved me, but they grew tired of this continued pattern in my life.

Addiction is not in my family tree, and I never understood how I became so engulfed. Most of my family viewed my problems as being caused by my weakness and lack of will power to stop. I believed addiction to be a disease I never wanted or expected. It is hard to say exactly when I became unable to stop.

I know I was drinking close to a gallon of vodka a day and would wake up sick and shaky until I got liquor in me. This vicious cycle was going to kill me, and I honestly wished it would. Those were my feelings then.

Active addiction is also a dark place for those who care and love the addict. When I think of all the hurt and pain my addiction has cost the ones who matter most to me, it's often more than I can bear. They try and want to help me, but it's not always known what that looks like.

My oldest brother, Jeff, and I have a history of sorts where drugs and alcohol are concerned. He walked away from them for the most part. He somewhat understands who I am, and who I am not. My other brothers and I call him a bull among other things, because he has so little patience and no tact whatsoever. I had been trying to get into a treatment center for several weeks; and because I was not court ordered or even on probation, there were a lot of obstacles standing in the way.

> *Active addiction is also a dark place for those who care and love the addict. When I think of all the hurt and pain my addiction has cost the ones who matter most to me, it's often more than I can bear.*

So, Jeff shows up one morning with a hair-brained scheme to cut the treatment red tape as it were. It was something only he would think made sense. He had purchased two large bottles of vodka, and he told me to jump into his car and slam these bottles on the way to the hospital. He was banking on the hospital cutting the necessary red tape to land me in a treatment center instantly.

I told him over and over, it was the stupidest idea he had ever uttered. I don't know if it was his arguing, or the vodka bottles, but I started pounding them just the same. By the time we reached the hospital, I had downed the second bottle, and it's the last thing I remember.

I woke up ten hours later in a place I did not recognize. I had been taken by ambulance from the hospital to a detox center several miles away. They asked me to breathe into a breathalyzer and to everyone's dismay, it read .71 which is nine times the legal limit for driving. Levels about half the amount of mine at .40 tend to poison people, and they die. Alcoholics like me who have been drinking heavily for days, weeks, even months at a time with no interruption, develop tolerances allowing them to drink insane amounts without passing out. The poisoning levels kill many with lower blood alcohol content. Detoxing our bodies of alcohol can be very dangerous and potentially lethal which is why it is advisable to have medical supervision.

I was administered medications to keep my vital signs stable as the alcohol left my body over the next few days. I was discharged from the detox place no closer to being admitted to a recovery facility. My brother was trying to help me back in 2015. Regardless of the way it worked out, I know Jeff's heart was in the right place.

The reason I described my relapse on paper is because I want folks to know how dangerous and powerful addiction is. When raw emotions rule the day, at times things are said we can't take back; and actions are taken that cannot be undone.

The reason I described my relapse on paper is because I want folks to know how dangerous and powerful addiction is. When raw emotions rule the day, at times things are said we can't take back; and actions are taken that cannot be undone.

In February of 2016, I was blessed with a New Beginning of sorts. I spent forty-one days learning the twelve steps of Alcoholics Anonymous. It was not the first time I learned them.

Also, while there, my memories of second and third grade came into focus, and the ugly nightmares began. I was treated for addiction, and the treatment was the twelve-step program with little else considered. I am not bashing the twelve-step model of recovery; but it is my contention it is lacking because it does not recognize the mental health aspect and the healing process connected to it. It would be several months before I found Hope by the Sea.

CHAPTER 25

I did a lot of writing last night, but the nightmares robbed me of my sleep once again. At daybreak, just as the sun is breaking the dawn, I see something majestic. Hundreds of small birds are flying right at me and over the house, and it is as if they are flying right out of the ball of the sun. This is a sunrise I will remember always. I'm also looking forward to reading these letters today. They were hard to write, but I usually feel better after I read them in class.

In class, I ask Frank if we can do letters in the first hour today. I have a little more anxiety than normal. This letter is a little different as it's about my brothers and parents and life before seven.

Life Before Seven Years Old

November 3, 2016

Growing up in southern Minnesota, darn near in Iowa, was quiet and not a lot went on. Everyone knew one another – the cars they drove, even the dishes at the pot luck suppers were an identifiable way to know who could cook; also, what dishes to avoid.

Our family lived in the country on the land my grandpa grew up on. Grandpa owned the farm land around the five or so acres we owned. He had about 200 additional acres all within walking or biking distance away from our home. Grandma and Grandpa lived less than 2 miles away, so we saw them often.

Dad and Mom built our house in 1971, and it was a nice home. When I was around four, Dad worked nights. During the day, Dad was finishing off the basement and taking care of me; and I can remember the scrap wood and little area he gave me to saw or hammer as I wanted. A big deal to me! Mom was working at a bank in town, and Grandpa would come by and help Dad some or pick me up, so Dad could get more done.

At ages three, four and five, there was no school so both planting and harvest seasons could be spent with my Grandpa in the field, and those were some of the fondest memories of my life.

We went to Sunday School and church every week with few exceptions. Both Mom and Dad were Sunday School teachers. Dad filled in for the pastor and preached the sermons sometimes when the pastor was on vacation.

The family vacation every year was going to a place called Cedar Falls Bible Conference in Iowa. I don't think it was until I was four years old that I remember going along. Before that time, I spent half the week with Grandma and Grandpa Foss and the other half with Grandma and Grandpa Gilbertson who lived a couple of miles away from our home. Grandma and Grandpa Foss were nice and always very loving to me. I didn't have the bond with them though like my other grandparents, probably because they lived in town twenty miles away, and we didn't see them as much.

I learned how to ride a bicycle without training wheels when I was four. My Big Wheel was fun, especially on the newly poured cement for the garage. My brothers could all ride and could go up and down the road, through the ditches, and over ramps.

I watched my brothers ride and studied every movement from how they got on and off, balancing, pedaling, pretty much everything but stopping, as it turned out. Our driveway had a slight down slope to it, then grass, gardens and trees all around. The bike had a banana seat with a sissy bar and no gears.

So, there I was, on and pedaling and just ahead I was running out of driveway, fast! About then is when I realized I didn't know how to stop!

One day while my brothers were at school and Dad was mowing the lawn, I pushed the bike to the top of the driveway. I began going over all I had remembered. I couldn't touch the ground from the seat, so I had to stand on a pedal and swing over while moving to keep balanced. So, there I was, on and pedaling and just ahead I was running out of driveway, fast! About then is when I realized I didn't know how to stop! My Dad caught a glimpse of me tottering down the driveway and started running toward me from across the lawn. On the grass, the bike slowed down, and in a panic, I jumped.

I went left, the bike went right, and we both tumbled a bit. Dad was there, and I was grinning ear-to-ear and laughing as if being tickled. Seeing I was okay, he taught me how to stop and turn easier. With a seat adjustment, I was a real pro by the time the bus dropped my brothers off from school.

When I was five, I attended a preschool called Children's Garden five days a week in the same town Mom worked. This was a lot of fun, and the teachers were very nice to me. Dad would pick me up, and we'd have lunch with Mom at a place called the Midway before going home. I remember this time of my life well because one-on-one time with Mom and Dad, having three brothers, was scarce.

I remember being excited for school in the Fall. I went to school at noon and rode the bus home with my brothers in the afternoon. The first thing I noticed about kindergarten was no farm toys. How was I to learn without tractors, disks, plows, and combines? I played with the semi-trucks and hauled blocks around at recess. So far, kindergarten was pretty good.

Mom and Dad usually hired a babysitter for us boys when they were out for the evening, grocery shopping, Bible study at the church or visiting friends. As we grew older though, when Jeff was fourteen, they would sometimes leave Jeff in charge of Dan, thirteen, Joe, eleven, and me, eight, when they were going to be gone for a short time. Little did they know that as soon as they left the yard, Jeff and Dan would start to get under each other's skin. Sometimes their disagreements would be more than just verbal banter. They would start to smack each other around. Being very young, to me, it was brutal. No one ever was hurt badly, but nevertheless, it was not pretty to watch for me.

After they were done sparring, Dan, Joe and I were threatened by our big brother, Jeff, not to tell Mom and Dad, or we would be sorry. Jeff was very big and strong for his age and so was Dan. He and Dan were very athletic and worked for the farmers baling hay and pitching manure to make some extra spending money. They were both very strong in their upper bodies and Joe and I knew better than to mess with them. Joe and I were never much for the fist-a-cuffs. We just kept our mouths shut about the fighting Jeff and Dan did. Mom and Dad never knew until we were all grown up.

CHAPTER 26

Frank said, "Okay, how was it?"

I said, "It was different at first to write about so long ago. Then, things just popped in my head, things I hadn't thought about for a coon's age. I think I learned to not tell my folks about stuff on those nights and other times when being told not to tell or else."

"That might be it," he uttered. After a few moments rubbing his forehead, he added, "But, yeah, let's keep writing; don't worry if you repeat yourself. Good job."

I don't know if it's impatience, anxiety, or because the purpose of this writing tool, as it pertains to recovery, is a lot clearer to me than it was even a week ago. But, since arriving here, I must have heard Frank tell us fifty times addiction is not the problem; it never was. I haven't had a craving for drugs or alcohol for over two weeks. The only reason I can account for is the feelings I used to get and drink to numb with alcohol, still exist inside me.

Every day, sometimes more than once, I write in my journal checking in with myself. For me, this is the most intimate writing I do. I process my feelings in these entries. I pray, I cry, I get mad, sad and happy on any given day. I allow myself to hurt, feel pain -- the emotional kind I have suppressed all these years. The entries are no less than twenty minutes of dedicated writing with no distraction or interruption.

> *I process my feelings in these entries. I pray, I cry, I get mad, sad and happy on any given day. I allow myself to hurt, feel pain -- the emotional kind I have suppressed all these years.*

The letters are an extension of the check-ins allowing for detailed specific work on issues. In my case, I have my childhood trauma and everything forward to sift through. As my past plays forward, I will eventually be down to the daily check-ins and gratitude work.

I believe my new neural paths are being established with every new day, and will continue to be strengthened as feelings, or problems are handled with the processes I have learned and demonstrated here. Eventually, my new pathways will dominate the old ones and my addictive behaviors will be gone for good. A great deal of work remains. I have no doubt about it, because I do believe some light may be visible in the tunnel of my darkness.

CHAPTER 27

On Thursdays, we meet for only two hours in Alternative Track because we have psycho drama from ten o'clock until noon. When Frank asks if anybody has any letters at the beginning of hour two, I waste no time and speak up. This is the second letter from my 1981 self to my current self.

Nine-Year-Old Self to Current Self #2

November 3, 2016

Dear David,

At home things are normal I guess. Goldie and the other dogs are always waiting to play when I get home from school. The bus ride bothers me because of all the shouting. It seems I look over my shoulder constantly, because when people are close or touch me, I become very tense. I often hold back oceans of tears on the bus because if I cried, I'd be teased more than I already am.

My stomach always feels like it is full of butterflies, and I always think I am in trouble. I feel I can trust very few with what happens in school. It hurts to ride bike often because of what Mrs. F does to me. Why is she so mad? Why is she so mean to me? I try to think what I do to deserve this reality.

There are a couple of places at home I can go where nobody can find me or bother me. My brothers built a fort out of fallen timber. It is well hidden in the woods and is decayed a little more each time I go there. The other place I go is the bent woods in the wooded swamp area. The trees grow to full size horizontally. This solitude is shared by Goldie and

> *When I am at these isolated places I can cry and feel sorry for being so bad, sorry for not being good enough, sorry for not being like my brothers, sorry for not fitting in.*

me mostly. When I am at these isolated places I can cry and feel sorry for being so bad, sorry for not being good enough, sorry for not being like my brothers, sorry for not fitting in. I'm sorry my Mom and Dad hear how bad I am at conferences. I'm sorry I am not a better son, sorry I am not better.

This makes me worse; talk like this. Maybe I believe I am the bad, evil boy she says I am when she hurts me. Why do I feel shame and think people will know I really am bad?

She is the only one who hurts me with electrical shocks; hits me; tells me I am stupid. I can't bear losing my parents if they find out just how bad I am. My brothers seem to enjoy school; did they not have Mrs. F as a teacher? They have friends and happiness in their lives it seems. Why do I live in this dark void all the time alone and scared?

There is an I-beam in the hallway that I shoot spit wads of paper at. My desk faces the hall and has walls on the sides and front, and it is away from all the other kids. Mrs. F said I was no good and can't be by the other kids.

One day this tall man with glasses was in the hall with the principal. This man saw the spit wads and glared right through me; and I thought he looked like he wanted to kill me. He took the teacher in the hall and the three of them huddled, each periodically would glare in my direction.

I didn't know what was going to happen to me next. I wondered if the principal and superintendent knew the evils that went on here, could they? A week with no recess for the spit wads, the longest darkest week of my life.

Sitting at my desk, I jumped a foot off the chair when anybody came near. I believed more and more hurt would follow any interaction I had with an adult at school. What did I do that this is happening to me?

On Friday nights in the Fall, we go to football games. My brother, Jeff, is a linebacker, and we go to most games home and away. A lot of times I get to be in the fields with Grandpa and don't have to go. When we aren't in the field, we watch the Dukes of Hazzard and Dallas.

I must say that driving a combine in the harvest time is amazing – so many moving parts. This is a big deal to be in control of a machine so magnificent and joyful as any I believe. If only this was my school room.

David

Frank asks me how it is and paused for a long time. He finally said, "You're doing a better job connecting to your feelings. It is understanding and processing them that will allow you to be able to release the negatives."

I said, "How do you know when it's time to release things? When is it time to forgive folks, or even myself?"

Frank said, "You'll know when forgiveness is to be. I ask you to trust me on that one. In a few more letters you'll be ready to release everything with the teacher and burn it all. Then, you will only have to deal with new things or nightmares, and you can work that out in the daily check-ins."

"Will the process in terms of letters be the same as the teacher with the other issues in my life?" I asked.

Frank said, "Each person, place, or thing is going to be unique and has its own feelings, and you need to process each one. Start with the negative feelings and write about them. What you will find from purging the negative completely is positives that can then and only then be identified."

Thinking about what has just been said gives me some pause. The idea of finding something positive regarding Mrs. F. by releasing my negative, crippling emotions and finding forgiveness within myself for her, is possible I feel at some point down the road; but, positive anything now seems unrealistic to me.

I said, "I will have to take your word on the positives right now, because right now I have some doubts."

Frank answered, "If you continue to put the work in, it will happen. You have plenty of stuff to work on. As far as the teacher goes, we are close to the end, so let's continue to keep those letters the top priority."

"Okay. I'll keep at it." I said.

CHAPTER 28

Psycho drama is something that is offered twice a week at Hope by the Sea. This class is not track specific. Once the track specific classes are concluded for the day, we are split up into Group One or Group Two for the remainder of the day. We are designated to be in one or the other upon arrival and remain in the group until discharged. So, we spend a lot of time and develop close bonds, like those we form in track specific groups.

Psycho drama was first developed in 1921 by Jacob Moreno who described it as the scientific exploration of truth through a dramatic, actionable method to explore the past. This type of therapy is favored by treatment centers because it is often a group method consisting of eight to twelve people. This group dynamic is like a tight knit community consisting of varying degrees of trust, friendship and respect.

One method of psycho drama we do is called Family Sculpture facilitated by Jane, one of the Therapists. This group session focuses on life situations of one individual with group members taking on roles to play as needed. Since no two people have the same family or people they are closest to, each of these sessions is unique and often quite emotional for the individual. These sessions take about an hour each. Because two hours are allotted, we can do two per day.

Jane instructs the individuals to pick their family members from the group. The individual then talks to each member arranged around the room by how close or distant the individuals are. These are conversations that likely have never happened; things a person has wanted or needed to say are often the context of these interactions. It takes remarkable courage to be vulnerable in front of your peers. The level of trust is also considerably high in this group.

The other psycho drama group is facilitated by Frank and Kelley who is another Therapist at Hope by the Sea. This group uses a mirror method to allow us as individuals through Facilitator guidance to see ourselves in various situations at different times of our lives. One individual sits in a chair at the front of the room, and the chair across is the mirror who is a person from the group selected by the individual.

I select my housemate, Anthony, to be my mirror. I have been observing these psycho drama mirror sessions for weeks now and decide I had better face my fears head on, face-to-face as it were.

I begin talking to my younger preschool self and focusing on my fond memories of farming and riding my bicycle. I talk about my parents and grandparents being loving and providing for all my needs as a child. Frank says this is no different than the writing, meaning there is no right or wrong way to do psycho drama. What is important is doing it to the best of your ability.

I am drawn to second and third grade like a magnetic force. I know it is going to be a difficult hour, especially because Frank knows everything there is to know about me and facilitates. Talking about Mrs. F to myself I suddenly am overcome with emotion, and the tears begin to flow. Frank tells me to talk to my eight and nine-year-old self as if I am trying to help. It is like the letters and nightmares are alive in these moments.

Kelley tells me to be my eight and nine-year-old self and talk to you, my current self. I begin asking why does she hurt me? Why am I so scared? Why am I so sad? I feel so alone. I am so overcome with emotion I can barely speak. I want to curl up and die. Why does nobody stop her? Why is she so mean to me? Do I deserve this?

> *Frank tells me to talk to my eight and nine-year-old self as if I am trying to help. It is like the letters and nightmares are alive in these moments.*

Am I really the bad person she says? I feel if I am not bad, then someone will help me.

What seems like a few moments is, in fact, over an hour in length. Afterward, I feel a sense of accomplishment. I have taken a step toward overcoming the fear living in me for so long. Still, I believe the more I can face and confront my past, the closer I will be to my past not being able to sabotage my today and tomorrow.

I am moved at the way my peers respond to my psycho drama with such positive support. I have never been one to show much in terms of feelings, or really any part of my life in public. This is another first for me. Trust has always come hard for me. The staff and clients of Hope by the Sea have helped me to accomplish a great many things, trust among them.

CHAPTER 29

Case Manager Meeting with Kim November 7, 2017

Meetings with my Case Manager, Kim, have been smooth and productive. For the past couple of weeks, I have been devoting most of my free time to letters, journaling, and gratitude work. I did not complete the other assignments, most notably the Smart Recovery book.

Kim asked, "How has everything been going for you?"

"Things are going okay." I said and continued, "I have been doing a lot of writing, trying to work through things."

"Your Mom said she will be here for family weekend coming up in a couple of weeks. She's looking forward to seeing you. She is a very nice lady, loves you very much I'd say." Kim said smiling.

I said, "Mom is looking forward to coming, and I am looking forward to seeing her too."

Kim has many years of clean sobriety under her belt, and I am sure there is a great deal to be learned from her. I wish there was better communication among the Alternative Track, Case Manager and Therapist. With eighty to ninety percent of the work coming from the writing and sharing, it is difficult at times to see the wisdom behind some of the work done with Kim.

She asked, "Have you completed the assignments on your treatment plan?"

"I have read some of the Smart Recovery book, but that's about it. I have been doing a lot of writing in Alternative Track, and it is difficult stuff I am working through." I reply.

Kim mulled that over a bit, then said, "We, as a clinical team, have been a little concerned you may be focusing too much on negatives and not seeing the positives around you. What do you think about this?"

I carefully considered what she said and replied, "Is that Frank's assessment too?"

She didn't like that answer based on her body language, tensing up. Leaning forward, she said, "Frank is not involved with the clinical team meetings."

I said, "I find that remarkable because the fact of the matter is I receive eighty to ninety percent of my treatment from his classes. I don't mean to sound rude or insensitive, but how could any realistic assessments or conclusions be considered without an understanding of the nature of the work we do in Alternative Track?"

Looking a bit deflated, Kim said, "I'm not discounting or minimizing the work done in the Alternative Track; in fact, the alternative to the twelve steps was a defining factor for me coming to work here. My job is to ensure your wellbeing throughout the treatment process while making sure we are achieving the goals you have for this experience."

"That sounds fair enough," I said.

"I want you to recognize how well you are doing. It is noticed by staff and clients alike, and you should be proud of this."

I never know what to say in these situations. Compliments and praise have never been easy for me to accept or believe. So, I said, "Thank you. I appreciate that."

"I get the distinct impression that you are not comfortable with compliments."

"I would agree. I don't really know how to react," I responded.

Kim concluded, "We are about out of time. Is there anything else we need to discuss today?"

"No, I think we are good." I said.

She said, "Okay, David. Have a good rest of the day, and we'll talk soon."

CHAPTER 30

Sunday mornings at Hope by the Sea you can either go to church, an AA meeting, Yoga or do some writing. This day, I decide to write in the park as it is a beautiful, sunny day, and it warms my face.

I am writing at a picnic table when I see someone wearing a back pack come off the trail which runs parallel to the park. As he got closer, I can see the many things he has attached to himself – old, soiled blankets, clothes, even a saw and some rope. I say, "Hello," and invited him to sit down.

We make introductions, and we just start chatting away about football. Being it is Sunday, I have my New England Patriots jersey on. It soon becomes apparent my new friend is not a Patriots' fan. Nope, the man who calls himself, Hayword, is an Oakland Raiders' fan.

As we jump around from topic to topic, it is becoming clear Hayword is a homeless man. He was born in Lincoln, Nebraska, and has been in California for more than thirty years. He must be all of sixty, maybe even a speck more.

We eventually get around to talking some politics being the election is so close at hand. Of course, wearing my Donald Trump hat tipped my hand to my horse in the race. Hayword isn't exactly a liberal, yet, he doesn't seem all that conservative either. What is apparent, is the remarkable optimism I hear from this man I have just met.

it is becoming clear Hayword is a homeless man. He was born in Lincoln, Nebraska, and has been in California for more than thirty years. He must be all of sixty, maybe even a speck more.

I tell Hayword I am a patient at a treatment center, and I am being treated for alcoholism, methamphetamine abuse, PTSD, anxiety and depression. I can't say why I told this near stranger these highly personal things about myself. Maybe it is the happiness that seems to radiate from this man. He is unfazed by the treatment center thing; if anything, he seems impressed a person would invest in himself in such a way.

Before we know it, two hours have passed, and it is time for us to go. I shake Hayword's hand and thank him for the nice fellowship. He does the same and, quick as a wink, he is gone.

I thought about Hayword that night while I was writing in my journal. This man had no home, little or no money or worldly possessions, and still this man had a much healthier outlook on life than I did. How could this be?

I never saw Hayword again; however, I would have liked to have seen him once more, because I learned much from talking with him. He taught me a strong lesson in what is important in life. Showing kindness to others and being nonjudgmental were among the pearls revealed to me on a Sunday afternoon in November.

CHAPTER 31

People have a lot of letters to read today in Alternative Track. I often get so caught up in my own trauma and problems I forget the other men and women have issues every bit as difficult as mine. Abuse, molestation and rape are too real in this world. The pain and anguish are horrible for us and to numb it, we take refuge in drugs and alcohol.

For many of us active in our addictions, it is rarely, if ever, clear exactly when it was our lives veered out of control. The mental sickness afflicting us is only enhanced by a life of drug and alcohol abuse. At some point, the numbing or medicating of our pain no longer is enough to take our pain away or even provide the respite, if only for a short time.

Those of us who don't die from the substances we put in our bodies have a void that isn't much better. The busted relationships and family turmoil causing so much pain to all involved are not always repairable. Others go to prison, often because they hurt someone, or even killed someone, under the influence or in a blackout with no memory of the events resulting in their punishment.

> *When I think only a few months ago, I was near death and welcomed it, the gratitude is considerable for this chance to heal.*

Then, you have the lucky ones who made it to a facility like Hope by the Sea. I see myself as blessed by God to have the good fortune of being here among these men in this place of healing. When I think only a few months ago, I was near death and welcomed it, the gratitude is considerable for this chance to heal.

The first letter I read today is my Good-Bye letter to Alcohol and Drugs.

Final Good-bye to Alcohol and Drugs

November 11, 2016

Dear Drugs and Alcohol,

Your arrogance is amazing; to think I allowed you to be the centerpiece of my life for over twenty years reveals to me a great deal about me. Living apart from you has been a good thing; maybe the best of things for me. My vision is clearer each day as the fog in my brain dissipates.

I almost posted your bail at the store a few weeks back. I figured I could sneak you into my room and love you 'til the pain was numb. The pain is never gone with you; it pauses briefly, only to come back with razor sharp precision cutting deeper and as cruelly as possible.

No more! Today your reign of evil is over; and I am prepared, finally, to say goodbye forever. You will no longer control my pain. I need my pain. I need it to recognize my demons, my shortcomings and my betterment opportunities.

At Hope by the Sea, I am learning to live free of you. Finding out it is okay to feel sad, ashamed, vulnerable, hopeless, worthless or depressed is becoming my strength.

For all these years you have been my love, my values, my therapist, my father, my mother, my uncle, my brother, my conscience; and, of course, the medicine forming the masks to hide my shame.

No longer will your services be necessary. I have found a way to begin to accept me for who I am, rather than who I am not. Simply put, I am not you -- the destroyer of happiness, the thief of potential and the wrecker of relationships.

You do not possess one redeemable feature I find worthy of me. So long Witch, may you thrive in the deep chasm of Hell.

Affectionately,

David Foss

Frank seems to like this one as he is wearing a rare smile. "All right, you can burn this along with the other two on the subject."
I said, "You literally want me to burn the letters?"
"Safely," he said and continued, "Yeah, release it and be done with it. We don't write these letters for others; we write these letters for you, and when the feelings have been dealt with, and the negative purged, it's time to burn it and move on."

I didn't burn my letters at the time because I was beginning to consider the merits of writing a book. I see the symbolism in burning them, the release and forgiving of what needs forgiving. I can also understand why a lot of the guys have said someone finding or reading them would not be good.

The next letter kept me up a while last night. I was working at it at the dining room table with my head phones on as usual. Stan had to go to the hospital to be treated for severe back pain so Pong, the head driver at Hope by the Sea, came by to fill in until Nick could get back to the house. He sat across from me, and I looked up with eyes full of tears which was often the case when I write about Mrs. F.

He told me to come out and have some cake with him in the kitchen. I like talking with Pong. He makes me smile and laugh and has been a real friend to me since the day I arrived.

When Nick got to the house, Pong asked me if I'd like to go to Tommy's with him to get some chili burgers and fries. It is good to get out for a bit. I mention Mom is coming out to Family Weekend and asked if he could recommend some restaurants. He said he would be glad to do it.

Pong has worked for Hope by the Sea for almost four years, and prior to them, he was a client. He and Frank are tight, so he understands a lot of what I am going through. We talk about anything but treatment; it is a much, needed respite, and the food is good too.

This next letter is a reversal of a letter to Mrs. F. This one is from Mrs. F to my 2016 self.

Mrs. F to My 2016 Self

November 7, 2016

David,

You are the most rotten, dumbest, misguided little boy I have ever had in thirty years as a teacher. I am a tenured teacher and am, therefore, entitled to do as I please with anyone at any time with no consequences ever. I knew you were going to be trouble the minute you set foot in my classroom.

It wasn't even a month before you were causing trouble making it necessary to hit you with erasers and magazines. The fact you were so damn stupid made it more fun to eventually break you. It took all my skills of deception for your parents to understand you were simply a bad apple, and that without discipline you would spoil the batch.

Birthplace of Addiction

I needed the rush of hurting you, so I began hitting more and more, even in front of the class. I told you how rotten a boy you are. You deserved nothing good; you needed me to beat you and shame you for your own good. You needed me to make you keep still and straighten up. You and your parents are trying to discredit my noble profession. I don't get why they think you are good when, in fact, you are the worst boy I have ever seen. You disgust me, you remind me of a cockroach that must be smashed and broken into a million pieces.

You are frightened of me, petrified and this makes me feel great inside. You will never amount to anything; your parents know how rotten you are and approve of my hitting you. They only want you gone, quiet and forgotten. You are no different than a retarded child; you are a piece of trash. You don't run or resist when I shock you, and this tells me I have broken you, and I can control you at will. The fear in your eyes is intoxicating and just makes me feel giddy within.

I am a teacher because I like to prey on boys and make them suffer. Truth be told, I have never had anything in my life that satisfies my desires like controlling and punishing young boys. When I put you in the closet, I dream of ways I can hurt you more. I get adrenaline rushes when I squeeze the breath out of your neck. I don't know what I enjoy most. Is it the fear in your eyes? The tears or the silent screams? I get goose bumps at the memories.

I live in an old house alone with my thoughts dreaming of boys to sabotage. You, David Foss, embarrassed me as a professional by scoring so high on the academic tests. For that I will see to it that you do not perform anything well again. I will keep you in as much as possible from recess, so I can make you hurt more.

In second grade I did not teach you to fear me enough. Third grade I knew I must scare the smugness out of you, so your defeated eyes will return. I rarely have opportunity to have boys two years in a row. The fear and shame you wear to school every day makes me realize my job is being done at a high level.

I decided over the summer that I loathed you and you disgust me. I must make you realize that you are the worst boy in the entire school. Being stupid and never having a life will be your legacy. Your days may be numbered with me, but the impact and damage last now and even in 2016, I control much of you.

Likely, you have become a pile; a no-good member of society. You are as big a disgrace as a man as you were as a boy. You still know I can hurt you; you are still pathetic. The rotten self-worth you harbor is simply who you are. I recognized this and made it my mission to make you suffer.

I have long since retired and may even be dead and buried, but I live through you and many others whose lives I have touched. Maybe that was the point all along -- to continue the hopelessness. I hope you die lonely and empty, that would be just fine with me.

Mrs. F

After a long pause, Frank looked up and asked, "How was it?"
"It scared me a little writing as her; it felt like I was breathing life into her with every word," I said.
"I suppose it is exactly what you were doing by allowing the feelings in; fear is what we all face when we really pull the blinders away. Facing fear is the key component of healing and learning to live with yourself. Then, we can focus on positives; your whole life has been dwelling on negatives; and because your conscious didn't remember, you never knew why," Frank said.
I said, "It feels like the center of my universe, my whole life. I can trace it all back to this. My fears and my addiction were all born in her classroom, in the closet where my innocence died."
Frank said, "Let's respond to it and wrap this up. I also want you to list ten positives about the experience with the teacher." "Don't look so confused, David." he began, and continued, "This is what we have been working toward; you won't find it as hard as you think. I want you to trust me on this."
I said, "Okay, I'll get started tonight."

CHAPTER 32

The process of releasing is a concept I don't quite comprehend. The act of letting go of something, when not understanding the glue keeping me clinging to it, is difficult. The letters I have written and the feelings I am learning to recognize, and process are beginning to change who I am. Discovering who is behind the fear and shame that have defined me for so very long creates a new fear. The unknown is something different; a picture that has not been drawn; or a field yet to be planted. To fear the unknown is natural to a point, even healthy.

I feel a void within me I didn't have when I arrived in California. This feeling of loss is strange to me. For decades, this negative cancer has been an enormous, influential part of me; and now that it is beginning to pull away one piece at a time, I find myself missing these pieces.

Replacing these with something else causes me considerable anxiety. My thoughts gravitate to negatives like is the new worse than the old? Is it better the devil I know?

It is a moment by moment challenge to not fall back to negative thinking, to my self-loathing defining me for so long. It is requested I use this new writing tool daily – writing three to five things for which I am grateful and thankful and why; writing ten positive occurrences in my life in the last twenty-four hours; and writing a quality I admire in myself and why. Some evenings I don't want to do *The Work*; I must force myself to complete it. If I cannot do it here, I won't do it when I leave. I am certain of that.

I feel a void within me I didn't have when I arrived in California. This feeling of loss is strange to me.

I can see the wisdom behind *The Work*; I truly can. I see the challenges as I let go of more and more of my negative thinking and strengthen the new neural pathways in my brain by continuing to write. I am optimistic because I see and feel the change in me in the short time I have been following the writing process daily.

CHAPTER 33

Now that I am nearing the end of the letters to Mrs. F, I am looking forward to moving past it. This is the response to the reversal from Mrs. F.

My Response to Mrs. F's Letter to Me

November 8, 2016

Mrs. F,

You sure paint a noble portrait of yourself, don't you? I have been curious how you were going to spin these evil deeds of yours. I expected more from you as strange as it sounds.

You validated the twisted sociopathic tendencies I knew you possessed these past several months I have spent in thought. What a petty person you are; how insecure you must be.

It occurs to me that you are a lousy, pathetic excuse of a teacher for many reasons. Your seniority, your union, and inept administrators allowed you to do whatever you pleased. The endless torture and horror took place in a school where everyone's job was to keep me safe. The lies and deception to mask your acts are nothing shy of disgraceful.

You stole my life, robbed me of my innocence and unrealized potential. When I think of all the hurt you inflicted on me and who knows how many others, I become sickened with disgust. For the first time in my life, I can see an avenue to eradicate you from my life. I have an army of people who care about me at Hope by the Sea who will help me destroy you for keeps. I may not have the strength yet, but my resolve has never been stronger.

One day soon you will burn in a ball of fire and your ashes will diminish into nothingness. Perhaps the best and only revenge here is finding a measure of accomplishment, a life of happiness free of the likes of you!

If I were you, I'd grow eyes in the back of my head. Make no mistake about it, I'm coming for you, you ugly lizard; and Hell is coming with me!

David

Frank said, "All right, how was it?"

"This one was easier than some of the others. It flowed like water out of me, and it felt good," I said.

"Okay, let's wrap it up with a final good-bye letter and then let's write ten positives you can take away from this."

I couldn't help thinking how the devil is it possible to pull positives from this horrible stuff? This will be difficult. So, I asked, "Doesn't ten seem like a bit too many?"

Frank said, "People on death row were asked to pull positives from their life from living on the row. They came up with as many as 100. I think ten in your case is doable, don't you?"

I said, "All right. I'll work on it."

CHAPTER 34

Sitting at a picnic table in the park watching a couple people shoot hoops nearby, I reflected on my past years of life. Looking for positives in my second and third grade torture seemed ridiculous. Harlan, smiling as always, sat down with his clip board at my table. If anyone could understand this absurd situation, surely, it would be him.

I explain I am preparing to write a final letter to Mrs. F along with a list of positives to take away from the experience. "How in the world can positives of any kind be taken from something so awful?" I asked.

He considers it for a moment, and then said, "The same way you identify them in your daily work, don't make it so complicated."

"I'm not complicating it," I bristled. But, I am unable to see anything positive whatsoever in being tortured for two years by a teacher."

He said, "Really? I find myself wondering if you have even tried. How many times in the time you have been here have your views, beliefs, or values changed, or at least made you view life differently?"

> *I really love this man, Harlan; except times like now. I am having a perfect pity party over here, and here he comes to bust it up with common sense!*

I really love this man, Harlan; except times like now. I am having a perfect pity party over here, and here he comes to bust it up with common sense! "Maybe I better give it a try and see what happens." I said.

"If you would get out of your own head and stop over-thinking this, you just might learn something about yourself."

I said, "That is no easy thing these days. My mind races with thoughts of what if? They often consume my day and night. Things about my life; about how things go back to those years; and what is left is what you see here today."

Harlan considered my dilemmas and answered, "Regrets are common as you become more clear-headed. It is important to discard these regrets; they will only hurt you and endanger your sobriety. In the end, what you have is today and beyond, yesterday has happened and cannot be changed. Learning to live with it by forgiving yourself is all we can hope for."

I replied, "I get what you are saying, and it makes sense too. Perhaps, that is why it is so difficult to let go of all the guilt and shame. It becomes too much at times and overwhelms me."

"It does do that," he said.

CHAPTER 35

Writing a final letter to Mrs. F is stirring up feelings I am not expecting. I have been discovering since my writing began almost every piece of me has her intertwined in some way. Therefore, even as I write my letter, I feel at some point more will be required. Yes, I have released a great deal of hatred, guilt and shame surrounding Mrs. F these past weeks. But with wounds, especially ones this large, they are bound to still cause pain and leave many permanent scars.

This is my final letter to Mrs. F

November 10, 2016

Dear Mrs. F,

The time has come to file you away; to leave you in the darkness as you did me. No longer are you going to define my life – now or ever again. You will be a chapter in my life that happened and is closed. You see the time has come for me to give up hope for a better past. It is time for me to forgive, not the actions, only the person.

This will likely be the last time I write directly to you. You have been center stage in my life long enough. The best justice I can think of is to live a happy, fulfilling life. One where I am comfortable in my own skin. A life with joy and serenity; the kind of life you have never had.

Despite all you have done to me, I find you to be a pitiable woman. Forgiveness is for my betterment. You will atone for yours, and God will judge you. I will begin a new life free of your tentacles, free of your lies, and free of the fear you put into me.

I will have adversity in life going forward. This is how I discover what is wrong and what isn't. Processing such things as I did, you will bring empowerment and enrichment to my life. My journey has just begun, but yours has come to an end.

Old and washed up is how I felt a month ago, best days behind in a mess of good intentions. A squandered life doomed to a miserable death. Today, I have a much different view. I have hope for a better life today. I have resolve and a burning desire to succeed and experience the joy of life, love and happiness.

The work I have begun is far from complete. Thirty-five years of wreckage that is my life, my identity, and all I know must now be sifted through. Good can be built upon while the negative is processed accordingly.

One day I will look upon this chapter as "the birthplace of my addictive behaviors." At the same time becoming the birth of new life for me. I will write a book for all the kids you have hurt; all the lives you have ruined. May families and victims alike find what I have found – Hope! Addiction is a mere symptom of a greater hurt, a trauma or a loss.

Some will, with a bit of faith and hard work, identify their own birthplace of addiction, and take back their lives as I have. I am taking back the power you held over me since I met you. I am turning the tables and locking you in the smelly, dark closet to perish.

Now I must say good-bye for my time at Hope is short, and the work load is tall. I have waited long enough to take my life back.

Sincerely,

David

Ten positive things resulting from my trauma.

1. Ability to express the hurt in a way that isn't destructive any longer. Writing has allowed me to better understand myself.
2. I have been blessed with positive memories in my discovery of this trauma along with the negatives. These memories would have likely never been realized with such clarity.

3. I no longer wonder "why me?" I have now come to an understanding of what happened to me at the young age of innocence; and it has empowered me.
4. I have gained a better understanding of my life and how it has unfolded. Looking at life in this way is enlightening, and I believe few people have this kind of opportunity to better themselves.
5. I now look at my memory restoration as an amazing gift that had to happen this way now in this place, for me to be where God wants me for His purpose.
6. Had it not been for my experiences at a young age and forward, I would not have the privilege of meeting these amazing people from across the country.
7. I have a sense for the first time in my life that I really can improve and build a life free from the need to put intoxicants into my body. I also believe soon the feelings of desire for such things will be eliminated altogether, allowing me to soar in life as I never have before.
8. Identifying character defects and past sins are more appealing now because now I know how to process things and how to gain strength in the process.
9. My future is unwritten and will be whatever I want it to be. These are words I never believed until now; I said the words but did not believe them.
10. I do not love myself at the time of this writing, but there is a desire to do so. I will learn to do this in time as the work continues.

"Okay, how was it?" Frank asked while he was doing the forehead massage thing.

I said, "It felt pretty good writing the letter; it made me feel I had accomplished a little bit. The positives were a bit slow starting but then came together okay."

"Positives always take longer it seems than the negatives." Frank opined and continued, "Most of us can write page after page of negatives in a very short time while coming up with a half page of positives takes several hours. That is why I write positives every single day, even when it's the last thing I want to do."

"I feel strange about all of this," I said and then after a long pause continued, "As awful as the teacher was, I feel strange about letting it go. Feels like a huge void in me, I mean this stuff has been there for so long, it still stings."

Frank said, "Feeling that way is to be expected for a trauma like this. It's not magic; there will be feelings unresolved; nightmares to process; and even more recovered memories. All this can be monitored in your daily check-ins."

"What about letters? Will I need to write more of them about the teacher?" I queried.

"If you are doing the check-ins daily and still have unresolved feelings or something that needs more work; then yes, you will write letters. You will know when you need to take that step." Frank answered.

I thought about this for a few moments and it made sense, as long as the check-ins and gratitude work are done daily. "Thank you," I said, "That makes sense to me."

Frank requested, "Let's write again to your eight-year-old self again from a more enlightened, optimistic viewpoint. Let's see how that goes."

I said, "All right. I'll start working on that right away."

CHAPTER 36

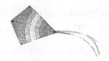

The Horse Shoe House is also referred to as the Executive House and generally does not have clients under the age of forty. Among other privileges, we have our phones and computers without restrictions, except they must be turned off during class.

It is important in the treatment experience to have yourself 100% focused on *The Work*. Trying to be home, at work, or any other place than Hope by the Sea results in a poor outcome. I decided before coming to California I would have minimal contact with the outside world and devote myself entirely to the task at hand. For many at Hope it is an impossible undertaking. Many clients are stressed out every day over the lives of loved ones at home; however, constant daily communication often creates even more tension between them.

For many of us the stakes are literally life or death. For me, I probably have another relapse in me, but what I may not have, is another recovery. I can cheat death only so many times. When my time is up, I'll be dead. Addiction does not discriminate by age, race, gender, status or lack thereof.

How many of us are given thirty, sixty or ninety days in life to work solely on the betterment of ourselves without work, a wife, kids, a girlfriend or any outside entity taking up our time? No one ever wants to become an addict or to put their life on hold to go to a treatment center. Working on mental health issues that cause many of our addictive behaviors takes courage and perseverance to have a chance at healing.

When put into proper perspective, ninety days of hard work to free me of addiction so I can live the rest of my life with out drugs or alcohol, makes perfect sense.

Having low self-esteem and thinking I was not worthy of goodness most of my life, is a significant barrier for me. Helping others is easy, helping myself is more difficult, impossible at times. I was a real mess when I arrived at Hope riddled with depression, anxiety, nightmares and sleep deprivation. I did not believe there was any chance I could feel normal, whatever that was. It is nothing short of a miracle, being surrounded by people like myself, that any healing takes place at all.

Nevertheless, I find it remarkable how much laughter and happiness exists at the Horse Shoe House. We all seem to be gifted story-tellers, often making ourselves the butt of jokes. We have come from different places and our lives are all unique, yet strikingly similar in the events leading us to this place. We had made hundreds of sincere promises to quit, and they were all broken. For a time, it would look as if addiction was in the past; and then, eventually it kicked us in the teeth again. This never-ending cycle yields a wake of wreckage in our families, and it cuts deep.

My own life has seen plenty of consequences from a life of addictive behaviors. I never understood why I would repeat this vicious cycle again and again. Addiction did not run in my family, and I came from a loving home. In my darkest hours, I cried and prayed for answers that never came. Legal, marriage and employment troubles were prevalent for more than twenty years. Everything goes back to the dark, awful closet in the domain of Mrs. F.

> *We had made hundreds of sincere promises to quit, and they were all broken. For a time, it would look as if addiction was in the past; and then, eventually it kicked us in the teeth again.*

CHAPTER 37

The work surrounding Mrs. F has all been a difficult, arduous endeavor. I struggle most with letters that force me back to the time when the torture happened. My memory of that time is quite clear now, and when I write about that scared little boy it often overwhelms me with tears. No matter how much I write, or how many years have passed, Mrs. F's impact and control over my present life remains.

Progress has been made in the last several weeks, and I am grateful for it. I have come to a place where I have pulled positives from the experience. I certainly never would have believed it could be possible mere months ago. The nightmares remain, but they are less frequent now.

I found this letter to my nine-year-old self from my current self to be enlightening and perhaps, something I would have welcomed in 1980-81.

Letter to nine-year-old self from current self

November 10, 2016

Dear David,

I wanted to write to you again because understanding some things about second and third grades has helped me a great deal. Most days you are pretty much clinging to life, but I am there with you; believe me, I am there with you.

Over the last month I have been reliving what happened in the classroom, in the closet, at gym and at home. I sure am happy you have our dog, Goldie. I miss Goldie. You are wise to trust her. She will keep you from harm. Grandpa is very good for you. He'll always be there and will never let you down.

David, one day all of this will stop. You won't be hurt by her any more. Life will advance and you along with it. You have remarkable strength; reliving everything now has shown me how brave you are. You have some wonderful times ahead of you, and you will overcome adversity.

Always know that you have abilities that provide fortification allowing you to conquer your fears. One day not so far away you will be a father and will be able to have a relationship that will define and enhance your life. All the hurt, sadness, and feelings of worthlessness you feel now will be transformed with an empowerment you can't yet imagine.

Aloneness, fear, and thoughts that everyone is against you will pass. You will make it. You will live, and things will get better for you. What you endure now will give you incredible power and insight that will allow your purpose in life to be revealed.

You are loved by many. Mom and Dad love you completely. I know you cannot tell them, and I understand why. You will realize in time that it's okay, it's totally okay. Writing to you like this, it is so real. I understand what you're going through at this moment.

You are scared, and you can't sleep without the terrible nightmares. I get it. You are a little boy I admire; a boy I love; a boy that will grow to be a man. You are so good. I know she tells you that you are not, and others do also. I can tell you, David, that we are good; we are deserving of goodness, love and understanding. I am here today, and that means you will be okay; you will persevere and become the man you are meant to be.

> *I can tell you, David, that we are good; we are deserving of goodness, love and understanding.*

The nightmares will end and be replaced with dreams of puppies one day. The thing I can give you right now at this very instant is hope. Hope is a real thing; it is tangible, and you can submerse yourself in it. Hope you will have a life of dreams, not nightmares. Dare to dream, David, for you can reach for the moon; even if you miss, you will be among the stars and the heavens. You know what, that is amazing!

David

"That was very nice, how was it?" Frank asked.

"It is always difficult to write about that time of my life, but this one was much easier than some of the others. It could be that writing about this is winding down, or maybe I am more accepting of the past," I replied.

Frank said, "It is both of those things, and you are now seeing some positives out of the whole experience. It does not mean the negatives are eliminated altogether, but the work you have done has begun to pay off because of the positives you see now that you didn't see before. Make sense?"

"It does, not sure what happens next; it feels a little empty. I guess the negatives only left scar tissue inside me," I concluded.

"That's one way to put it, I guess. Now, let's do a gratitude letter focusing on the positives you have learned. So, write a thank you to the teacher, and we'll see how that goes and where we'll work next," Frank agreed and requested.

I said, "All right. I'll start on it tonight."

CHAPTER 38

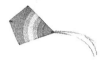

The skepticism I harbored on arrival here has all but disappeared. *The Work* over the last several weeks has shown me how to process feelings -- the very ones that had led me to seek solace in alcohol and drugs my entire life. The journey has only begun and much work needs doing no doubt. What I know for certain is the processes I am learning, I have sought my whole life.

The writing tools we use in the Alternative Track are a major component of my new optimism. The rest of the curriculum at Hope by the Sea balances things to make this program all-encompassing to my overall recovery. The individual sessions with my Case Manager, one-on-one sessions with my Therapist, the psycho drama, the group therapy and the peer support at the House and Center all work together as a whole to make this place so special.

I look at my restored memory as a gift, not a curse, as I did before coming here. I have been able to look at my life from many different perspectives and at different stages, and this I find to be empowering despite the vulnerability it also creates.

> *The writing tools we use in the Alternative Track are a major component of my new optimism. The rest of the curriculum at Hope by the Sea balances things to make this program all-encompassing to my overall recovery.*

Most people live their lives trying to avoid vulnerability because it is often viewed and perceived as weakness. People like myself, who have suffered traumas in their lives, often have trust issues. For me, my inability to trust at the age of seven never went away. Throughout my life, I never allowed people close enough to expose the vulnerabilities everyone has.

I simply did not want to be hurt, and it caused me to harbor fear of exposing the shame I have lived with since second grade. Strangely, the vulnerability I have feared all these years is playing a vital role in the healing process. I never considered I would have to be humbled by life and in a place of rock bottom spirituality to be broken enough to realize I needed fixing. This describes any given person addicted to substance who finds himself or herself realizing he or she is sick and tired of being sick and tired.

In moments of undivided attention in life, we are treatable. I have discovered strength in vulnerability I never expected. It is unlikely I would have found this amazing contentment at my lowest. If God be with me, I will learn to trust, and even love another.

Birthplace of Addiction

My mind is busier than it ever has been when I reflect on my life up to now. Everything builds off events, choices and environment; and any way I slice it, it goes back to my young years. To have my life irrevocably changed and forever altered at the innocent age of seven, eight and nine, and watch my life playout is the only way I can describe what I feel now. I am beginning to realize living a happy life free of the chains of the past, will require me to learn to live with all my past.

Working out my past has been done upstairs in Alternative Track with Frank. My therapist, Nancy, and I have been working on the here and now and the recent history of my life. Since nobody comes here on a winning streak, it means lives are unmanageable and down-right chaotic. For me, this is true. Legal issues, family issues, and broken relationships are among the things I work through in therapy. Nancy also works with my PTSD, depression and anxiety disorders.

It is easy to become overwhelmed with all the different thoughts occupying my day. There are so many things to work through, and ninety days is too little time to do it. With the alcohol and drugs completely out of my system now, it is easy to see addiction never was the problem. It is a symptom of the mental health disorders from which I suffer. I am in no way minimizing addiction, and the many destructive attributes of it. What I am saying is: "If all I focused on was treating addiction, and not the afflictions that feed it, it would only be a matter of time before it would gain traction and destroy me yet again. Any treatment not considering mental health has a high possibility to fail.

> *Regardless of how we have come to terms with our life and with the past, all can agree coming to terms or finding acceptance are fundamental to any recovery or happiness in the future. For me, I want God in my life.*

My past had to happen is something my Therapist said to me. Because if it did not happen just the way it did, I wouldn't be me today. The why things happen like -- why would God allow someone like Mrs. F to exist and do horrific things to me? I do believe in God, my Therapist does also, and she told me the why and why nots of life are God's business. For some, these last statements are not applicable; and that is okay, to each his own in matters of faith. Regardless of how we have come to terms with our life and with the past, all can agree coming to terms or finding acceptance are fundamental to any recovery or happiness in the future. For me, I want God in my life.

Things to work on while here at Hope by the Sea are abundant. Where to begin is often a source of procrastination. I am grateful to the folks here. Many were clients or come from recovery and empathize with current clients well. Some days I am quiet and only absorb and relate to what others say. I find the fellowship of the House to be most helpful when I feel like this. With all the expertise of the staff here at times, it can be the closeness of another client with a similar circumstance to mine who I find helps me the most.

CHAPTER 39

Gratitude is a key component to a happy life and successful recovery. So, when I was writing a thank you note to Mrs. F, it stirred up a strange medley of emotions and feelings in me. Being thankful to someone doesn't mean you agree with their actions, and it does not mean approval. Trying to be mindful of these things, I wrote the following:

Thank you Letter to Mrs. F

November 11, 2016

Dear Mrs. F,

Thirty-five years ago, you perpetrated unspeakable acts upon me. The kind rarely seen in the light of day except in therapy, and often not even then. So, the idea of thanking you for anything, ever, made me question the strategy of Frank who has been helping me sort everything out. Several hours later, it occurred to me if I hadn't lived through the horror of Hell that is you, Mrs. F, I would not be here at this place at this moment in time.

You see, I choose to believe everything happens as part of a Divine plan. That is why I am here in California writing this today. A great many things have been bestowed upon me because of this trauma -- positive things and in some cases, life changing for the better. Much has not yet been realized at the time I write this. The goodness that has trickled into my life is only the beginning of what lies ahead. One day the trickle will become a river of fortune, and it will be a glorious day indeed.

The truth is I want to express gratitude to you for the influence you have had over my life. I never thought I'd ever say a thing like that, and I doubt an old bag like you will hear these words again. Let's be crystal clear on this. I am in no way saying your actions are admirable somehow, because frankly, I find them disgusting and deplorable.

I cannot deny I am in a place today that has allowed me to come alive again. A fire I believed was long gone is beginning to roar inside me once again, and you are in no small part someone to thank for who I am today.

I must admit no other person has had such an impression on who David is. You set in motion things nobody could have predicted except God. Since God created you and me, He can now tend to you. I'll say good-bye and thanks for the life that is ahead of me.

David

Sharing this letter makes me feel as if progress is being made. For six weeks, I have been focused on this evil teacher. Now I feel as though an enormous weight has just been lifted from me. A void is inside me where all of this has been living so long; yet, at this moment I feel a sense of accomplishment I have not felt in a long time. Frank must have sensed this because he was wearing a rare smile when he asked, "How did this one go for you?"

For six weeks, I have been focused on this evil teacher. Now I feel as though an enormous weight has just been lifted from me.

Smiling a little myself, I said, "It was good. I know there is more work to be done, but now I am ready for it."

He said, "All right. Now you can burn them and be done with it and start writing about other areas that need tending to."

"There is no shortage of work." I said.

CHAPTER 40

Hope by the Sea offers a family weekend as part of the client's recovery program. Family members spend three, eight-hour days learning about addiction in general. The clients participate in only one of the days; therefore, for sixteen hours, family members meet with various addiction specialists without them. With most of my family not talking to me, except my seventy-two-year-old Mom, I was certain she would not be making the trip from Michigan to California for the family weekend. Boy, was I wrong!

Since arriving here, I had not called Mom often. I called no one else either, choosing to stay as engaged and as focused on programming as possible. I figured I needed to absorb as much in this short period of time as I could. So, when I called to say, "Hi," she informed me she would be making the trip. She also said she was bringing a friend along. Oh, yeah, almost forgot, the friend is someone I had never met or spoken to in my life.

After I inquired who she was bringing to a bound to be stressful emotional ordeal, I would think! Mom said, "Oh, it's Cherylee. You have never met her, but she lives up the road from me and has been praying for you

No, not so much as "Oh, you don't mind if I bring a friend along, do you?" or "By the way, I have a plus one to add to the classes." After I inquired who she was bringing to a bound to be stressful emotional ordeal, I would think! Mom said, "Oh, it's Cherylee. You have never met her, but she lives up the road from me and has been praying for you. She goes to Celebrate Recovery which was started at the Saddleback Church out there."

"Well, in that case, everything is just fine then, isn't it?" The sarcasm laying on thicker with each exchange. "I'm not sure they will let her participate, what with her not being family and all." I uttered.

Mom said, "I'm sure it'll all work out; and your birthday is the day after the family weekend, so we will leave the day after on the twenty-second. Maybe you can find something for you and me to do on Monday, the twenty-first, on your birthday."

Since it was becoming more and more apparent Mom's bubble was not to be burst, I didn't tell her about the rules around here they loved and cherished so much. Things like not going to the store on Monday, Tuesday and Thursday, or no Monster energy drinks, ever! So, I decided to save the *Passes on Saturday and Sunday ONLY* for another time. So, I said, "Can't wait to see you in a few days," and that was that.

I love my Mom very much and without her love and support along with my stepfather, Thad, I don't know where I would be right now. The more I think about it, the more I am looking forward to seeing her and spending some time together. The Cherylee thing, I'm not going to lie, is kind of, well, weird, but I'm guessing it's got to be weird for her, too!

CHAPTER 41

Saturday at the Horse Shoe House means up at six o'clock and down to the Harbor for a seven o'clock morning AA meeting. This gets us out of going anywhere following the ten o'clock morning group at the Center and giving us free time until Sunday morning.

We spent a good part of our weekend time talking among ourselves. We talk about life before and after Hope by the Sea. We all share at least one thing above all else. The common thread is fear -- fear of the unknown, of failure, of relapse and of dying from our addictive behavior which has put us together at the Horse Shoe House.

We all have experienced great losses. Loss of a job, a marriage, freedom or losing it because of a pending legal matter, are all too common and many are permanent, but there are a few exceptions. The loss of respect, integrity, love and honor keep many of us awake at night. Some of us are weak, and we pray for undeserved forgiveness.

My friend, Angel, lives in the same house I do; and we have had many laughs, but we have covered serious ground, too. Angel's eyes light up every time he speaks of his wife and children. He has told me many times how much he hates being away and feels great shame for his addictive behaviors. Angel is a passionate and emotional friend who wears his heart on his sleeve.

Of course, in some cases passionate people become agitated or even angered rather quickly. In Angel's case, lines across his forehead completely radiate, "I am a bad one, and if you don't get in check now, there is going to be a fight." This is completely oblivious to him. In fact, he is stunned how others fear him when this happens. So, if you, my friend, are reading this, I hope the lines will be missing from your forehead and only a smile or a laugh are seen or heard.

It helps all of us to talk about difficult topics. The House fellowship is some of the best treatment at Hope. We live coast to coast and in different environments at our homes. These men will always be special to me; but as much as we all talk about staying in touch, I know I will never see or hear from most of them again. It is the way recovery life tends to unfold. I will miss all of them and have immense gratitude for their love and friendship.

Down time is nice on the weekend. The pace during the week is go, go, go! Rest is welcome, and a nap is a common way to spend an afternoon. It also gives time to think and reflect. Since none of us came to this place at a high point, the reflections and thoughts are full of regret and sadness. No one is spared a moment when he does not want to give up or succumb to his demons and get a bottle or a fix.

For me, the time came about two weeks after arriving when I was writing about Mrs. F almost every waking moment. The pain I felt when writing about her was worse than anything I have experienced, except when I was seven, eight and nine, and she was unleashing Hell upon me.

Listening to loud music in my headphones is usually what I do when I write, and tears running down my cheeks is very common when I am writing. Well, on this Sunday, I guess I had reached a breaking point and was ready to numb my pain as I had so many times before.

Looking across the valley and leaning over the iron fence by the pool, I was hatching a plan how I could get my hands on some vodka. I was certain I could organize a trip to Wal-Mart or the local supermarket where I could grab a couple pints, smuggle them back to the house and down them in my room without anyone knowing it. Yes, it would be a piece of cake. I went back in the House through the kitchen, and my Angel started talking to me about issues he was having. I was trying not to stop, but Angel kept right on with his problem. He poured us each a cup of coffee, and we sat down at the table. I couldn't tell you what we discussed at the kitchen table. What I can tell you is after our talk, I no longer had a desire to drink. I doubt my Angel knows how close I was to a drink. I never told him. I believe there are situations like mine happening often throughout the Treatment Center where we help one another through crisis times.

CHAPTER 42

Upon my arrival in California, I began writing in my journal again. Looking through it today, I find my gratitude has been steadily rising. It makes me happy I have been able to express gratitude even with all the negatives and adversity with Mrs. F. coming to light. I am now at the half way point of my ninety-day program, and I am seeing growth and betterment.

Gratitude is something we focus on every day in the Alternative Track. Many of these exercises are written and shared in the classroom on the same day. Feedback is not generally a part of these activities and is kept brief in those rare times. Frank said this week and into next week we would be doing more work in this area than usual. This is a thank you letter to my drug of choice. For me, that is alcohol.

Thank You Letter to Alcohol

November 16, 2016

Dear Alcohol,

I am writing to thank you for expanding my knowledge of life and giving me more awareness going forward. This process of shedding you from my identity has given me opportunities to rid myself of other negatives in my life. These are negatives I certainly and ultimately would be turning over to you to manage and medicate. Relationship stresses, loss, and fear are among the things of which I speak. Fear, in general, was your forte for far too long in my life.

I am now forced to deal with things I had never thought necessary to sort out. It was easier to absorb your goodness and trust it was the best way to handle life. I've got to hand it to you though, I am alive today and in reasonably good health. Without you, I likely would have never faced my childhood trauma, never would have known the truth of what happened. I never would have been able to find positive results from something so horrific.

You numbed my pain of marriage by allowing me to live and function in depression and regret. A band-aid fix as it turns out is better than no fix at all.

Now that I choose to be abstinent, I experience the humility of knowing what it would mean to return to the behaviors you love so. Today, I have gratitude that can only come from God. I am learning that even the worst of experiences have positive things to be learned if you let it.

Alcohol gave me confidence when there was none to be had. This allowed feelings of euphoria I likely would have never felt at those times in my life. In closing, I will say I don't want to relive anything with you ever again. I will say thanks for the memories; there was some good along with the bad.

Sincerely,

David

I realize many would say having a positive outlook on addiction is ridiculous. I find myself recalling adversity throughout my life which defines me now. I have accepted my past had to happen for me to be the person I am today. This radical acceptance is a necessary component of beginning to heal from a life of addiction and the traumas of other hurts causing me to take solace in alcohol and drugs.

Today, I have gratitude that can only come from God. I am learning that even the worst of experiences have positive things to be learned if you let it.

Radical acceptance is not something that is going to be possible in a flash of thought or an *ah ha* moment. It requires a large amount of work, desire and commitment. The kind of work I am doing here needs professional guidance and direction. People like me who have dual diagnosis considerations must be treated to have any chance at living a life free of addiction, and the opportunity to live with the mental health issues like PTSD, depression, anxiety and trauma.

If I were to leave Hope by the Sea now at the halfway point of approximately forty-five days, I believe I would eventually return to addictive behaviors. I find myself wondering if in ninety days I will have enough healthy neural pathways to resist more than twenty-five years of addictive behaviors.

Hollywood and the bulk of treatment centers believe twenty-eight days, also called *spin dry*, is an adequate time to resume life free of addiction. Many people have succeeded in this model, but too many do not. I believe anyone who can recover and live without substance has been in a good program. I guess you could look at it as an *all the above* approach.

Detoxification is the first order of business at any treatment center. People often come to treatment heavily impaired from drugs and alcohol. For many it requires a week, or even two, before the fog in their brain has cleared away enough to take an active role in their treatment. Most people are too sick to get out of bed, and **irritable** is putting it mildly in terms of temperament. This phase of the process for me was done with my vitals checked hourly. Medications like valium and phenobarbital are some of the medicines used to keep heart rates and blood pressure at a safe level. The reason for this type of care is many people die from detoxification.

When I look at one to two weeks to become functional, and the program is only twenty-eight days long; it isn't hard to understand why the *spin dry* model is ineffective for most cases. Programs like these are all over America. Some have as few as ten percent success rates after one year. I have been to programs like this and believe them to be lacking. For many of us, trying to heal from addiction which took a lifetime to develop into something requiring in-patient solutions, ninety days seems like minimal time, and less time feels like no time at all.

There is no easy answer to what treatment program is right or wrong. There are individuals who are willing to try to be healed, and those who simply are doing time with little intention of doing anything other than using again when they leave. These are but two of the scenarios in treatment centers today.

After all the hurt, pain and failure, one might expect treatment would be a welcome blessing. I have made promises to quit, to seek help and go to a treatment facility. In the end, it comes down to a couple basic questions

> *For many of us, trying to heal from addiction which took a lifetime to develop into something requiring in-patient solutions, ninety days seems like minimal time, and less time feels like no time at all.*

that sound simple, at least simple to someone not suffering from addiction. Have I spent enough time in my life hurting? Am I ready to hang up my shot glass, or put the pipe, straw or pill bottle down? It certainly sounds simple enough, right?

Dozens, if not hundreds of times, I found myself defeated and feeling completely broken. It is in these times of adversity, I made promises to stop using and work on living a life free of drugs and alcohol. Each time I meant what I said, and I had no intention of breaking my word to those who love and care about me. Every addict the world over has lived the same vicious cycle in their family time and time again.

I didn't need the drugs and alcohol, I needed to stop the pain and suffering. Most of my life this pain had no identity. Unlike a broken leg which can easily be treated and ultimately will heal, I grew up with a pain I could not identify or name. I only knew I wasn't like everyone else. I guess I can describe it like this -- when my brothers or anybody picked on me, called me names or hurt me physically, it hit me with a force 100 times harder, and I would turn it all inward.

Today, it is easy to identify this pattern thanks to my restored memory and the help I am receiving here in California. Before this, it wasn't because I did not want to be free from the chains of addiction that treatment was not successful, quite the contrary. I did not believe I could be healed, or ever live a life free from the negative baggage I had lived with for so long. Now, I do.

David on Vacation

David

Chelsey, David and Grandma

David and son David, fun in Florida

David and son, David

David and Peggy

David and Chelsey in Chicago

David at Harvard
Business School

Daddy's girl, Chelsey

David's beloved grandpa

Mom, Dad, brothers & me 1979

Mom, Dad, my brothers & me 1991

David a moment of laughter at work

Brothers 4, Jeff, David, Dan, Joe

My brothers – Joe, me, Dan, Jeff

Brothers together, June, 2017

CHAPTER 43

Family weekend starts today, and I will see Mom after programming. The family members participating have a class schedule for eight hours per day with only Saturday being joint with the residents. I have been nervous about this for weeks. It has been about two months since I have seen her. The anxiety of real world things, and life after here have made for a lot of stewing I guess. And, of course, there is Cherylee whom I have never met, but who has been praying for me for many months. I am taking all this in stride, I mean what is the worst that could happen?

Others who have family coming appear a whole lot more nervous than I am which is always a plus. There are two men from Alternative Track and four women who are having family here -- two of them are Alternative Track also.

Cherylee is a hugger and quite a pleasure to meet. I am also happy Mom has a travel companion. So, Pong, who you may remember as the guy who drives for Hope by the Sea, moonlights as a restaurant critic and while he finds most places to be *nothing special*, he does have some picks that are ***special***. Tonight, Mom, Cherylee and I are off to Lucy's for some barbeque Pong highly recommends. It is also in route to Saddleback Church where we decided to attend *Celebrate Recovery*. CR is a Christian based twelve- step program that was founded at the Saddleback Church where we are going after dinner.

This dinner is the first time I have seen Mom for more than a minute or two since she arrived in California a couple days ago. The food is great, and it is nice getting to know Cherylee and visiting with Mom. They both enjoyed the day of programming, and they learned quite a bit about addiction. They are looking forward to the next two days.

I have never been to a CR meeting in California. Those in the Christian Track at Hope by the Sea, however, attend every Friday night. The Alternative Track spends the evening journaling and catching up on other writing assignments. The auditorium at Saddleback Church is large, and tonight more than 500 people are in attendance. The CR experience is four hours long -- hour one is a meal, hour two is praise and worship, hour three is break-out groups based on the type of addiction or hang-up you have and finally, hour four is coffee and fellowship. We came for the praise and worship and break-out sessions.

There is a large stage at the front of the auditorium with a band and singers. The sound system is amazing, rivaling any professional set-up anywhere, and lyrics on the monitors allow the audience to sing along. The praise and worship conclude with someone sharing their testimony from the podium. This is moving and emotional. CR encompasses an array of hang-ups, hurts and habits including: chemical, sex, gambling, abuse and other addictions in our lives.

The break-out groups are separated by gender and topics and are in various rooms throughout the facility. In the smaller settings, people share with others in the group what their addictions or hang-ups may be to help one another. This part of CR is like other twelve-step programs similar to AA. The primary difference is the array of groups, and the Christ-centered focus within everything. Cherylee is a regular attender back in Michigan, and she wants me at the session for first time attendees since this is my one and only time at a meeting here. I simply want to go to the substance addiction tent, but Cherylee is having none of it. We locked eyes, and Mom said the temperature dropped twenty degrees.

> *I simply want to go to the substance addiction tent, but Cherylee is having none of it. We locked eyes, and Mom said the temperature dropped twenty degrees.*

Cherylee and I, according to Mom, are both accustomed to doing things our own way -- period! Having been taught to respect my elders, naturally, I agreed to go to the new-comer group.

Fellowship with people is one thing the Alternative is lacking, and it is a good resource to be involved in for that purpose alone. It appeals to a wider base by attracting people with issues other than addiction. I can absolutely see the value of the Christian fellowship as it is something my life lacks and needs.

Heading back to the Horse Shoe House I thought would be uneventful as we all are tired and looking forward to a good night's sleep. The thing is though, I seem to have forgotten where the house is precisely; so, a bit of aimless driving needs to be endured before arriving at my home. I have lived at the Horse Shoe House for almost two months and apparently, I cannot find it when it is dark. The House Managers take us everywhere we need to go in white passenger vans we affectionately refer to as *Druggie Buggies*. Obviously, as a passenger I didn't pay enough attention to details like where the house is. I enjoyed myself and I think Mom and Cherylee did too; I am hopeful tomorrow will be good as well.

Saturday is spent in family programming with a group of other families along with Mom and Cherylee. This is the day I have been anxious about ever since I heard Mom was coming to California. I have had feelings like this for as long as I can remember regarding what others may or may not think. The only difference now versus past years is I am now learning the how and why of my fears in life.

Birthplace of Addiction

I decide to let Mom read some of the letters I have written since I have been here in California. It is a hard decision given the subject matter, and the last thing I want is for Mom to blame herself or shoulder guilt. Sometimes, it is easier to throw all the information out there instead of playing twenty questions the entire time she is here. She stayed up most of the night reading the letters I had flagged for her to read. She seems to be okay with things, but it did create some feelings that troubled her. It is probably a blessing we have programming all day to keep our minds busy.

The morning class consists of a long power point presentation covering various addiction topics. Five out of seven families in the room have loved ones in the Alternative Track, so I am surprised it is almost all focused on twelve-step programs. I am not going to say it isn't useful, but it seems to be exclusively tailored to that program. On break, some people express anger and frustration because no Alternative Track programming is mentioned. This surprises me, because Hope by the Sea is so meticulous about almost everything.

After lunch is over, we shift to a much more intense exercise for the afternoon. The room is set-up with chairs along the entire perimeter of the space. There are four chairs in the middle of the room facing each other, two on each side. The instructions are each family will take a turn in the *hot seat* to talk to one another about obstacles and challenges beyond treatment. Emotionally charged is a mild description of what the afternoon has in store. The facilitator's job is to guide the conversations between family members to a positive conclusion if possible.

The families of clients in addiction treatment are plagued with tension and adversity often throwing wedges into their relationships with one another. The tiresome cycle of failing to overcome addiction and broken promises is only the surface of the hurt lying beneath. It ceased being about right and wrong, or who did what to who long ago. What remains are families who are here today repairing relationships, and realizing, maybe for the first time, recovery is life or death.

There is a closeness among the clients in this place which is unspoken yet understood. It is as if we have known each other for years. Perhaps, it is the similarities existing in our adversity or the hopelessness we have felt for so long. The Alternative Track clients write about the most intimate details of their lives. Terrible traumas, rape, molestation, and acts of unspeakable violence are among the things shared daily. Learning to live with these events in our lives is why we are here at Hope by the Sea, and for many, this is our last chance to have a meaningful life.

My Mom and I don't have a whole lot of things to discuss in terms of resolving differences or unresolved anger. If not for Mom, I never would have been able to be here at this amazing place where healing happens every single day. I am very grateful to her and my stepfather for believing in me, and for all their help in ways I doubt I can ever repay. Mom expresses regret for not being able to protect me in the classroom of Mrs. F, and this brings a lot of feelings and emotions to the surface for us both. All I can say is my past had to happen, or I would not be me. I would not be in this place now with a future; and, for the first time, I can remember, I can dream what I dared not dream, because I believed it did not exist. I am speaking of hope.

What I observed this afternoon with these people at Family Weekend is nothing short of miraculous. By the end of the day, we all felt as if the difficulties and challenges experienced here, were shouldered by everyone in the room. In so doing, it takes some of the burden away from all of us. We walked into this room for the most part as strangers, and several hours later a bond is cemented among us all. Fittingly, the day ends after the last family is finished. It is a day we surely will not soon forget.

Overnight passes to stay with family are made available to those who request them. Pong recommends a restaurant for dinner called *The Chart House* located above Dana Point with a view of the Pacific. The food and company are great, and we talk of normal things. I get to know Mom's friend a little better over dinner. After we arrived, before being seated, Cherylee left to locate the restroom. In the meantime, Mom and I were seated. This should have caused no difficulty, except I made the reservation using my full name, David Foss, not realizing Cherylee only knew Mom's last name, not mine. Cherylee came out of the restroom and did not see us where she left us. Not missing a beat, she asked where the rest of her party was. When they asked whose name the reservation is under, she said, "Uh, I have no idea!" This is a large upscale restaurant, so wandering around looking at everyone is a bit irregular. She found us, of course; and we all had a needed laugh at the situation given the day we had all had.

The last couple of days have been pretty action packed with a lot of information learned and discussed. Family weekend is at an end for me, but for Mom and Cherylee, it will end tomorrow at four o'clock.

Mom and Cherylee are staying at a nice hotel in Laguna Hills not far from the Horse Shoe House. Everyone is a little worn out from the day, and a good night's sleep will be welcome. Nevertheless, I must find out what the story is with Mom's friend, Cherylee. The fact someone, whom I have never met, would want to come to California and spend three days sitting in a room at a treatment center still amazes me. She was immensely interested in learning about addiction and taking a lot of notes today, not to mention the intense emotional baggage of today. Yes, there's more here than meets the eye, and I need to learn the rest of this story.

So, I ask why she is so inquisitive about the subject of addiction, and she told me she has an addiction too. The look on Mom's face is truly priceless. It turns out, gambling is her poison of choice. This addiction can be every bit as destructive on a person's life as substances. The destruction of the family, feelings of hopelessness and obsessive compulsion destroy lives. I am glad Cherylee confided in us, and that she made the trip. I am looking forward to knowing her better when I get back home in January.

With my mystery solved, I had sweet sleep that night at Mom's hotel.

CHAPTER 44

Mom and Cherylee dropped me off at the House on their way to their final day of the Family Weekend. It is early, and nobody is up yet, being a Sunday and all. I walked out on the patio, and I am anxious to get caught up on my writing. The following is the check-in I wrote in my journal on that morning.

November 20, 2017 Journal entry (daily check-in)

Last night was nice. I went to a place on top of Dana Point called the Chart House for a wonderful steak dinner with Mom and her friend, Cherylee, from Michigan. The family sessions left us tired and ready for some relaxation.

When we got back to the hotel, Mom and I went down to the lobby to talk awhile. She wanted to see more letters than the few she had already seen. I hadn't planned on being so open with my writing, but maybe it is fine. She seems to be coping well with the content. I sensed some guilt and regret as we read through a few more letters. The last thing I want is for Mom to have feelings of melancholy over what went on all those years ago.

I felt myself getting antsy, or maybe anxious is a better word, over conversations about life back in the Midwest. Anxiety over leaving there is high for me, and each time the conversation went in that direction my feelings spiked. *The Work* that has and is being done makes processing feelings possible.

The families accomplished some healing yesterday, and it was nice to see. I gained insight for my own situation by seeing these things in others. The format of the Family Weekend was focused heavily on twelve-step principles having little content related to the Alternative Track.

It feels good to know I have made progress so far, and I am looking forward to the remainder of the program to work on things that need attention. It is made clear at Hope by the Sea that things creating the most awkwardness within me, tend to be among the most important to address. This morning I had a craving to write, and a craving to process on paper. That felt good! Onward and upward!

I have been assigned a new Case Manager because Kim quit for personal reasons and her cases were divided among the other Case Managers. I could not be more thrilled to have Harlan as my Case Manager for my remaining time at Hope by the Sea. I have spent more time with him than any other staff member here, and we know one another well. I am looking forward to formally meeting with him this week. Informally, I will see him later this afternoon in the park.

Gratitude is a component of a core philosophy in *The Work* we do in the Alternative Track and in other recovery areas as well. We are continuing *The Work* in this area this week by doing another gratitude letter to our addiction substances.

Gratitude to Alcohol and Drugs

November 21, 2017

Dear Alcohol and Drugs,

If someone were to ask me: Which friends have you spent the most time with? Who matters most in your life? Who do you miss and think about the most? What person, place, or thing makes your eyes radiate and mouth water the most? The answer is you on all accounts. Even though, we are only pen pals these days, it is not possible to dismiss all the happy times or feelings of grandeur that are in my memory always.

I struggle today to find methods or means to occupy myself without your domineering presence. Your loyalty has been true; always being there to celebrate the good, bad and even ugliest of times. Be it vodka, cocaine, oxycodone, methamphetamine, or heroin, you could be found at my side as if you were always there.

You are to be commended for your resiliency in surviving and making it through various storms designed to eradicate you. No matter how much I neglected you, sometimes for years at a time, you remained as faithful as a Golden Retriever. It never mattered how broke, rich, tired, happy, sad, mad, glad, depressed, anxious, proud, ashamed or guilty I was, I never had to wonder where your allegiance was. You were ready to numb my feelings and dull my senses, so life's problems could be put at bay for another day.

Sometimes days, weeks, months and years would pass with you in my system. No matter how sick or shaky I was, you stood ready to keep me spun. The affection you show me is soothing and in a sick way nurturing. Wrapped in your blanket of death is often my happy place, and at those times, death is my friend. Thanks for the nostalgia.

David

It might seem a little strange to write gratitude to something as awful and damaging as addiction. It kills thousands each year and is the culprit of an infinite number of broken families. When I arrived about six weeks ago I was in pain, a terrible, mental anguish that made me physically ill. I found gratitude to be in low supply in my life, and I couldn't tell you how long I had felt this way, only I did.

The first day in the Alternative Track, I arrived after class had begun due to meeting with the doctor. Frank didn't like tardiness. Everyone was writing three things we were grateful for and why, ten reasons the last twenty-four hours were positive and one quality in ourselves we respected and admired. I could not think of enough to complete the work in the time allotted. When people, one at a time, started sharing the assignment, I was stunned at how easy this exercise was for everyone to do. I remember thinking these people must have been here a while.

> *It took a certain amount of humility to discover I needed help. I learned a good life free of substances requires a balance of these two things — gratitude and humility.*

Centric to the Alternative Track is learning how to be grateful. For some of us, this is the first time in our lives we are learning this. Addiction tends to make people self-centered and often lacking in humility. For me, it took a certain amount of humility to discover I needed help. I learned a good life free of substances requires a balance of these two things — gratitude and humility. Perhaps I should clarify, it is a formula for a happy, meaningful life that is often elusive.

It's simple enough to mesh gratitude and humility to perfection and boom! your happy, right? It took me years to uncover and deal with many mental issues going back to elementary school and there is more to do. Each day I complete *The Work* asked of me, it is creating new neural pathways in my brain. When I leave here, I will need to continue it without being asked. It is how the new neural pathways will become stronger. I do *The Work* not asked of me, because I believe in what I am doing, and in Frank who teaches me.

CHAPTER 45

Harlan, as per normal, took a seat at the picnic table in the park that has become my favorite place to write. My conversations with him are invaluable to me. I have been here seven weeks, and in that time, Harlan has become a large part of my healing process that I never expected. I consider Harlan a dear friend, and I hope our friendship gets even stronger in the years to come.

I asked Harlan if he felt blessed by having the honor of being my Case Manager. He began to chuckle and said, "When I learned of this, I demanded a substantial raise for having to put up with you," and he smiled and chuckled again. Then, he asked me how Family Weekend went, and if I had learned anything new about myself?

I said, "Turns out I was stewing these past weeks for no reason at all. The weekend was enlightening; and I learned my Mom is tougher than I thought. I was humbled by the other families after hearing some of their stories and by the healing power of the group."

"How is everything else going? What are you working on now?" He inquired.

"I am beginning to write and process other things now that the teacher is disappearing into my past. I am discovering my life after third grade was not unlike a design of dominos tumbling down, and my youth was the catalyst setting them in motion. Does it make any sense to you? I can't say it any plainer," I reflected.

I asked Harlan if he felt blessed by having the honor of being my Case Manager. He began to chuckle and said, "When I learned of this, I demanded a substantial raise for having to put up with you,"

Harlan thought about that for a minute and said, "I never heard it put that way before. It sounds like you have a plan to get where you can move on in life and stop living in a sea of yesterdays. I advise a little patience and realism in your expectations; this kind of work can take a bit more time. I have been at this for decades, and I still don't have all the answers. What you have are more and more reasons to keep at it and never give up."

Harlan is correct. I may never have all the answers to the many questions I have in the realm of whys and why nots. Rarely do we have a hundred percent clarity in anything; there is generally room for one more opinion or course of action to consider. Here at Hope by the Sea there are three different methodologies for the treatment of addiction. Christian, Traditional, and Alternative Tracks all have the same exact goal, being each promotes a life free of willful addictive behaviors. It is left to the clients to decide the one best suited for themselves. My view is each Track has benefits. I believe those fully committed to defeating addiction and the mental health afflictions that plague their lives, will find attributes of each in their personal journeys.

I ask, "Do a lot of people who come here stay less then ninety days? Seems a lot of people have been leaving after thirty, forty-five, or sixty days here."

He said, "For some it is about their insurance company being unwilling to pay for the entire program; for others, it is their decision to leave. As I am sure you are aware, not everyone takes their program seriously."

"I have noticed people have left and come back in the short time I have been here. Others come here, and it is their second or even third time in treatment in the last twelve months," I said.

"Son, I have been doing this for a long time, and it seems to come down to a willingness to say good-bye to the addictive behaviors. Have people been hurt enough? Have they been hurt for long enough? This is not the same for everybody as you know all too well. For some, it is under-estimating the sheer power addiction and undiagnosed mental conditions like, depression, PTSD and trauma that people have lived with for years, have over us. Until recently, addiction and mental health afflictions were not discussed in the same breath. Many treatment centers still do not. Count yourself blessed to have landed at a dual diagnosis (co-occurring) facility." Harlan stated.

"I am among the lucky, and not a day goes by I don't thank God for being here. Having met so many people who are like me has given me a sense of gratitude I didn't have prior to coming here. It is fitting to feel this way the week of Thanksgiving as I have so much for which to be thankful. I have a lot to learn and a long way to go, but I feel good about *The Work* thus far," I said.

Harlan continued, "In the end, all we can do is our best to live a life free of all the things that brought us here. When you leave here, I can assure you there will be trials to test you. I believe you will be prepared and will overcome all of this," he said.

"Thanks!" I said.

I'm taking off early today, and I'm going with Mom for the rest of the day. She is leaving tomorrow to go back to Michigan, so we will go to the Ocean and enjoy the views before dinner.

I have a pass to not attend the evening activity because it is my birthday. Luck is with us and Mom and I made it to the ocean, and we will watch the sunset later. We spend a little time chatting at the park by the Pacific about nothing in particular; it is good to have a nice visit alone without any Family Weekend activity. The sunset could not have been more beautiful that lovely day on the Pacific coast.

Since Mom has only been in California for a few days, and I have been here a couple months, it is established almost immediately I will be the navigator when we are out driving around. Up to now, outside of a couple irregularities that may have taken us on a couple of side trips; *i.e.*, driving on a toll road and we had no clue as to how we got on it, or how to pay said toll, or even exit the tollway. Nevertheless, we have survived my superior navigation skills. By this time, it has gotten dark outside, so I decide to keep things simple and go over to the ice cream shop near the Horse Shoe House. This would be perfect as I had been there before, so nothing could go wrong, right? Long story short, neither of us got any ice cream that night, and to this day the California Highway Patrol is still looking to collect an unpaid toll. Without any further direction assistance from me, Mom and Cherylee, checked out of their hotel, drove to the airport, returned the rental car and flew home the next day without incident.

CHAPTER 46

Gratitude was again the focus in the Alternative Track. I asked, "How come I am expressing so much gratitude on substances that have become a source of considerable negative influence in my life? I could sit and write about the destructive wake it has left in my life and not be in jeopardy of running out of material for decades."

Frank said, "You wrote about your teacher and focused on your feelings, mostly the negative ones. Then I asked you to write some positive things that exist because of the trauma. If you can learn to express gratitude for addiction like you did for the trauma, you will be in a place to release all of it and burn the letters. Make sense?"

I said, "I think it is beginning to."

He said, "Those things occupied a lot of your thoughts over the years along with the substances; it would have had to have perceived value, or you wouldn't have kept using it. People often get into a cycle of confusing the right or wrong aspects of this. Don't go there. An example would be when promises are broken people will say things like: You should be *ashamed* of yourself for what you did! Maybe you should be. I don't know, but it is not what we are doing here, attaching morality and consequences are something else. Here, it is: what hurt or was too awful to face that required you to bury your mind in these substances? Again, if the substances didn't serve a purpose or a respite from something, you wouldn't have found it necessary to use. David, do you understand the exercise now?"

I said, "Yes"

The exercise being a third gratitude letter to our addictive substances and here it is.

November 22, 2016

Dear Alcohol and Drugs,

The ride we have been on together has had some definite positive times. The insight I have into how my brain works on a micro level likely would not have been discovered without this courtship of ours. Your power is considerable and shouldn't be underestimated, for you push the boundaries of survival and go to extremes to succeed.

I have found strength and hope at times when there was not any. I have found light in darkness. In many ways, you have enhanced and empowered me to fight for what I believe in and to win at any cost. My ability to adapt to people, places, and things are exceedingly high, and I owe most of that intuitiveness to our relationship.

People say you're all bad and evil, the devourer of those you seduce. I believe without this thing of ours, a lot of the qualities I deem desirable would be weakened or lost altogether. I owe a debt of gratitude for the gifts that have been bestowed on me.

I never would have learned the value of adversity or the strength in vulnerability. These along with failure are often viewed negatively in our society. The strength realized from these things brings a level of clarity that few in my experiences have attained.

So, even though we are no longer a thing, and never will we be rekindling either, I choose to embrace the good; and release, or learn to live with all that is bad. The rest of my life is bright, and I will finally be able to realize my potential free of many of the obstacles that always had my worst interest at heart. Thanks for the memories,

David

CHAPTER 47

Active Addiction, Denial, Acceptance, Recovery, Denial -- the vicious cycle can end

One of the things I am learning about myself through writing is drugs and alcohol have been my best friends throughout my life with few exceptions. The soothing attributes of alcohol served to dull the pain which many times could not be identified other than it hurt. My alcohol use began in adolescence and drugs followed a short time thereafter. They initially took all my problems and made them small. Drinking and drugging gave me confidence I never had, and I wasn't afraid anymore.

Alcohol, being the most insidious of all drugs, seduced me into believing I never had a problem; and I was, therefore, in control of my life. I convinced myself and others I did not have a drug or alcohol problem, because I supported my family and always went to work. There was no shortage of rationalizations and justifications for my addictive behaviors.

Denial essentially is a defense mechanism providing a false shield that makes me believe I do not have a problem. There are literally infinite reasons I am able to convey to others which proclaim I am in control, and drugs and alcohol do not control me. As the layers of denial are built by me over many years, it becomes an alternate reality for me to always preserve my secret at any cost.

Addiction is described by many as cunning, baffling, and powerful. I was living in active addiction, and I was cunning, and I could be described among other things as baffling. I would pursue efforts to supply my addictions as powerfully as necessary. Throughout this cycle at the core of every thought for every action and consequence is denial. Despite causing the very pain, hurt, and destruction the drugs and alcohol once medicated, the denial remains.

Denial is not exclusive to those of us in active addiction. Some examples of denial in others include: our employers, family, and friends who are often in this denial cycle as much as we are. Often it becomes easier for them to pretend it doesn't exist. If they ignore the addictive behavior, then it is not a part of their world. This happens in the workplace often where it is not uncommon for addiction to thrive for many years before the behavior is addressed.

Family members can fall into denial of addiction existing in their home. Emotions run high in the immediate family unit and often result in family break-ups including divorce. Where children are involved, it is certain the entire situation will be traumatizing. It isn't a lack of love in a family creating the tension. Most families aren't equipped to deal with what is happening with their loved one. The denial by the family and their employer tend to enable the addict. Addicts in active addiction can be very manipulative in getting what they want, and they consider everything fair game in pursuit of their substances.

As someone, who is and has been addicted to substances, I can tell you it is difficult to accept a problem exists in your life; and that it isn't someone else's problem. Accepting it, however, puts the substance in charge (*i.e.*, alcohol, street or prescription drugs); it is the only thing numbing the pain, and, what I have come to require in my life. I have little understanding of the only thing that makes sense to me, and it delivers what I perceive to be medicine to alleviate my pain. I know without these substances, my pain is greater; so, doing anything that will remove what reduces my hurt is insanity to me. Logic or anything resembling common sense does not resonate with someone who is in active addiction.

> *Addiction is a result of the pain caused by the trauma I suffered as a child. My birthplace of addiction is in the dark, stinking closet in Mrs. F's classroom.*

I had many periods of abstinence from drugs and alcohol. I learned recovery begins when denial becomes acceptance, and recovery ceases when denial picks up where it left off. The substances leave my body in a matter of a week or two once abstinence begins. What does not leave is the pain and hurt the substances have numbed. As a victim of trauma and many mental health afflictions, the vicious cycle will continue until we treat the pain and hurt. Addiction is a result of the pain caused by the trauma I suffered as a child. My birthplace of addiction is in the dark, stinking closet in Mrs. F's classroom.

Knowing why, when and what happened to me all those years ago is the information empowering me to treat the pain and hurt. Writing all the letters surrounding the trauma is a beginning to allow me to uncover, discover, and discard the negative and to build on the positive of coming to a place of accepting my past had to happen. This allows me to not live in fear of today or tomorrow. This has been made possible by Hope by the Sea. The Alternative Track working in concert with individualized and group therapies is why I believe in *The Work*.

CHAPTER 48

Many years ago, I went to a treatment center in Iowa. It was my first time in a residential setting and it lasted twenty-one days. The twelve steps of Alcoholics Anonymous along with Narcotics Anonymous made up the program. No mental health component was available. I was at a place in my life where I was ready to stop all drugs and drinking. I wanted to live a normal life free from addiction.

I had a job and was a top performer in the home remodeling field. The jobs were being sold responsibly, and the boss was thrilled I was making over a hundred thousand dollars a year for his company. I was drinking a lot and did drugs often. When the owner called me up in December to fire me, I was shocked and afraid it would ruin my family's Christmas. I met with my boss the next day, and he shared with me he had stopped doing drugs and alcohol. It was why he was letting me go, despite the big sales contracts I was closing.

I called and thanked that boss when I was half way through my treatment. I was working the twelve-steps and learning a lot of information on addiction science. I was discharged from that place after twenty-one days, and I was feeling good. I began attending meetings and got a sponsor to help me work the steps. Sober and clean, I was eager to resume life believing addiction was in the past.

I was abstinent for more than three years when I did not find it necessary to take a drink or do drugs. At the time, I was married with two children in their teen and pre-teen ages. I was running a large remodeling company, and I got along with my family better than ever. Life was good. The stage was set. I made a lot of money, and I considered it a dream come true when I earned an equity stake in the company I had helped grow to its pinnacle of success. I enjoyed the work. I told people I never wanted to return to the life of an addict. What I didn't know was why I continued to have a feeling of not being good enough or deserving of a life of happiness.

My conscious had blocked the memories of the trauma that had shaped my life. My sub-conscious recorded a complete record of my life including second and third grades. I have learned I am what my sub-conscious projects. The hurt and pain inside of me for thirty-five years had no face recognizable to me; and, I discovered once again, it couldn't be soothed. I put more and more drugs and alcohol in me to numb my hurts and to tame the raging beast within me. It has been a malignant presence for as long as I can remember.

Periods of abstinence for me have always ultimately resulted in a return of denial, killing any recovery that had taken place. It is important to understand how easily and rapidly this return of addictive behavior can begin to creep into your life. Denial and feelings of grandiosity began to slowly extinguish the gratitude and humility that kept me clean and sober for three plus years. This process is insidious in nature, taking many months or even years before a person uses a drug or takes a drink. The relapse happens often long before the substance use.

> *Denial and feelings of grandiosity began to slowly extinguish the gratitude and humility that kept me clean and sober for three plus years.*

For us who have suffered traumas in our childhood, in my case unbeknown to me, self-medicating is a necessary part of survival. Because it is the case for many, nurturing denial is equally necessary to live. I could never figure out why I am the way I am; nobody else could either. With my recently restored memory, the answers to very difficult questions are beginning to unfold.

I was working what I considered my dream job, and in almost every way, it was. As I had countless times, I began to self-sabotage my success. Several months before I began using drugs and alcohol again, I was beginning to think I could handle drinking and drugs in a controlled way. I began to create scenarios in my head how it could be done. I didn't want my family or my associates at work to know about it. I decided to only let the demons out when I was out of the state on business; then, nobody would know. I had worked very hard to get to where I was, taking on challenges and reaping the rewards of being the best at what I did. The *Great I* had returned in my life, pushing gratitude and humility aside, meaning destruction would follow. It was an absolute certainty.

About two years passed, and everything was gone. Again, I found myself broken, worse than ever. I never recovered from what began with drinking and drugging in other states. In this same time frame, my eighteen-year marriage came to an end, straining relationships with my two children in the process. This relapse began in 2012 and did not stop until late 2016 with my admission to Hope by the Sea.

One moment I was grateful and humble for the gifts bestowed on me in my life. The next thing I knew, I cannot say exactly when, the denial took over. Broken promises, ruined or strained relationships, financial

> *The hope keeping me going and willing to put in The Work comes from my daily relationship with God through Bible study and prayer.*

stress and legal issues are some of the many things existing in a lifetime of addiction. Overwhelming circumstances and emotional fallout come with getting clean and sober again, and suicides are common. I never considered myself suicidal, although I would have welcomed death at many points of my life.

My addiction is a result of something else entirely, but there is no denying the pain and destruction. The mental afflictions surrounding my childhood made me ripe for substances to help me cope. The failures in my life only validated my low self-esteem and feelings of worthlessness that were hard-wired in my early childhood. *The Work* necessary to sort all of this out will probably take the rest of my life. The hope keeping me going and willing to put in *The Work* comes from my daily relationship with God through Bible study and prayer.

CHAPTER 49

Harlan is my Case Manager now, and it makes us both happy. These past seven weeks we have gotten to know each other. It was like I have known this man for years and his experience when it comes to addiction and overcoming it, is something he gives to me freely. His thirty-five years of sobriety speaks for itself in my mind; and because of that, I do what he asks even if I don't agree or see the wisdom of it right away.

Today, we reviewed my treatment plan. I immediately discovered his style was more informal than my previous Case Manager, Kim. He explained some of the assignments we will be working on between now and December 31 which will be my last day at Hope. He said we will begin working on what life looks like after I leave. He called it brain-storming, a name I thought reflected my mindset. I need his help preparing a plan for living day-to-day without the need for drugs and alcohol.

Coffee is not available at the Treatment Center, only in the houses. Consequently, to get your daily caffeine requirement, it is necessary to bring a thermos. Harlan, however, has a private coffee pot inside his office. I refill my thermos each day after lunch to remain attentive for afternoon programming. I believe Harlan likely drinks a gallon or more of coffee each day. It reminds me of my Dad.

Harlan became clean and sober using the twelve-step program of Alcoholics Anonymous, and it has kept him sober more than thirty years and counting. I believe when I cut through the bull, any program a person can find that works well for them and their family, is a good one. All the above is what I am doing for myself, selectively enhancing the Alternative Track methodology by embracing my Christian faith in Celebrate Recovery, incorporating some of the principles of AA and utilizing Smart Recovery processes. I am not a twelve-stepper by any means, but I enjoy and desperately need the fellowship of these organizations.

I will probably ruffle a few feathers out there in recovery land due to how I write about them, but I don't think utilizing one program exclusively is wise. I asked Harlan if he deviates from the core text of AA, and he had this to say, "There is flexibility in every recovery program; there has to be. The lived experience of people is going to be different from one to another; we are all perfectly imperfect human beings seeking recovery in programs designed by same."

I said, "That is interesting to me because many people here, staff and client alike, seem to be rather defensive when deviations are discussed."

He said, "That doesn't surprise me for many reasons. The way I believe is based partly on experience; and at my age, I really don't care what others think, nor should you, if you take your recovery as serious as I do."

I believe Harlan to be passionate about everything we discuss because he has walked in my shoes and understands what the residents of Hope by the Sea are going through. He gave me a couple of assignments to begin working on. One was about acclimating to life when I leave here. Legal matters, family and employment to name a few. The other one he calls, *Willful Neglect,* also known as relapse prevention. Harlan doesn't believe in relapse; contending, for one to occur, your program is being neglected. No one forces anyone to neglect their recovery program; therefore, making it willful.

Both assignments had numerous pages, and as I was thumbing through them, it became clear they assumed a twelve-step program was being followed. I pointed this out to him, and he agreed to let me adapt them to the Alternative Curriculum I had learned from Frank. I told him, "I will work on and complete these in time for our meeting next week."

Tomorrow is Thanksgiving, and it begins the holiday season. I have heard it called the silly season because it causes many families to be stressed in some fashion, and Christmas bears most of it. Thanksgiving Day through New Year's Day are among the most troubling for those plagued by addiction and other mental health afflictions. Suicides, relapses, overdoses and arrests for impaired driving all see increases in frequency. I decided to stay here in treatment until the holiday season is in my rear view.

Frank told us to be mindful around this time of year and write about the feelings it stirs up. He said it is important we learn to express our feelings on paper as they are happening to us. When we leave here, this is the kind of work it will require if we seek a fulfilling life.

Today Frank asked us to write a letter, and the content will be: this is our last day to live, and this is the last writing anyone will ever hear from us ever.

The following was what I wrote:

November 23, 2016

Hello All,

Today is my last day to live in this world, and these are the final words anyone will ever hear from David. Life is short, and I feel a heavy lump in my throat along with some powerful emotions. I simply am not ready to leave.

I want my children to know I died alcohol and drug free, and I died trying to better myself, so I could be there for them. I would say they should not hate or bottle up emotions and feelings as I have in my life. Express and process things; get the weight lifted from your hearts. Understand life is a gift; it is precious, and your lives have barely begun. Be good to each other and realize you have more in common than either of you would admit. Build the lives of happiness you deserve, learn to forgive and demonstrate compassion in all your affairs. Express gratitude and be humble, these are the two qualities that are essential to have fulfillment in how you live life.

To Mom I say thank-you for being my Mom and a light for me in some very dark places. Do not blame yourself for any part of my life. My life had to unfold as it did for me to be the person you now know. I would not have found Hope by the Sea by myself. Hold your head high and know that you are exactly what God had in mind as a Mom.

To my brothers I want to express love and regret for any stress or embarrassment that I brought to your lives. I wish we had more time because I really don't think any of you know me. This place has allowed me to realize the negative, awful things inside me. I am at peace with myself; it is new and different. I feel this incredible calm and know that everything is going to be okay.

Tomorrow will happen, and I will be gone; all that remains are some words in my journals along with my children to show that I was ever here. Live today and make it count, do this each day for tomorrow is promised to nobody. I am grateful and thankful for the knowledge of knowing today is my last. I am glad I wrote this and know that life is not something I regret. Good bye.

David

For whatever reason this writing is emotionally charged. Almost everyone is visibly emotional upon sharing. I have been focusing most of my time processing events from three decades ago, and this exercise strikes a lot of nerves in me.

As always, Frank took a few moments to gather his thoughts and said, "The good news is everything you wrote does not have to be. It isn't the end for any of you, because tomorrow is whatever you decide to make of it. The only thing ever holding you down is you. Addiction is not your problem; it is a symptom of something else altogether different. That is why we write, to sort out and deal with the negative;

purging it from us by releasing it. Then, we can start recognizing positives we never saw before now."

I realize the previous paragraph may seem redundant. I write it over and over, because it is how I learned. It is how I realized the vitality of what Frank taught countless others and me. Tomorrow is Thanksgiving, and I am spending the day with my housemates in lieu of programming at the Center. I have much for which to be grateful this year.

I have been looking forward to Thanksgiving for weeks now -- the meal, fellowship with my housemates and maybe a little football on television. I decided not to do any writing. All the Houses at Hope by the Sea are on lock down for the day. Nobody can leave on passes, and, there will be no activities. Some people grumbled, but I think most, including me, appreciated the time hanging out with nowhere to go.

Ringo, a good man to have as a friend, is a Chef who prepares lunch each day at the Men's and Women's Centers. Thanksgiving dinner with all the trimmings including dessert is being delivered by Ringo to every House. Ringo takes good care of us and putting all that food together and delivering it to the residences, must have been a pile of work. The meal is excellent, and in some ways, it is better than with our own families. It is quiet while we eat. I think most of us had a shot of depression along with the turkey and gravy.

When I was growing up in the farming community back in Minnesota, I remember having a lot of family over for the holiday. A lot of traditional dishes and nobody ever went hungry. Alcohol was never a part of the holiday experience, even when my brothers and I had homes and families of our own.

Talking to the guys in the House, we have similar holiday stories, times of stress and heartache around this time of year. Life for someone in active addiction always is more stressful when we are spending time with family. Plug in some holiday time, and the unrealistic expectations create a great opportunity to fall short. We all agree Thanksgiving is a practice run, building to the big kahuna in a month. I am happy to be here in California this holiday season; I don't believe it would have gone well back home.

Turns out Ringo brought enough food to the House to have dinner twice. Surprisingly, everybody could load up two plates full of turkey and assorted side dishes, and of course, more dessert. I personally ate so much I was downright uncomfortable; my brothers would have been jealous! So overall, it was a nice day with good fellowship and great eats.

CHAPTER 50

Something I did early in my treatment was start a list of people, places and things. I felt it may become necessary to write letters in these areas at some point in my recovery. I realize, it will take a lot longer than ninety days to process most of my life. It is challenging to write letters to my Mom, Dad, Grandpa, Grandma, Son, Daughter and Brothers because they strike a lot of nerves that were not there thirty plus years ago.

When I write about my peers at Hope by the Sea I only use first names. When this book is read by these folks, it will not be easy for anybody else but them to identify themselves. When the writing is about my family, it is next to impossible to mask their identity. This is something with which I struggled, and I did a lot of soul searching to find the right way to proceed. This is a work of non-fiction, and there isn't a way to bring my lived experiences with the traumas of second and third grade, and the consequences thereafter to life, without talking about them.

The writings thus far have seen plenty of family references both in the letters and creative writings as Frank calls them. What is different going forward is much of the writing will include letters to specific family members.

The thing about writings that involve family is if you write about one, it almost always involves another. Our family, perfectly imperfect as the next, has a real closeness and kinship I have always felt even in times of adversity and despair. I have not spoken to anyone in the family other than Mom since July of 2016. I have respect for my family, and in my lowest places, I never meant to hurt or disappoint anyone and do not wish to with my writings.

It is good to be back at the Center the day after Thanksgiving and get back to business. Frank told me writing to my Mom is going to be necessary. I am not sure how to begin, so I just began writing and kept writing.

This is a letter to Mom

November 24, 2016

Dear Mom,

Fourth grade you would think would have been better than the last two years, and I suppose it was. There was no violence or torture at the hand of Mrs. F. I could still hear her teaching and yelling, the whole school could.

I didn't know how to act in school anymore. I didn't know what was right or wrong and really didn't have any friends. I had a deep-seeded hatred of school I didn't understand; it consumed me. Mrs. M, my teacher, didn't yell or hit me, but she seemed to have the low down on me. I believed I was bad and thought everyone else felt as Mrs. F.

What bothered me at the time is you and Dad seemed to think that everything was going to somehow magically be fine again, and I would revert to the person I was before second grade. I don't know who that is. That child never saw the light of day again. That kid died in a dark closet two classrooms down the hall.

I found myself being despondent and uninterested in pretty much everything. I did not believe school could be anything but terrible. I rode the same bus with the same people, and I had the same principal. I saw Mrs. F every day, and despite not being in her class, I was still terrified. I trembled, and my chest became heavy whenever I saw her.

I had no interest in learning anything in that school, and I didn't want to live anymore. I am still seven years old in maturity. I didn't progress like everyone else, and I didn't understand a lot of things about social situations or friendships.

I still loved farming and Grandpa was letting me drive the tractor more and more. It was with him I received positive reinforcement that I believed. You see, Grandpa didn't ask about school he knew I was miserable and hurting. He knew I devoured information about farming as fast as he could talk about it. When we would go to tractor dealerships, I would know as much as he did.

I knew you and Dad loved me in fourth grade. I was routinely in trouble. I was bored and probably deeply depressed. The first month or so of fourth grade was a time of melancholy at best, and of being on the verge of a psychotic breakdown at worst.

There was a new kid in our class today, and he lives in our neighborhood about two miles away. His name is Jeremy as you know. I don't know why he seemed okay to me, maybe it was because he was awkward too. Jeremy and his Dad stayed at his Grandparents' home, and you would take me there to play sometimes. This began a friendship that lasted fifteen years, ball park. He hurt. I knew it. He knew I had issues, but we never talked about them, not ever. Might say we were a bit strange, and on the bus and in school we often became the targets of kids making fun of and picking on us.

I don't know why or how, but school had one ray of sunshine because now in addition to Goldie, there was Jeremy. This helped in ways most wouldn't comprehend. I have never spoken of this before as to why this bond seemed to happen by itself.

In the neighborhood, at Sunday school, even on vacation each year, there was never any kids my age to play or hang out with. Joe had Bruce; Dan had Joel; and Jeff, had the Davis boys Kevin and Kirk. *FINALLY*, there was someone my age and grade on the bus and in the neighborhood. This may seem like a small thing, but to me it was everything. He hated school like I did and was a bit off socially like I was.

I don't know how much longer I could have made it in school if Jeremy hadn't of shown up when he did. I am realizing now I was suicidal in fourth grade. I hated my life, and I was convinced everyone thought I was a bad person. I was sinking into a vat of endless despair and hopelessness. I fought back tears on the bus going to school and cried most nights in my bed.

This is fourth grade, and things were supposed to be different. Truth is, it scares me to think what would have happened if things hadn't changed.

I think it must have been sometime in this time frame when I blocked out everything that happened in second and third grades. It must have been my brain's way of preserving my life, a survival mechanism of sorts. What remained is a person who had a lifelong feeling of never being good enough, often hating myself. It was what it was I suppose…it was what it was.

David

Frank said, "How was it?"

"Writing to Mom was more difficult than I thought it would be. Going back there from this perspective, even though it is content I have written a lot about, it is somehow much different, not sure if that makes sense?"

He answered, "You have feelings that are more charged emotionally, and it isn't unexpected when writing about parents. We need to write about the feelings surrounding the second and third grade teacher. There must be some anger, resentment because nobody rescued you. No?"

"I don't blame my Mom or my Dad for what the teacher did. My Mom and Dad are and were loving parents."

Frank said, "That isn't what I am talking about David. I met your Mom and have no doubt of her love for you. Feelings are what the writing is all about, we need to write and bring the negative out and deal with it; then, we can focus on the positive."

I asked, "Are you saying I should write from the perspective of when the trauma was happening in the classroom?"

"Less story and more about the feelings in the moment, is what will get you to the place where you can release the toxic feelings and build on what is not, but you will not get to positive unless we deal with the pent up negative feelings and emotion. So, keep writing to Mom," Frank said.

I said, "Okay, I will work on it over the weekend."

My Mom is the reason I am here in California, and I am very grateful for this. I completely get what Frank is asking me to write. It is like some of the Mrs. F letters format-wise anyway. I know Mom would want me to do whatever is necessary to make myself well. There is zero doubt about that. My Mom has thick skin, and perhaps a couple extra layers, being Mom to my brothers and me.

The Work gives me evidence of success, sometimes instantly upon sharing. I mean I feel better. It is emotionally charged, and it takes a lot out of me. I am finding feelings I didn't even realize I had until I wrote about them. I recognize my writing will require much more work in the coming months and years, and that is okay. I am a believer in the tools I have been given here.

CHAPTER 51

Harlan's office had a comfortable couch and fresh coffee in the pot. The letter this morning drained me a little, so something containing caffeine was just right. Pecking away at his key board, Harlan asked, "How is the assignment on *Willful Neglect* coming along?"

I said, "I put some time into it, and brainstorming through it is what I think it requires before going much farther in the process."

He said, "That is what the assignment does, it makes you think and consider your life and what is necessary to succeed. So, what do you have to start with?"

I said, "The Alternative Track operates on a premise we are not powerless over addiction. It empowers and really emboldens, assuming the necessary *Work* is being done. The daily writing exercises identify potential toxicity of feelings and emotion that, if ignored, will result in failure. I am comfortable and feel good about the simplicity as long as I do the writing. Should I be concerned there is not a lot of people in this particular program?"

Harlan said, "Isolation is historically problematic for those afflicted with addiction. My concern for you would be how loneliness, depression and loss are part of living. I have seen too many friends, men and women, I thought as strong in their recovery as I have seen, relapse, even die from these things. You are right to question this, it could be a real trouble spot in your recovery."

I immediately thought about my Dad, Grandparents and many other losses over my lifetime. Drugs and Alcohol use always increased in stressful times. Would having a larger network of human interaction or cemented relationships have made any difference?

I said, "I have never had a healthy relationship, only a few friends, and our family gathers primarily on holidays, weddings and funerals. My tendency to keep people at arm's length is as hard wired in me as a primal instinct. Most twelve-step groups, be it AA, NA, even out-patient programs have relapse ratios as high as ninety percent. Many, including myself, often relapse with people from one of these programs. When I talk like this to those in twelve-step programs, many become combative or defensive accusing me of not wanting recovery badly enough and refusing to work the steps with a sponsor. I worked the steps with a wonderful man who sponsored me when I quit alcohol and drugs for more than three years. I have tremendous respect for any recovery program or combination of programs that help people break the chains of addiction. All of the above!"

Harlan has these facial expressions and mannerisms that are priceless, yet insightful at the same time. A good two to three minutes passed before he responded, "I think you lay out some legitimate things to brainstorm. Why do you believe you need to have people involved in your recovery, when it sounds like you don't really like them all that much? Tell me about this," He said.

I said, "I have great difficulty with trust. I fear hurt and rejection. Allowing anyone close enough to get to know who David truly is, has never been something I have ever been able to do. It isn't something I am even aware of most of the time, if ever. My whole life, vulnerability has been another word in the dictionary; I never knew it has infinite empowerment attributes. Even now, I only know fundamentals and basics."

Harlan said, "Low self-esteem and feelings of worthlessness are all too common in addiction and trauma. What it is going to come down to is: now that you have found the reasons for a lot of these things, and how they have been controlling every aspect of your life; what are you going to do differently? When are you going to start? How are you going to maintain the changes? I can tell you from my own experiences there is little you will do in the coming months that will be easy. It does get better, a lot better. In fact, you will find happiness. Don't you think it's high time for it, you're a young man with your whole life ahead of you. Make it count."

I said, "I must admit for the first time in my life, I believe it may be possible to have a positive life and put aside the demons that have defined me."

Harlan said, "This was good brainstorming here today. We still have a month to position you for success when you leave here. Have a good weekend and try get some rest and have a little fun. You need to learn to do that as much as any of these things we discussed today. I will see you later; now get out of here."

"See you next week," I answered with a smile!

CHAPTER 52

Between the letter this morning and meeting with Harlan, I am ready for the weekend to begin. In a month, it will be time to get on with living and see about finding some happiness in my life. Strangely, thinking about what that may look like, I'm not sure if it bit me, I could identify it. Anxiety and fear are the feelings I have for what is next in life. I am not who I was when I arrived here. When I think about the void inside me which previously was occupied by the feelings and emotions I have released here; strange as it may sound, it is the source of all my fears.

Fear is often what is masked by other negative and even some positive emotions. Shame is a self-loathing feeling that cripples a person's life. It consumes confidence, joy, even love. My shame had no face or beginning I could uncover. I only knew I was a person who was bad and deserved to suffer. Thirty-five years is a lot of time to develop protective measures so no one could discover my shame. Masks literally became reality to a level where it was nearly impossible to know what was real and what was masked behavior. I was trying to protect myself by burying everything deep inside and projecting the masks necessary to guard the truth.

Therapists at the Center facilitate most of the programming in the afternoons. Shame is a commonality shared among the residents at Hope by the Sea. It is difficult to realize masks are more our reality than anyone cares to embrace or accept. Everyone wears masks from time to time. An example could be family reunions where everyone is always fine and a little bit better than reality. The same could be said at work when we are *fine* or everything is *good* or *great* to anyone who asks, "How are you today?" The person asking the question does not want to hear about your bladder infection or colonoscopy you had last week. Yes, everyone wears a mask from time to time.

Some people think wearing a mask is being dishonest, and anyone wearing one is a liar in some way. If your spouse or significant other asks you, "Do these pants make me look fat?" Most people who have been married or involved in a serious relationship for more than thirty seconds, realize it is one occasion in the interest of all to be shall we say, idealistic? These are every day little white lie situations of life where we find ourselves now and then.

Growing up, when I was often the target of relentless teasing, I already felt I was a bad person. Teasing was most likely received by me with a lot more malice than was intended by those doing it. If I liked a girl, my fear of rejection was off the charts; and I would never tell the girl or anyone else my true feelings. After third grade, my brain was messed up; and after I had no memory of it, it left me with no answers for why I was like I was.

People wear masks sometimes to misdirect perception to others. For me, it was more of an automatic defense or protection mechanism than anything else, guarding my shame so nobody would know what lay just beneath the surface. If I succumbed to crying when I was picked on, I would have felt in danger, vulnerable to more hurt. I already harbored feelings of hatred toward myself, and believing I was bad in everyone else's eyes was easy. When people hurt me, be it emotional or physical, it only validates my deep-seeded truths.

Traumas in childhood alter the development of the brain centers that soothe pain, discern what is right or wrong, develop trust, determine risk assessment and cause the traumatized person to be extremely vulnerable to chemical and behavioral addictions. Mental health afflictions and addiction are the norm for people who have lived with their traumas; many of us for years, even decades, with no memory of the traumatic circumstances. For some, the memory recorded perfectly in the sub-conscious of the brain will never reach the conscious level where it can be processed. I lived in darkness for thirty-five years before I remembered anything. This gift of memory is a conundrum for me. I have gratitude for the opportunity to heal; yet frequently, I experience a hatred beyond understanding, and it scares me to wonder how long this dark emotion will cloud over me.

Mental illness tends to worsen and intensify when alcohol, drugs or other destructive addictive behaviors are added to the equation. Speaking for me, they tend to feed off one another. Alcohol and drugs primarily addressed pain in my life both physical and psychological. Alcohol is a depressant and tends to worsen clinical depression. It is difficult to find someone who struggles with addiction who is not struggling with mental illness.

CHAPTER 53

I didn't sleep well last night. It wasn't due to nightmares, and I am grateful. The family letters are striking nerves and my mind races, and I become anxious. Frank says to keep writing when this happens, because feeling this way is an indication I am writing about what is important.

The following is a second letter to Mom.

November 28, 2016

Dear Mom,

I have been working through what happened in second and third grades at the hand of Mrs. F. The amount of pain and hatred I endured is beyond comprehension. I was eight, you were not. How could you not know that something horrible was happening in that classroom? She beat me and tortured me for two years. You were supposed to protect me and keep me safe from harm.

> *She beat me and tortured me for two years. You were supposed to protect me and keep me safe from harm.*

I do not know why I couldn't come to you and Dad; my compass of right and wrong, or who to trust was grossly wrong. You should have dug more, pushed me more. Why in God's name didn't you get me out of there before third grade? Half of me died in second grade, and when I learned she would be my teacher another year, the rest of me was lost for good.

I think back to the first time she put me in that awful closet, and it still scares me; it still gives me nightmares. I can't stand being confined or locked up. I go crazy and have suicidal thoughts. Mostly, it takes me right back to those years in Mrs. F's. classroom.

Didn't I ever have marks around my neck, dried tears, or lifeless eyes of complete defeat? I was convinced I deserved everything that was happening. I wish I could have been saved before I lost myself. I had no idea who I was after first grade.

You and Dad would go to conferences and want me to talk about school stuff when you got home. It was as if you accepted anything they said at face value. I know that wasn't the case, but when you and Dad asked me questions, it felt like an interrogation. I can remember sitting in the kitchen, more or less cornered, and I felt you were both on her side. That belief made me sink deeper and deeper into darkness.

Being with Grandpa was the one place I really felt completely safe, and now I believe because he never asked me about school was a big part of that security I felt with him. I hated it when you would come to the field and make me come home, and say I needed to sleep so I could be ready for school. Sleep was the last thing I wanted. My nightmares were frequent. Didn't they wake you? Sometimes, I would sneak out and go back to the field where Grandpa would let me ride some more. We talked very little on the combine; it was therapeutic.

The farm toys I would get for birthdays and Christmas allowed me to create Grandpa's world at home. It was there I found a measure of peace. As you know, I wasn't interested in a lot of things throughout my life, finding it easier to keep people, places, and things at arm's length. I believed if I let anybody in close, I could and would, be hurt. My brothers in those days were not all that bad as far as brothers go I suppose. My perception though validated every measure of my low self-worth.

I was different from other kids and my brothers. I suppose anyone would be that walked in my shoes for a bit. You had four of us to juggle, and you and Dad both worked so avoidance was easy. I didn't want to deal with life, so I hid anywhere that felt safe. I spent my childhood in a lake of despair that in many ways has never left. Later in life, I learned to numb or at least reduce it with drugs and alcohol. At age eight and nine, I had no way to soothe or numb my pain.

In third grade, I took a bunch of pills from the medicine cabinet and some other kids did the same. I took hands full of unknown drugs that day. I became sick and threw up and was very sick. I know now that could have easily resulted in my death. God has spared my life more times than I can keep track of, and I think there is a reason unbeknown to me now.

I don't blame you for the terrible things that happened when I was young. I know you love me, and I love you. I don't want you to be hurt from my hurt.

Love, David

Frank said, "That was nice, how was it?"

I said, "Writing to Mom is tough for me, I don't have malice surrounding any part of my life where my Mom is concerned so some of this gives me feelings of guilt and shame."

He opined, "Having feelings like that are good because it means you are beginning to come face-to-face with the negatives surrounding your early childhood. Remember, David, and all of you here, this isn't a letter you are going to mail today or ever. We air our feelings on paper to heal us, not to bring heartache or adversity to those in the letters or anybody else. I say this often because it is that important. We write, we share, and then release the negative, then we can bring positives into our life that you cannot see now because of the negatives. Keep writing to Mom."

"Okay I will," I said.

The writing exercises we do aside from the letters in the Alternative Track, are like the negative memory Frank has asked us to write today. We are given twenty minutes to write this negative memory about something we have guilt and shame about. This style of writing is completely off the cuff.

Negative Memory

November 28, 2016

When my Grandpa Gilbertson died, it hit me hard, and I had a difficult time with it. For as long as I have memory, he has always been there and made me feel safe. He was always my friend and on my side. As I grew into my teens and adulthood, I saw him less and less. I didn't go spend time with my Grandpa as much as I should have. He was always there for me day or night. He never failed or disappointed me, and that is amazing.

At his funeral, I did not deliver or write any part of his eulogy; instead, relying on my brothers to hold up my end. I was full of selfishness and self-centeredness, and it showed in my relationships with many loved ones at this time of my life. With Grandpa, I feel an overwhelming regret of not cherishing the time. There would be no more boat or sportsman shows to go to as we had done every year together. When I visit the cemetery, these feelings make me cry in regret for not spending more time with him. The guilt and shame eat me from the inside out.

As his grandson, I think I was his favorite due to the many hours spent on the tractor or the combine in Autumn harvest. I think about him almost daily, and Grandpa has been gone over a decade.

I wish I could go back, if only for a moment, to tell you how much I love you and how grateful I am you were my Grandpa.

I wish I could go back, if only for a moment, to tell you how much I love you and how grateful I am you were my Grandpa. My Grandpa loved me, and he would not want me to be troubled like this. He was the most selfless man I have ever known, only one of his many, loving qualities.

Love, David

Negative memories are among the most emotional for me because there are many things I could write about. Frank said, "It is vital to write them." When I asked, "Why?" He said, "How good do you want to feel? How fast do you want to reach the happiness you seek?"

"For a man of a few words, you sure make them count," I said.

CHAPTER 54

It's getting closer to the end of my time here, about thirty days to go, and the anxiety and fear about going back to the Midwest are starting to surface. Like most of the clients, coming to Hope by the Sea is an escape as much as it is to find help. My world imploded in about every area in the months leading up to arriving. My job, my relationships with my kids and most of my family, my home and my spirit were all broken; some permanently, I thought.

The following is a journal entry:

Talking on the phone to Mom last night about normal things made me feel a bit stressed and overwhelmed. The things that are piled up to be dealt with seem enormous right now. I know in the end I have no control over most of it, only how I respond is under my control. I know things will work out the way they should, and God willing I am ready to accept what happens.

Anxiety, I guess, is what describes my feelings best when it comes to unknowns. What I am referring to is legal issues, my kids and the first 100 days of 2017. There are a lot of things troubling me. Living in Minnesota would apply pressure to my life that isn't easily explained. The status of the relationships with my brothers and my kids has a likelihood of stress I cannot have in my life right now. There is no need to force anything as I have not heard from any of them. I think it would be fair to believe they may not be ready to talk about things either.

I need to keep up with the work when I leave here, especially the gratitude exercises. I know I will have a life of meaning. A life in service to others is predicated on adherence to what I am doing here every day.

I also wonder how long I will continue to have the nightmares. They drain me. When I wake up, it is as if I haven't even slept. This fatigue makes it difficult to focus and be attentive throughout the day. Last week I had nightmares nearly every night. I am on medications that are supposed to make me not dream. I hate to think what they would be without the medicine.

I have begun to transform my life and thinking in this place. When I came I thought it was likely to not be helped. I am so grateful for this program, I no longer believe I cannot be helped. Today is good.

CHAPTER 55

My mind has been racing more than usual creating more and more anxiety. This happens when I have idle time or am trying to sleep. Writing seems to temper feelings as they are processed on paper. Attempts to soundboard verbally with a peer or Therapist seem to get stuck. Overwhelmed with rapid thoughts and emotion, I cannot seem to articulate the words as fast as my mind generates them. I spent a lifetime deflecting or simply burying the feelings in my head; projecting to others what I believed would guard my shame. Through much work I have begun to change.

Last night I did a considerable amount of writing, family letters primarily. It is difficult to process feelings so emotionally charged. Letters are about purging the negative before things turn the other direction. Forgiveness, release of the toxicity one harbors and finally acceptance. This creates a measure of peace that permits the worst adversities to become livable, sometimes even wonderful.

The following is a third letter to Mom

November 30, 2016

Dear Mom,

My mind has been a flurry of activity with all the writing about so many things. Talking on the phone about regular things gives me a sensation of butterflies in my stomach that at times can be overwhelming. It isn't only when talking with you that this occurs. When I speak of leaving here with my Case Manager, Therapist, even my peers, the anxious feelings are there.

Facing uncertainty in many arenas, including legal, kids, brothers and what the future holds gives me great anxiety. I guess I am hating myself for again being in legal trouble. I am ashamed at the number of times this pattern has played out. The way people in the family look at me, and the way they think are all hard to process. My kids don't have any respect for their Father which is not a new development. It probably goes back to the end of 2013 when I left their Mom, maybe even longer. The fall out of that, the death of Uncle Mike and my loss of livelihood all in the same span of a couple weeks created enormous turmoil and despair.

Every feeling that had a negative impact came back seemingly at once and is having a crippling reaction. It feels as if I have done no work at all, or it has no meaning. I return to the same dark place that is familiar and strangely comforting. This is the place in my mind where I am not worthy of anything good, the place of hopelessness.

That dark place is me, it has been my identity for better or worse my whole life. Despite all the work, I am scared to let it go. Letting go would leave me empty, desolate with no identity. I am terrified of the unknown. I fear things that are likely good and places where I am not a bad person. I realize this may sound crazy; truth is I need this pain. It is part of me, and therefore, difficult to just cut away.

There are a lot of reasons I suppose for thinking as I do. At the same time, I cling to this pain, I work tirelessly to kill it and be free. I am working harder to inject gratitude into my life; diligent letter writing and the other writings necessary to win my battle to overcome darkness have got to be done. Only my relationship with God will be first in my life.

Besides the legal stuff, I see a big mess financially and in relationships that will take some doing to right. Who knows when or even if the ships with my brothers and kids can be righted. I don't know what to tell you on that front. Maybe someday things will work out, maybe not.

Simply put, if I had not started drinking and drugging, this tension probably wouldn't exist. The relationship with the kids would still be strained as opposed to no relationship. I own this, you do not.

As I look back at life through the years, I experience a lot of anger; feeling somehow robbed of the life I should have had and didn't. I speak of a life without second and third grade. The other side of that coin is, I wouldn't be who I am without the lived experience, adversity and all.

All I can do is put the negative aside and build a life of meaning. A life that is genuine, rewarding, and happy with yesterday staying in the rearview and blue skies ahead.

Love, David

"Ok, how was it?" Frank asked.

"Writing about the here and now causes a lot of unexpected anxiety and emotion. Thoughts about what will happen when I leave seem to be what I felt the need to write about as much as the things from so long ago."

He said, "There seems to be a lot going on in this one. You are doing better connecting with the feelings and that is what needs to happen. Have we done a reversal with Mom?"

"No, not yet."

Frank said, "Let's write a reversal and start writing to Dad and Grandpa to."

I said, "Is there a certain perspective for my Dad and Grandpa. Specific time of my life?"

He said, "Just write, pick what you deem important, and we will see where it takes us. Feelings are what you want to bring forth, especially negative aspects going on that can get you to a spot where you can release everything and burn it. Closure only happens when the feelings are dealt with like with the teacher. Make sense?"

I said, "It does, I will get going on this right away.

With the amount of time left to work on these things here, a lot needs to be done in this last month. Frank knows this too and is pushing me to stay focused on *The Work*. I also need to do a lot of work with Harlan to feel good about my discharge. I need to talk to him about these feelings I am having concerning my discharge.

CHAPTER 56

I am down at the horse corral giving Topper a couple apples. I do this each day at lunch hour. Today, I decided to go again after the afternoon classes. Topper got extra apples out of me today. Topper eats them out of my hand. He takes a bite that is nearly a perfect half of the apple, then returns to the hand to get the other half. This way Topper never eats out of the dirt. He is obviously a smart horse. He lets me pet him on the face, and he smiles. I have brought new arrivals down at lunch to see if they want to let a horse eat from their hands. The townies are all afraid to do this, but the rural community folks appreciate me showing them.

On the walk back to the park, I spot an empty picnic table in the shade, and I start walking towards it. I sit down, pour a cup of coffee from my thermos and get my journal out and begin working on gratitude exercises: three things I am grateful and thankful for and why, ten positives in the last twenty-four hours and a quality in me I respect and admire. I am about half way through the work when Harlan sits down. I was hoping he would stop by, I can finish this work later tonight.

Harlan knows I am all business today, and he is just settling in waiting for one of us to blink. Today, I feel I have pressing work to be completed before going home and am hoping he can help me prioritize things.

I said, "I am feeling like there isn't enough time to get done the things that need doing."

Harlan said, "Where is this coming from, you've been doing great. Still thirty days to go too. What is the issue?"

I said, "My mind is moving at warp speed with negative things I cannot control. I guess I thought I had moved past things like that. Learned how to accept what is and what isn't."

He said, "What I am hearing is someone inside his own head trying to play God. I will ask what I asked when you first got here. How long did it take for someone from the Midwest to come two thousand miles to try and right the ship?"

I said, "It isn't that, I have discovered a lot of things about me and bettered myself. It took many years to get here to answer your question."

Harlan is just sitting over there with a big fat smile on his face. Two or three minutes passed before he said anything. "Over the years I have heard your response literally a thousand times. The first time was out of my mouth when I was sitting at your side of the table. It still, makes me happy to hear."

"Well, you don't have to enjoy it so much," I said and continued, "So, what are you telling me here?"

Harlan said, "You know full well you will need more than a few months to transform what took years to create. I wanted to fix my life with a quick easy magic pill too. If I had one, I would hand it over to you. You need to build on positives; negatives in the recovery world are non-starters."

I said, "I know your words are spot on; how do I deal with the fear I have of leaving here? I have a lot of fear of living."

Harlan said, "You know full well you will need more than a few months to transform what took years to create

He said, "That is the most honest statement I have heard from you today. I experience fear; everyone does; at least anyone that is trying to live life. Risk (fear) is also called living a life in the pursuit of happiness. There are no guarantees, never have been. Accepting that is a necessary component if you truly want to be free to live the life you want."

I said, "Thanks for being you; I appreciate these talks we have."

He said, "So do I, son."

CHAPTER 57

Matthias is from Alabama and one of the residents at the Horse Shoe House. Matthias is convinced there is a ghost living in his room. I realize there are some who believe in this sort of thing; as for me, I don't really have a view one way or another. At first, I didn't really pay much attention to the talk, content to just watch. That didn't last very long.

Out by the pool each evening there is a feeling not of a Treatment Center, but more like sitting by a campfire as a boy. By that I mean the laughter and kidding are at times constant. The House Manager discovers a kitchen knife in the bathroom in Matthias's room, and according to Matthias, *the ghost* placed the cutlery in the cupboard beneath the sink Matthias utilizes. With that jewel of information some of us more immature and mischievous residents of the house begin to conspire and plot, as to how to keep this *ghost*, shall we say, *lively* in the mind of Matthias.

Donavon is from Maryland and Peter is from Indiana. These two and I decide to purchase a pair of two-way radios thinking Matthias' *ghost* can use a voice. Peter and Matthias share the same room, so, inside Peter's luggage we place one of the two-ways. I don't believe any of has any intent but a laugh or two. Matthias is well liked by everybody at Hope, residents and staff alike. Despite my mischievousness in all of this to Matthias, I value him as a friend and respect him as a person.

> *Laughter is something most of us have not experienced for a long time. In many ways, laughter is the best medicine.*

When Matthias was telling us about hearing his *ghost* on the way back from shopping one day, it tickled me to the core. Unbeknown to me, Peter wrote Matthias' name in the steam on the mirror while he was in the shower and right below it, he wrote BOO! Matthias brought it up during supper one night, and we couldn't contain ourselves any longer and burst out in laughter. We told Matthias that to go to such length and expense to pull a prank on him, the man must be an all right person.

There are many pranks around the House, other Houses too, as far as that goes. Laughter is something most of us have not experienced for a long time. In many ways, laughter is the best medicine. Being here is a serious thing, and I don't want to imply it isn't. I am sharing this only to show that learning to laugh again and being part of a sober community is important too.

CHAPTER 58

I got some rest last night for a change. I attribute this to the talk I had with Harlan in the park yesterday afternoon. This morning in Alternative Track we begin the day with a positive memory.

Positive Memory

December 1, 2016

My son David and I took a trip to Des Moines, Iowa, to attend WWE's Friday Night Smackdown. WWE being World Wrestling Entertainment. It was 2010 and David was ten. For the most part, the two of us had never gone anywhere alone. Wrestling being a favorite for years, he was excited to be going.

Des Moines is a three-hour drive from the Twin Cities, and we arrived at the Embassy Suites Hotel around three o'clock only a couple of blocks from the arena. David was impressed with the hotel, smiling from ear to ear. We had a nice dinner at the hotel restaurant before walking over to the event.

It was everything it was supposed to be and more. As good as the wrestling was, I think for David, having room service might have been more impressive. I suppose it was a toss-up.

Before heading home Saturday, we stopped to see my Uncle Larry, whom I had not seen in a long time. Neither David nor I had been to his house before, and he was happy we stopped, and we were too.

Road trips are great ways to get to know someone. That may seem strange to say about my son, but is it? At home, we both had routines and hanging out just the two of us was rare. I have been on more luxurious trips in places more elaborate than Des Moines, Iowa; but this trip with my son will remain among the best for me because it was the first.

Writing about good memories is not more difficult as far as writing goes. Coming up with positive memories not involving drugs or alcohol is the challenge. This must change; all this work must not be in vain. For too long, I have been either miserable or living behind masks. In the years ahead of me, finding some happiness in this life must be a priority. Every time I am asked to write about something positive, I struggle to find things. Negatives are a different situation all together.

CHAPTER 59

Listening to my peers read letters is as emotional as reading my own at times. The amount of pain in the written pages of this group is a somber experience at the very least. The closeness of the group has healing properties as we share the intimate details of our lives that have not been spoken aloud until this room.

Mom reversal:

December 1, 2016

Dear David,

When you were born, I was so happy. I came close to losing you during pregnancy making you even more precious to us. You were the happiest child and so curious. Your Dad and I loved you very much as a baby.

I am very sad for the sufferings you endured in second and third grades. I only wish you would have told us. I would have protected you. I blame myself and that awful school. I want you to know that I tried to fight for you. I was so torn up inside, and when you had Mrs. F for a second year I knew you were troubled; I failed you; and I am so sorry.

I have always been proud to have you for a son. I may not have approved of some of your choices or behaviors, but my love never faltered. I do believe now that everything you were doing growing up, and as an adult, is connected in some way back to those awful years so long ago.

I am elated you are at Hope by the Sea getting help, the help necessary for you to move past this. I want you to have a life free of addiction. You are so talented and blessed with so much goodness; I have seen

Birthplace of Addiction

it time and again throughout your life. I hope and pray that you can begin to see these things for yourself.

You have so much life yet to live and have an abundance of gifts that God has given you. I believe the help you are receiving will make all the difference in the world going forward.

I know life has been hard for you, especially your school years. I can see now that it was Hell on earth for you and nobody ought to go through such things.

Seeing you and participating in Family Weekend showed me a fire in you that didn't exist when you left for California. It is all going to be okay now. I am so proud of you.

Love, Mom

"How was it?"

"This I found easier than any of the other Mom letters, maybe, because it was positive!" I said.

He said, "I could see that being the case, you wrote about the negatives in the previous letters, and you found it difficult to bring some of those feelings out. Now, in this one you are writing about positive emotions and feelings and found it to be easy. This is good because we generally struggle with positives. When I asked you to write positives about the teacher, you initially thought it impossible. Do you see what I am talking about?"

I said, "I have been able to work through the negative feelings and emotions surrounding Mom. Because of that work I was able to come to a place where I could write about positives."

Frank said, "Right exactly, this is how it is in life too. When you leave here, it will be necessary to continue to process things. Some past things will resurface and new feelings from living life will inevitably require work. Options are to process or not, ignoring them would almost certainly return you to a life of addictive behaviors. It is necessary to write daily so you can identify the things that require attention."

I said, "My priorities will include daily writing similarly to how much I write now. I have already realized value in the work done thus far. It gives me incentive to continue."

"That's good you realize the importance. You can write more to Mom if you wish. It is up to you. Now I would like you to write Dad and Grandpa. You can close out by burning the Mom letters or however you release and move on to Dad and Grandpa."

"Okay."

CHAPTER 60

Afternoon classes cover the topics of trauma, relapse, and anger management, just to name a few. Relapse prevention is the topic several times every week. It could be argued the entire treatment experience is built around this methodology. In the past few years that position has been challenged due to a shift in strategy. Mental health afflictions are the underlying factors feeding addictive behaviors. Treating one and not the other, with little doubt, is doomed to fail.

I find very few folks at Hope by the Sea are new to treatment. I mean this isn't their first rodeo. Some have been to treatment as many as ten times. I believe some folks aren't ready to give up their addictions, and I also believe some simply cannot. Drugs and alcohol for the addict are about relieving pain. The pain is deep inside of us. Sometimes it is intertwined with suppressed memories as in my case. Sexual assault, molestation, violence, and torture are often suppressed in children, and the pain follows into adulthood. By this time, we have been blaming ourselves for many years, convinced we are bad people and deserving of misery.

The lived experience is going to be different for everyone, and the traumas experienced in childhood are also unique. Because of this, it is necessary to treat the mental illness in concert with addiction treatment if there is going to be success. Individualized therapy is a necessary component and demonstrates there is no one size fits all or even most in treating addiction.

> *Individualized therapy is a necessary component and demonstrates there is no one size fits all or even most in treating addiction.*

It is becoming more accepted by the Medical and Psychology fields that addiction is but a symptom of something else altogether. This explains why, earlier in 2016, I was unable to stay clean and sober. My Therapist, Nancy, called it in the first session I had with her here at Hope by the Sea. Essentially, she said that only the tip of the iceberg was addressed, leaving the bulk of it to do further damage shortly after I left a Minnesota facility in early March of 2016.

Relapse is a return to old thinking and behaviors that ultimately end in using again. It is important to note a relapse does not begin with the use of the substance, but with changes in our thoughts and attitude. Weeks, months, even years can go by before the use takes place. In my experience, this cycle has repeated itself hundreds of times in my life because the only thing I treated was a symptom of the core problem.

I was a resident of a treatment center in Minnesota for forty-one days of in-patient care in early 2016. This was a twelve-step program that also offered some Mental Health Services. About twenty-five percent of the program was in mental health and was in a one size fits all approach. The remainder was devoted to addictive substance disorders. I felt I received valuable care there, and I believed if I adhered to the twelve-step principles, I would be able to live a life free of alcohol and drugs.

My memory of second and third grade at that time was beginning to come back. The details of what happened were not yet clear. I remembered some of the yelling, hitting, and emotions surrounding that time of my life. One of my assignments while there was to write a letter to Mrs. F. It was the only assignment I had regarding that time, despite it being one of the main factors I became a client there.

The following is the letter I wrote to Mrs. F.

Letter to Mrs. F

February 13, 2016

Dear Mrs. F,

If I had the ability to change or erase anything in my life from existence, it would be having you for a teacher in second and third grades. In pre-school, kindergarten, and first grade I loved school and learning, and I received high marks from my teachers. This enthusiasm and zest for life I had then, were sucked out of me in your classroom in those formative years. Never again did I have the joy of learning or experience a healthy relationship.

You told me repeatedly I wasn't any good and never would be. You embarrassed me daily, hit me with erasers, rulers, and your hands with that rough dry skin. You told my parents and the principal I was slow and stupid with severe behavior and discipline problems. The constant yelling and shaming was more than my young mind could process. You have been a cancer inside of me for more than thirty years.

The rest of grammar school and school in general left me troubled, sad and convinced I was no good. I had no confidence with friends or girls causing me to isolate in protection. My family interactions, like school, made me less happy and more distraught. Why did you do these cruel and awful things to me? What did I do to deserve this? How can you have been a teacher of young children for so long?

Erasing this from my life is not an option, since this has been in the dark far too long. I suppose learning to live with what happened is the only option available to me. The intimacy defects that live in me and feelings of low self-worth are things I must come to terms with.

I hope one day I will be able to forgive you as you are a pitiable woman who must live in misery with all your sin.

David

I left the Minnesota treatment facility about two weeks after writing that letter. I had a temporary sponsor in Alcoholics Anonymous I could call if I needed to. He introduced me to a man named Tom who became my permanent sponsor in the program. I began going to two meetings a week while working the steps with Tom. I believed everything was going to be okay. I had a nice place to live with my two kids, David and Chelsey, and I had some job prospects.

Something wasn't right, going to meetings and working the steps had worked for me from 2007-2011, but it was not working now. I told my sponsor I was not able to achieve any measure of happiness, despite all the things for which I was grateful. We continued to work the steps and attended two meetings a week and days became a week and weeks became a month, then another month.

> *I was shaking the same way I did in third grade in that dark closet when I could hear her coming for me. I remember sobbing in the dark until daylight.*

Every morning I lie in bed and needed to convince myself to get up and face the day. I had an uneasiness at my core that can only be described as hopelessness. I went to work each day because my kids needed to eat and to keep a roof over our heads. I shared this daily when I talked to Tom. His response was things will get better.

Things didn't get better; they became worse. I began having nightmares that terrified me and made me afraid to sleep. They were my letters to Mrs. F coming alive in my head. Not sleeping takes its toll on a body and mind; it causes extreme fatigue and diminished brain power to name a couple. There was little I wouldn't have entertained if it would have quashed my nightmares.

I had little understanding of the shame and self-loathing feelings that accompanied my dreams unleashing a hurricane of emotions. The frequency of the nightmares was nearly every time I slept, increasing in severity each time.

I continued to attend twelve-step meetings and sharing with my sponsor what was happening to me. He was legitimately concerned, but ultimately had no solution or help for me. I wouldn't be eligible for health insurance through my employer until July; I earned too much for assistance, but not enough to afford psychiatric care for my nightmares. I doubted anything or anybody could help me, so I prayed.

I bought a bottle of vodka with the intention of reaching a blackout state to either eliminate or allow me to have no recollection of my nightmares. It had been several months since I had taken a drink. I still recall the warmth in my stomach as it absorbed. I slammed the 750-milliliter bottle in less than five minutes. I was sleeping within a half hour and slept through the night. When I woke up the next morning I didn't remember any nightmares. Encouraged by this, I stopped at the liquor store and made another purchase on my way home from work.

I sat on my bed and considered other options to stop the nightmares besides the one before me. I was aware what the risks are in drinking. I awoke in a cold sweat, two hours after putting the bottle down. I was shaking the same way I did in third grade in that dark closet when I could hear her coming for me. I remember sobbing in the dark until daylight.

It takes almost no time for alcohol to dig in its claws. A couple weeks had passed; I drank ten of the fourteen days; and the nightmares remained strong. I knew the alcohol wasn't doing any good at all. I also knew if I didn't stop, things would get bad. Still, I prayed.

I called Walt, and he answered on the first ring. We had met in treatment, and I knew he was going back to his street life including dealing drugs. I knew I couldn't afford cocaine, so I asked about some Adderall, an amphetamine I had taken in the past. He informed me that it was expensive and hard to get. He suggested I get some Methamphetamine (Meth) because it was potent and cheap. He brought me a big bag of it and charged me next to nothing.

I began staying up twenty-four hours seven days a week. My thinking was I cannot have nightmares if I am awake. It was my thought process for doing meth and things got out of control quickly.

Walt was always there to supply me; I started driving him places in exchange for more meth. In the beginning, I smoked it or snorted it with a straw. Then one day that wasn't enough, and the girl I was doing drugs with showed me how to inject this poison into my veins directly with a syringe. It was July 2016, and I was shooting drugs into me at a rapid rate.

Being awake was becoming a nightmare itself. When I couldn't find any meth, I got heroin. Another line in the sand crossed. At this point I didn't have much sand left.

I was barely hanging on to my job, and by this time, I didn't care about much except my next fix. I wasn't liking what I had become, and neither did anyone else. I did some speed balls -- Meth and Heroin in the same syringe. It can be cocaine and heroin, too. Nightmares continued to plague me every time I slept. Being awake was becoming a nightmare itself. When I couldn't find any meth, I got heroin. Another line in the sand crossed. At this point I didn't have much sand left.

With a good amount of this destructive behavior occurring at home, my kids were less than impressed with their father. Who could blame them? I had a mere four months ago completed a twelve-step program. At this stage, I wouldn't know where to begin in terms of explaining any of this to them.

It was July 18, 2016, and when I got home from work I needed sleep because I had been up for days upon days. I took some Ambien, slammed a pint of hundred proof vodka and passed out before my head hit the pillow. I woke suddenly at two o'clock sweating and scared. I took another Ambien and tried to sleep again, but it wasn't going to happen in my state of fear from my nightmare. I messaged a girl who lived about fifteen miles away and asked her if she wanted to party. I was out of control when I left the house that night.

I have no recollection of driving. I went a good twenty miles past where I was planning to go. When I saw the police rollers in the rearview mirror, I didn't know where I was, or how I got there. I was arrested for suspicion of Driving While Impaired (DWI), possession of Meth and possession of drug paraphernalia. I was taken to a hospital where I was required to have blood drawn to be tested for illegal substances.

I was booked into the county jail on felony charges. The felony was for being in possession of less than a gram of meth. The phones available to me were collect only and didn't work at all with cellular phones. I didn't see a judge until three days had passed, and by then I was terminated from my job for not showing up or calling in. Bail was set at an initial court appearance and because of the felony charges was $22,000.

My Mom paid the bail bond, and my brothers and children were against it, and told her so after the fact. They felt staying in jail was the way to handle someone who uses drugs. I felt their thinking was closeminded at best and malicious at worst. They are my family, and in time, I hope things will mend.

The question is when did this relapse begin? Was it the first bottle of Vodka? Second? Was it the first drug use? Or, is the answer none of these and something else entirely? If you are reading this book and struggling with addiction, this is a bad one to get wrong. **Does anyone think that the stakes are something other than life or death?** If that is the case and you have read this book to this point, please put the book down and find something else to read.

CHAPTER 61

In my experience, a return to denial and old thinking are present in all relapse behaviors. What I have become more and more aware of these past couple of months are my feelings. I guess the question is: what caused the return of denial and embracement of old thought processes?

The Alternative Track walks a different road than twelve-step programs. Through participation in the Alternative Track at Hope by the Sea, I came to the realization *alcohol and drugs are not my core problem.* I am not saying addiction to a substance is not problematic, quite the contrary. When addiction takes ahold, it leaves a wake of despair. In my case I suffered two years of trauma at the hands of a teacher when I was young. The effects of the trauma altered my life. My PTSD, Depression and Anxiety disorders are all rooted in those years. Suppression of feelings for most of my life led to low self-worth and fear.

Alcohol and drugs served to lessen the pain, guilt, and shame my life was built upon. My memories of second and third grade were suppressed, but not gone. The subconscious area of my brain preserved a complete record of all that occurred in those years. I had feelings of hopelessness and shame I could not explain. I had a social awkwardness that others did not have; I had tendencies to isolate myself from an overwhelming fear of rejection when it came to friendships and relationships. I had pain without a face, a name or explanation. Learning to process feelings and acceptance of the past are priorities in my life now.

> *When addiction takes ahold, it leaves a wake of despair.*

Relapse prevention plans are completed by clients in just about every treatment center in the world. They include things like going to ninety meetings in ninety days, changing your playmates and playgrounds, not driving by liquor stores, not driving in neighborhoods where drugs were once procured and building a network of sober people to keep you on track. I believe these are matters of common sense, but the real work is what is done in the Alternative Track at Hope by the Sea.

I have noticed already if I process life as life comes to me, and clean the slate of the past, I no longer find it necessary to drink or do drugs. I process life on paper every day. When I leave here, I will continue this practice. It will be something necessary for me to write letters to continue to right the past and deal with current challenges. I also plan to seek the fellowship of good, decent people, but not necessarily those who are in recovery. Don't get me wrong now; I don't oppose those fellowships. However, I think it is healthy to embrace a larger scope of people.

It is worth noting I got the meth from someone with whom I was in treatment; it was a simple phone call to score drugs. There were multiple people I could have contacted because treatment books are signed like high school yearbooks, and all list contact information. I cannot speak for everyone I met at the Minnesota treatment center, but the ones I tried to reach had gone back to addiction. Any relapse prevention or discharge plans need to consider what is being said here.

I think treatment is a wonderful thing, and it helps many heal and have a life of happiness. **However, what I am saying is when it comes to Relapse Prevention, a bad plan can be fatal.** I strongly recommend finding out what causes addicts to find it necessary to use; it is the right thing to do. Failure to address these difficult, often traumatic issues, will result in failure. If not for the hard work I did in the Alternative Track at Hope by the Sea, I would not have discovered my birthplace of addiction; I would still be in darkness. I still pray.

CHAPTER 62

The negatives in my life are abundant, so I get why we do the gratitude work every day. I am always stunned at how much easier it is to focus on the negatives and neglect the positives in our lives. It took time for me to understand the necessity of purging the negatives. Some people have told me to dwell on positives and push negatives under the rug. The shame that plagued me for most of my life was always buried and hidden. It was something I guarded as if discovery by others would annihilate me.

Frank told us we need to dig deep within ourselves to identify the feelings and process the negativity. Negative memories tend to be hidden deep within us. For the next several days we are to write negative letters to ourselves to address guilt and shame. The following is the first one I wrote.

Negative Letter

December 5, 2016

Dear David,

What an idiot you are! what a waste your life continues to be. You have pushed away anything and everyone who meant anything at all to you. What a loser! Your kids have needed you their whole lives, and you mostly chose work, alcohol and drugs over them.

You continually squander all goodness that has ever been bestowed upon you. What do you say to a person like you? How about you are a self-centered, inconsiderate human being who deserves to rot for the pain you have caused those closest to you?

How many treatments is it going to take to kill or heal you? Most could care less at this point as your credibility is zero. I mean, really, would you trust you? Would you love you? How many more chances would you give you? If the answer is anything other than zero, it would indicate you are the same miserable person you have always been and only care about yourself.

Honestly, I do not know why I even waste ink on you. Being what you are and have always been, is also what you will continue to be. I find you disgusting and goodness is wasted on you. Your legacy is a long list of disappointments and hurts you've inflicted upon yourself and those that matter most.

How does it feel to be such a pile? What is truly sad is the amount of potential that you continually left unrealized your entire miserable existence. You have brilliant children; so smart in fact, they want nothing to do with the likes of you. I certainly hope your precious alcohol and drugs are worth it. I hope it has been worth the endless misery and sadness because all you are is miserable and sad.

David

Writing negatively about me is always easy because what I write is an accurate picture of how I view myself. Shame is among the most toxic things a person can have inside of them. One of the reasons for this is it isn't amendable. Guilt is something that can usually be resolved by expressing remorse or by apologizing for bad behavior. I am not suggesting this is simple or easy, it can be the opposite.

Frank asks us to write about the feelings of guilt and shame as much as possible. These feelings are resolved one way or another through acceptance or forgiveness. Forgiveness was especially difficult for me to do, not only of others but also of myself. It is good I am here for ninety days. The writing tools and learning to incorporate them into my daily life is valuable, and I am grateful for this time.

I baked a carrot cake and shared it with one of the female houses. They made us a batch of frosted sugar cookies.

When there are a few minutes left in class before a break, Frank will have us do gratitude work. When we do writing of a negative nature, it becomes more urgent to do gratitude work on those days. Today, he asked us to write ten positive things that happened in the last twenty-four hours.

December 5, 2016
The last twenty-four hours are positive because

1. It was a gorgeous day in the park yesterday to sit at a picnic table and get some writing done.
2. We set up a Christmas tree at the house and had fun doing it.

3. I baked a carrot cake and shared it with one of the female houses. They made us a batch of frosted sugar cookies.
4. I enjoyed talking about nothing on the porch with my housemates.
5. I did some laundry so now I have clothes not requiring the sniff test.
6. I had a fantastic sandwich from Beach Hut Deli. Pong endorsed this place, and it is something special.
7. I went to a place called Top of the World in Laguna Beach and watched the sun set on the Pacific.
8. I enjoyed talking to a liberal named Evan, a House Manager who likes to spin his keys and enforce rules.
9. I slept well last night and did not have a nightmare.
10. The girls had Yoga class right by the picnic table where I was writing, and it made my morning a perfect one.

Some people would probably think the ten things listed here were somewhat mundane. When I arrived at Hope by the Sea I struggled to write anything when asked to do this exercise. I saw nothing when I looked at myself but hopelessness and shame. I didn't consider I was in treatment, and my Mom and stepfather's support made it possible. When looking for positives daily, one will seldom be writing down major, life-altering events. It will be things like helping a friend or enjoying a good cup of coffee.

Learning to see and appreciate things around us and expressing gratitude are among the very basics of humanity. Coming to treatment allows us to be vulnerable in a safe place. Victims of trauma and forms of violence fear vulnerability, particularly if those events took place during childhood development, what I call the age of innocence. As children, we trust others to not hurt us, such as: Parents, Grandparents, school teachers and others determined largely by our Parents. When this trust is smashed when we are susceptible, it makes it next to impossible for us to be vulnerable again. This makes intimacy, love, and even friendships extremely challenging if not impossible entirely.

Most of us come to treatment with little or no money, are unemployed and are either homeless or dependent on family for support. This makes us vulnerable adults which is not a good thing. My life long fear was being vulnerable to having my shame exposed. Fear of validation of my unworthiness to give or receive love, joy, or compassion. When I reflect on the past decades, I now see clearly the continuous fear hard-wired inside of me.

In my time here, I have been reluctantly learning vulnerability is not something I have to fear. I am learning ways of doing things I have never considered before, and it is a positive of being vulnerable. Writing has given me a strength I never thought could ever exist in me. I think of it as being humbled.

When humility is absent, it is impossible to experience the strength in being vulnerable. If I can remember, I have gone to great lengths to not feel anything. I numbed what caused the most pain with alcohol and drugs. Any susceptibility was numbed along with everything else, or at least I told myself it was.

With little exception, I won't let anything or anyone in close enough to hurt me. The dark side of the coin is nothing good can get close either. What I refer to are feelings of love, joy and happiness leaving me primarily alone. It is an absolute and final loneliness. This is the pain I have lived with my whole life, not understanding why until recently.

Risk is required sometimes in life, and the same can be said for personal health and happiness. If I never allow myself to be susceptible to being hurt, I will never be able to experience life's greatest gifts of being loved, expressing love or being in love. We all experience joy, a level of serenity and contentment with the risk of being hurt. Life will always have failures, pain and sorrow. I suppose perfectly imperfect is as good a way as any to describe living life.

CHAPTER 63

Writing a letter to my Dad last night, I felt like he was sitting at the table beside me. The memories of my life with him are vivid, and I know he loves me very much. The following is the letter I wrote to Dad.

December 5, 2016 First letter to Dad

Dear Dad,

Even though I think about you often, I find writing this difficult. I helped Mom take care of you as cancer took you from us in early 2002. Dad, I am in treatment again, and I haven't done a very good job with my life. The drugs and alcohol that have been in control of me most of my life have gotten a whole lot worse since you passed. I am sorry I disappoint. I am sorry for many things I've done that don't reflect the code you lived your life by. You were a gentle, loving Father, and I miss you dearly. I am going to write assuming you know everything I have ever done, thought, and experienced. You are in Heaven, and I am here in California trying to get my life in order, so I might live a better life.

When I was very young you worked at night, and Mom worked during the day, so it was just us at home while Jeff, Dan and Joe were at school. You would make good lunches like mac-n-cheese, and once you made homemade potato chips I can still smell after all these years. Memories of pounding nails and sawing lumber in the basement are good memories for me.

One day, Grandpa put grain wagons in the field just beyond our back yard. I snuck back there to check them out. I opened the hatch and would climb in and slide out. This was mega fun, and when I cut my head on the way out, it didn't even hurt until the blood was gushing out of my forehead. I was crying and tracked blood all over the kitchen floor. You came running and looked scared, but not mad. You fixed me up, making me feel safe.

I was happy to begin school, and aside from missing time on the tractor with Grandpa, I enjoyed learning things. Kindergarten and first grade were nice, and I had good teachers who taught us a lot of new things from reading and writing to how to tie our shoes. If only second and third grade could have been like the two previous years, but everything changed forever.

Mrs. F began doing horrible things to me. You know now the things I speak of. She locked me in a closet, and I was scared of what she was going to hurt me with next. You didn't come running like you did when I fell off my bike the first time. Nobody came and that's the awful truth of it. Why did you and Mom let her hurt me so bad? I never recovered from what happened in those years. My regret is not finding a way to tell you. She made me feel as though I was nothing, hopeless, and undeserving of good.

I look back and know you were a good Dad to me. You were kind and loving to Mom and all of us. You instilled a work ethic in me that I appreciate very much. I really couldn't have asked for a better Dad.

Jeff, Dan, and Joe used to pick on me, and I just didn't seem to fit in anywhere in the family. Jeff used to bully us when you and Mom were not home; he said he would do it worse if we told on him. I feared him before second grade; but in third grade I wasn't scared of him anymore, it turned to hate. The stuff I dealt with in school was far worse than anything he could dish out.

I began to detach from everything emotionally, and if I deviated, you might discover what a terrible son I was. I stuffed gallons of hurt and pain into the deepest recesses of my soul; and then I sealed it. I thought it would be gone forever. I can't explain it any better than that. Sometimes I would explode in uncontrollable rage, almost always at one of my brothers, mostly Joe. One time I went and got your single shot twelve gauge and went looking for Joe. I found him in the living room, and when he saw it, he began running and shouting. Dan was right beside me and saw the gun was cocked with the safety off; it was pointed at Joe at the bottom of the stairs by the front door.

I wanted to blow his head off. I was also scared at my loss of control and inability to stuff my feelings down inside of me. Tears were running down my face, and I was so incredibly angry.

I don't know what Dan said to me, but something inside of me broke that Autumn day. I gave him the gun, and he put it away. I cried uncontrollably right there on the floor for a long, long time; then, I felt nothing. Nobody told you or Mom. I guess, it was just the way of it. Jeff wasn't home that day. If he had been, Joe would almost certainly be dead. He didn't have tact for such things and not one drop of finesse.

When I reflect on that time of my life, I find myself wondering something over and over. I can't understand how it is possible a teacher could do what she did to me, and nobody got wise to it. The school rooms were wide open, not having doors. The yelling alone should have brought attention to Mrs. F, and it apparently didn't.

I felt as though I couldn't trust anything or anyone, so I sank deeper into loneliness and isolation. I felt a heavy blanket of shame; and it was swallowing me whole. Why didn't you and Mom get me out of that terrible school? Didn't you see I was dead inside? You're my Dad, and you are supposed to keep me safe.

Nobody ever came to the closet; nobody even noticed me. I was this weird kid that nobody liked much. I spent a lot of time alone in thought. In a room full of people, I was alone, trapped, and scared, afraid you and Mom wouldn't love me if you discovered how awful I was. I believed these things and a portion of me always will. I hate myself, and I don't want to any longer.

I am in my forties and still controlled by what happened then. I used to pray at night that I would never have to go to school again. My prayers were never answered or acknowledged. I wasn't a fan of God growing up and didn't like Church any more than I liked school. I needed to be saved.

I love you Dad and have difficulty writing this when you have been gone so long. I have fallen to pieces at your grave many times in the past five years. I have lost so much and so fast that I slipped into a fog; a fog that may never let me see light shine. I am glad you weren't here for much of what has happened. My family is in shambles and may never recover. I miss you, Dad.

Love, David

Frank took a minute doing that forehead thing before saying, "That was nice, how was it?"

"My Dad was an incredible man and writing about him brings some good memories. It also is difficult to talk about feelings connected with Dad and second and third grade."

He said, "Writing about a deceased loved one is always going to be difficult. When it is someone you cared for deeply, it can be overwhelming. You took care of your Dad when he was sick with cancer? How long did you care for him before he passed?"

"He was on hospice for about six weeks and died in January of 2002."

"We will need to do some work surrounding his death, and the feelings you had caring for him. It is also something that was taking place in the Christmas season. Being here through the holiday season will no doubt generate a lot of feelings you will need to process. Keep writing to Dad and work on the time you and your Mom were doing the hospice care."

"I know I am probably going to regret asking. What does taking care of my Dad in 2001 have to do with the big picture?"

"Because it is emotionally charged and even traumatic doing something like that. Look, even if you didn't have the traumatic life you've lived, it would be hard. You have spent your life not expressing feelings or processing emotion. Then there is grief. Do you think you have allowed yourself to grieve the loss of your Father after he passed? Have you grieved for anyone in your life who has died?"

Do you think you have allowed yourself to grieve the loss of your Father after he passed? Have you grieved for anyone in your life who has died?

I thought about if I ever have grieved for anybody or would even know what that looks like. The answer was obvious. I have never processed any feelings in a healthy way so something like grief was numbed with substances of alcohol or drugs, that is how I dealt with hurt.

"I never grieved loss in healthy ways, I only numbed the pain. I can write about Dad and cancer, and I can write about the hospice time and even his death."

Frank concluded, "Connect with the feelings and write about them, the story should be secondary to what you felt. I know you know this, David, yet I thought I would refresh it. Write to Dad and we'll go from there."

I said, "Okay, I will get going on this today."

CHAPTER 64

Coming back from feeding the horses a few apples, I see three kites flying. Harlan found himself some kite flyers. I take a seat at the picnic table farthest from the flying kite. I don't have anything against kite flying. I want to think about grief now.

Grief isn't something I have thought of very much in my life. Might say it felt natural, even masculine, to bury the hurt, guilt and regrets deep inside. It didn't take Harlan long to make it over to my table with that clip board of his.

He took a seat opposite me and asked why I wasn't over kite flying with all the normal folks?

I said, "Normal you say, that unsavory bunch over there are normal? What are you and I then?"

"We are the dummies who would rather sit and stew about things that most likely are out of our realm of control. So, what is it you are beating yourself up about today?" He questioned.

"It is entirely plausible, even probable, I am sitting over here writing about all the things for which I am grateful and thankful, ever think of that?"

Harlan said, "Sure, the first year I worked in the recovery field I used to have thoughts like that. Then, I realized almost everyone at your stage of recovery is telling themselves one of two things. They are the ones who think they are cured because they feel so good now that the chemicals are out of them, and regular meals are strengthening them. They also benefit from exercise and the therapies they have had thus far. Denial is already sprouting inside them, and they do not even realize it."

He continued, "The other is what you do, believing you have a ton of work ahead of you, and you do by the way. You often become overwhelmed; partly because you believe you can structure addiction treatment like you would a business. Workaholics like us, yes, I said us, believe they can literally write the plan, execute the plan, complete the plan and case closed. Most likely it is a good plan with adequate execution even. Am I getting warm yet?"

I said, "Probably more similarities than differences, I cannot deny it. Patience is something I find lacking; it creates anxiety in me, not the good kind either. Every time I feel I am in a good rhythm and progress is being made, something is uncovered showing me how messed up my life is, and I have no clue how I am going to deal with it."

He said, "I still have things like you describe happening after thirty-five years of sobriety. It is called life. I don't mean to sound insensitive but think for a moment about how drugs and alcohol have been as much a part of you as your hands and feet. You are going to have to learn a lot of new things and ways of living. How long do you think it will take to accomplish this completely? What is it that is cooking your grits today?"

I said, "It will take longer than it has been to learn everything I need to learn. I may never learn everything I want to. Frank asked me to write about the loss of my Dad, specifically when he was on hospice and dying of cancer. The topic of grief and grieving was brought up and how it is processed. I think it is safe to assume, I haven't grieved for anyone who has died who was close to me. Instead, I used drugs and alcohol to sooth my sorrow."

Harlan said, "I have never known one individual in addiction or recovery that didn't have unresolved grief. It is, after all, the opposite of soothing our hurt and pain. In processing grief, we are required to let grief in, and allow ourselves to hurt before we can come to a place of resolution. Death isn't the only area of life when grief comes up. Loss can be very problematic depending on who, what, where or when. Dissolution of a marriage or intimate relationship are things that require us to grieve. Loss of friendships or even jobs and careers can be very emotional, and sometimes take a heavy toll on us. The greater the loss, the more intense the grief. Left unresolved, it will stack up until something breaks within."

> *I was running with a kite attached to a string. This must be a top-notch kite. It was above the tree line in under twenty yards, so I stopped and let out some more line. I was enjoying this!*

I said, "I have a lot of reservation opening this can, I have spent a lot of time avoiding uncontrollable emotion. I am going there, but maybe I don't know where to begin. I am afraid of this, and I shouldn't be. When I write these letters, pretty much all of them, I envision the person sitting right where you are sitting now. Does any of this make sense?"

Harlan got up and motioned for me to follow. He said, "It will all be clear after we attempt to get a kite in the air." It annoys me when he doesn't answer my question and directs me in another direction entirely. Before I knew what was happening, I was running with a kite attached to a string. This must be a top-notch kite. It was above the tree line in under twenty yards, so I stopped and let out some more line. I was enjoying this!

CHAPTER 65

Frank said, "Today, we will be continuing the work of letters to ourselves in a way that expresses guilt, shame or remorse."

Yesterday, took me by surprise, and as a result, I wasn't in a good place last night. I felt I had been squeezed until there was nothing left. Sleep evaded me completely; so, not wanting a repeat, I did some gratitude exercises before coming to the Center today. The following is a second letter to myself.

December 6, 2016

Second negative letter to myself

Dear David,

So, I see you are processing your past, and I bet you think being here is something special, don't you? How is this any different from all the other times you have attempted this sober and clean stuff, or whatever you are calling it this time. Your life is in shambles. Your family and your kids want nothing to do with you, and who could blame them? You do not even know where they live.

Face it, you are and always have been and always will be a loser. We both know you will fail in this latest attempt to rid yourself of addictive behaviors. Misery loves you, and you love it. It is a dark place that seems normal to you. This darkness is what you have created for yourself.

You know full well you are an awful person, and you deserve nothing good. This is ultimately what will derail this latest attempt; you are never to experience goodness; it is wasted on you. You will lie to mask your treachery as always. At least you are consistent...consistently dumb!

Exasperating doesn't even begin to scratch the surface when thinking of all the times you've said, "This time things will be different." Guess what moron? Nobody cares anymore, except your Mom and stepfather. You have accomplished nothing but hurting everyone that ever cared a thing for you; and now you are alone. The loneliness that filled your mind so many years ago is home to stay.

I don't know why you don't just end it. Being you, I imagine you couldn't even kill yourself properly, could you? Do everyone a favor; when you relapse this time, please overdose, and do it right. It's not like you would ever be missed.

David

Committing suicide isn't something to be taken lightly. Addiction brings many to have conversations in their head about ending life. The darkness of active addiction is hard to put into words. The realization of failure is the moment when things fall apart. Sometimes this is a relationship or marriage ending, being fired from a job or death of someone for whom you care. Any one of these stressors can put an addict into a tail spin.

I write repeatedly in this book about things like denial and relapses because I want people reading this to discover how they can help themselves or someone they love. Every single day people lose people they care for to this awful plight.

I write repeatedly in this book about things like denial and relapses because I want people reading this to discover how they can help themselves or someone they love. Every single day people lose people they care for to this awful plight. Families hurt in ways that are like the addicted one. Suicide for an addict doesn't necessarily involve a bullet to the head or a slit of the wrist. It could be an accidental overdose, perhaps, even a welcomed one.

In my darkest hours, I would be remiss to say I never hoped for the end. Putting needles in my veins when I didn't know for sure what was in the syringe was a dark time. I have drunk more than a gallon of straight booze and didn't care if I ever woke up. Are these accidental overdoses, or a binge of drugs and alcohol? For too many, the answer isn't ever revealed, because dead is dead; and there isn't anything anyone can do to bring them back.

CHAPTER 66

When writing about the time Dad had cancer, I realized I never allowed myself to grieve for him. The clarity of this came in the following letter written last night:

December 7, 2016

Second Letter to Dad: Hospice

Dear Dad,

Fifteen years ago, you were on hospice at home, you were very ill. Several years of fighting cancer was coming to an end. I had just moved back to Minnesota from Missouri to help Mom with your care. I wasn't prepared for what that entailed. I recall the first night you were unable to make it to the bathroom without help, and that was hard for us both I think. Sadness overwhelmed me, and I realized you were dying, I never accepted that until that night. I had come home too late.

Mom told me to be strong, so I was. The pain you felt was enormous and some of the medical stuff irritated you, yet you never once vented that to me. I wanted so much for you to live and to have been with us these last fifteen years. Almost every day I think of you and have wanted to talk to you.

I was twenty-nine when you passed, and my life was in torment then as it is now. I didn't tell you this while I was caring for you, because I thought it would have been a selfish act to burden you. I was filled with guilt and shame for who I was, and how I lived. Much of it still lives inside me today as I write.

In so many ways I have wasted my life making one bad decision after another. I never wanted to disappoint you, Dad. I wanted to be the kind of man you were. You put God and family first, but not in words only. You never spoke of being Godly or religion in general. It was by how you lived that defined your character and your faith in God.

Christmas has always been a huge deal in our family. From the time I could crawl, I remember the tree, the presents, and joy that visited our home each year. Your last Christmas with us in 2001 was a more somber day comparatively. Without you as the rock of the family, much has changed, mostly not for the better. Christmas is the time of year that brings out the best and worst in people. My Christmas this year will be at Hope by the Sea. It will be a good holiday; the last couple have been difficult. There is an optimism in me this year. The sliver of peace and optimism inside me tells me I am getting better. Is this the presence of God in my life?

> Dad, I am sorry for a great many things in my life. At the same time, I am grateful for this place, and the hope in my heart now.

I have fallen short as a Father to both of my kids. I don't even know what their living conditions are at present. These are among the things I wish we could talk about. How do I reconnect with my kids after all that has transpired? How do I atone for a lifetime of being a bad father, husband and role-model for my kids? These are things I have trouble working out.

I am a better person today than the one who arrived at Hope over two months ago. I have been a friend to many in this place and with every passing day, I feel more right with God than the previous day. Dad, I am sorry for a great many things in my life. At the same time, I am grateful for this place, and the hope in my heart now.

David

I wrote eight positives going on in my life right now immediately after completing this letter. Writing about the last few months of Dad's life is not something I can do without a lot of emotions flooding me. When I go back to that time, I realize inside me live feelings, negative mostly, I haven't processed. This takes my mood to bad almost instantly, which is why I wrote these positives.

1. My brain is working at a high level despite the heavy amounts of drugs and alcohol I have put in my body recently, and this feels good.
2. I have hope in my heart and in my life that was not there a few weeks ago.
3. I can see a future today that can be anything I set my mind to.
4. I have a family who I think may be able to connect with me in time.
5. I feel challenged and a little motivated these days.
6. The people I have met here will always be a part of me, no matter how long I may live.
7. I have half my life yet to live, and that is a positive.
8. I am in reasonably good health, and I am grateful for this.

Frank said, "That was good, how was it?"

"Mixed feelings I guess covers it. Feelings of Dad are nice to revisit, but very sad because he isn't here anymore." I offered.

He said, "The more connectiveness taking place in the writing, the faster you will be able to move past the unresolved losses in your life. This was about your Dad, but the principles are the same for many things in your life, make sense?"

I said, "I am not sure I understand writing to Dad helps with other things?"

He said, "Feelings, mainly the negative ones, need to be dealt with before any positives will stick. Now, when you think about your Dad, it brings powerful emotions to the surface. Someone you admired, respected and loved. How come you don't just talk about the positive?" Not waiting for an answer, Frank continued, "Sadness, regret, guilt, shame, unworthiness and many other feelings exist more in a loved one's death than for someone else. People don't look at this as problematic, and if you don't want to numb, ignore or suppress, then it isn't. Is this making sense?"

> Frank continued, "Sadness, regret, guilt, shame, unworthiness and many other feelings exist more in a loved one's death than for someone else.

I said, "It is beginning to. I release feelings of guilt, shame, etc. to process the grief, loss or just unresolved conflict in general to come to a place where positive feelings and gratitude can now be incorporated. Is that right?"

He said, "Yes, that is it. Don't forget it takes work to accomplish a lot of work. Therefore, I give you the writing tool. When you leave this place, there will still be work to do. At some point, you will no longer need to write about the past, only life as it happens. Keep writing to Dad, write about the feelings surrounding his last Christmas, and his final day."

"I will get started right away." I said.

CHAPTER 67

Between three and four o'clock each day and during lunch hour, I can be found either feeding apples to the horses, or in the park writing. It is during these times I keep my writing on task. There are also the countless hours talking with Harlan. So, when a couple of clients decided to walk off during lunch hour to buy alcohol, the administration decided nobody could leave the building at lunch or during the three o'clock hour. This made a lot of people angry, myself among them.

I can understand management's position on this given the severity of relapse. At the same time, I believe it is a bit of overkill to punish the entire place over the actions of two misguided young men. However, I did discover upon further investigation a solution to my predicament.

It turns out, because of being here more than sixty days, I am eligible to move into a house that enjoys some considerations the rest of the clients do not have. Leaving the premises over lunch and being able to go to the park from three to four o'clock are among the privileges restored. Leaving the Horse Shoe House is the only negative, but most of the guys are leaving in the next week or two. Therefore, to the El Dorado House I shall go.

The El Dorado House has several men who are enrolled in the Alternative Track. The house is a five-minute walk to the Center. The Horse Shoe House is a twenty-minute van ride. This provides a lot of extra free time and is okay by me.

> The following is a journal entry.
>
> **December 9, 2016**
>
> Moved into the new house and my own room. My park privileges have been restored, and that makes me happy. The last several days, I have had ups and downs. Anxiety over leaving ranks number one. I know the time to fly the coop is fast approaching, and while I believe the necessary components are in place to continue *The Work*, doubts still exist.

Processing feelings is in its infancy for me, and the speed in which I process them is slow. I get stuck I guess is one way to put it. Burying and deflecting is much faster, and those tendencies are still alive in me. Talking to my Mom a couple times in the last week about my brothers, kids and normal life stuff was stressful and elevated my blood pressure. I know because they check it a couple times a day, and once, it was right after our phone call.

I feel it is probably best to not be in an immediate hurry to rekindle family relationships. The holiday season has tensions and stresses that don't exist in April or May. Right now, I need to continue to work on me. Selfish as it may be, I believe it is the prudent course.

Writing longer than normal check-ins has given me a heightened awareness. I recognize negativity within me, and what can happen if it is left unchecked. I enjoy writing in the positive here, so, making it a priority is a perk to me. Kind of weird but it is how I feel.

I wonder sometimes where the last three years or so have gone. The feeling of dark emotion and sadness have at times been overwhelming. I am cautiously optimistic the past going forward will not be a source of perpetual adversities any longer.

CHAPTER 68

The number of clients is low at Hope, and there are fewer new arrivals and more departures. I'm told after Christmas and New Year's Day the place is packed for several months. It makes perfect sense; in the meantime, class sizes are smaller. In the Alternative Track, it means more Work; it also means more feedback from Frank. Lately, he has been telling us that writing about the negatives and processing feelings is only the most basic part of what he is teaching.

Frank told me on a smoke break about how he first began writing. He pulled the shades in the house, locked the doors and began pouring out his soul on paper; terrible things that had been burdening him for many years. He kept writing for days and days working out the adversities of his life on paper purging the negative. It was because of that work, and a whole lot more no doubt, he learned to help others as he helped himself. Addiction being only a sliver of the scope of what this tool can do.

I see endless potential, such as my future projections coming true. The only obstacle standing in the way of those projections is me.

When I absorb everything Frank tells me, I see endless potential, such as my future projections coming true. The only obstacle standing in the way of those projections is me. For those to come true, I must clear out the clutter also known as negative feelings from within me. Then, it will be time to get out of my own way.

This morning, Frank said, "Now that we have talked about some of the benefits and positives possible with writing, let us do the third letter to yourself in the negative that looks at shame and guilt, and talk about those feelings."

Negative Letter to Self #3

December 12, 2016

Dear David,

You are by far the biggest saboteur in your life, you screw up everything you touch. I don't know how you live with yourself. The guilt, shame and regret only compound the *poor me* card.

I think wrecking yourself must somehow be, in a peculiar fashion, your mission all along. It provides validation to a core belief that you are a bad person worthy of nothing. You are rotten to the core; there is zero doubt; and everybody knows it. You are batting a thousand when it comes to destroying all the goodness your poor excuse of a life has had.

You found someone to marry you which is a huge surprise; she must have been as messed up as you. Then you have some kids who are radiant examples of everything you are not. Being the poor excuse of a father, you are; it's a wonder they are still healthy and well.

If hurting others and betraying trusts were an Olympic event, you sir, would have a room full of gold medals. Seriously, how is it you can still get out of bed each day? How can you look yourself in the mirror?

So many would be better off had they never heard the name David Charles Foss. The amount of hurt you have inflicted on others is beyond selfish and self-centered. Anyone else would have done everyone a favor and disappeared, since you are not man enough to eat a bullet. You are a coward.

You already know this latest effort at change will ultimately implode. Most with sense have long since turned away and good for them, it's about time.

You will likely be buried in a cheap, unmarked grave that nobody would ever care to find. You will not be missed, nobody will cry or mourn your passing. Congrats on a life squandered and wasted. Congrats on destroying the goodness given by others. Congrats for having no legacy at all other than a template of how not to live a life. Bravo!

David

CHAPTER 69

Frank reminded me to get another letter to Dad written for the next day's class. Writing about Dad remains difficult and emotional. I see the logic behind doing this kind of writing and the long-term benefits are becoming clearer every day. The grieving process I have never known is happening with the writing. I have never been comfortable talking about emotions or losses that are part of life. The following is a letter to Dad about his last day.

Dad's last day

December 12, 2016

Dear Dad,

The day you died was probably the saddest day of my life. Spending the last two months of your life helping with your hospice care was difficult for both of us. I had been up all night, and you weren't awake; it was apparent the end wasn't far off.

I went to sleep the next morning, and it wasn't long before someone woke me. I went out to the living room where Mom and my brothers were gathered around you. Then you stopped breathing. No opening of your eyes, no goodbye, and no tears -- just nothing. You were dead. I felt so helpless. Why did God take you away?

The funeral home came and got you. They placed you on a gurney and covered you with a blanket, head, face, body and everything. Then, they left, and you were gone. All the emotions from being strong for all those weeks began coming out uncontrollably. I suddenly wanted one more day, hour, even a moment to tell you how much you meant to me, and how much you will be missed.

Dad, I felt angry, anger toward God and toward the doctors who didn't save you. Simply put, I was lost and in complete despair. You made it through Christmas and New Year's. Now, arrangements needed to be done so we could lay you to rest. The obituary for the newspaper, and the service needed to be put together. I wrote a poem that I read to you before you died, and now it will be printed on the back cover of your funeral folder for the service. Mom said you and she had chosen the hymns for the services together.

You had two services; one in the Twin Cities and one in Deer Creek where we lived until 1988. My brother, Joe, gave your eulogy, and I have never been so proud of him. I had trouble with the services, not knowing what to say to all those people was hard. I don't like expressing my feelings to others; this has always been the case as you know.

You have been gone so long. In some ways, it's as if you just left, while in others, you have been gone a lifetime. I think of all the times I have talked to you at the cemetery, sometimes falling apart completely. When we put you in the ground, we sang hymns at the cemetery. The closure was there I suppose.

The months and years following that day were difficult, and I could never find sustained happiness. I have wanted to talk to you at least a thousand times. My emotions surrounding you are as fresh and raw as they were in 2002. I know you are in a better place, and I know you loved me.

Love, David

"How was it?" Frank asked.
"It was helpful for me to write this. Emotional as it was, I could see I hadn't really processed my feelings until now."
He said, "Grief in general is going to be a process and many of the dark emotions like anger, fear and regret can be released now, opening the way to incorporate the positives. What else are you working on?"
"The gratitude exercises every day along with check-ins. I have started writing to Grandpa and I have been considering the kids and brothers."
"Let's write to Grandpa and you can write to the kids also. Hold off on the brothers for now. Let's see where this takes us for now," He requested.
"All right, I'll get going on it tonight."

CHAPTER 70

Harlan had a fresh pot of coffee ready to go, and I am a few minutes early. Had a big lunch today so I needed my caffeine fix. I poured us each a cup and got settled on the couch, all ready for our one o'clock meeting.

He was still doing the two-finger shuffle on his keyboard when he asked, "How are things over at the El Dorado House?"

"I like it. Got my own room, and most of the residents are in the Alternative Track. Even the House Manager is good, my favorite liberal key spinner, Evan."

Harlan said, "That's great! I am glad we could accommodate your request so quickly. Well, we are at about three weeks until your discharge. I spoke with your Mom, and she is happy to have you coming back home."

"That's true. She is happy. How long did it take on the phone to discover this?"

"That isn't very nice, David. We had a good conversation. How are the assignments coming along?"

I said, "The *willful neglect* packet, I love that term by the way, It's much better than *relapse*. Over the weekend I worked on it for a few hours. I made some adjustments that make it more Alternative Track friendly. So far, my core daily, weekly and monthly plan is coming together. Not sure I am satisfied with it; it has some gaps. Do we have time to brainstorm, and poke some holes in it?"

"That's exactly why we meet each week." I passed the packet to him, and he began studying it intently. I wanted to see if he had the same observations as I did. He said, "This is a well thought out program you have written here. My concern for you is I don't see a lot of people here. Other than your Mom and stepdad, there aren't any." Harlan observed.

"That is what I see as well. The positive is I do not have any ties to cut including places and things. I recognize the need for fellowship with decent people, some could be in recovery, but I don't care about that. I want to associate with good, decent and law-abiding people. I'm not sure I know what that looks like right now," I said.

"Tell me more about the daily writing you are going to be doing. I want to understand it more, so I can provide better feedback," Harlan requested.

"That's fair. The gratitude exercise is writing a list of three things for which I'm grateful and thankful and why; writing down a quality in myself I respect and admire and why; and listing ten positives from the last twenty-four hours. Then, I write a check-in for a minimum of twenty minutes. This is where I sort things out in my life and pay extra attention to any negative feelings. I use it as a prayer journal also. These check-in's will identify things I can do better, or things that require further processing. I try to do this in a place where I can give undivided attention to it."

Harlan said, "I think that is a wonderful, detailed plan; and if you continue the work ethic you have shown here, I think it will be a powerful component of your overall well-being. Why is it you have a concern about not having more people in your life?"

"That is a really good question sir. I have tendencies to isolate from people. At some point in the future, I can't say when, I hope to enter a healthy relationship. I have difficulty with my personal life being social. In my professional life, it is easier to communicate. I realize I am all over the place. I believe I need to step out of my comfort zone by trying to do things that involve people. Don't know really what that looks like right now. I could throw stuff out there, but it would just be empty talk right now," I concluded.

"That actually sounds real and genuine to me. It isn't easy putting together a thought out, honest plan to avoid *willful neglect* of your recovery. Brainstorming helps with considering things you did not, or even looking deeper into components you already have. Let's table this until we meet again or in the park some afternoon. I think we have made progress here today," Harlan said as he wrapped it up for the day.

"That works for me, see you then," I agreed.

CHAPTER 71

El Dorado House has two guys who arrived at Hope by the Sea around the same time as I. Potter is from Maryland, and Andy is from Georgia. So, it seems we started together and now, we are going to finish together. Because we are all in the Alternative Track, we know one another extremely well. Andy had to fly home for a legal matter for a couple days and has just returned. He didn't look or act the same as before he left.

While we are sitting around the table eating some supper, Potter and I called Andy out, and asked him to bring us into the fold on his trip. He denied he had been using and stuck to his story for about ninety-seven seconds; then, he realized we weren't going to let up. He wouldn't look us in the eye, and the shame of relapse was apparent to those who have been in his boots. Andy's drug of choice is a synthetic opiate called Fentanyl, although Heroin, or any opioid drug would do. Fentanyl, according to the National Institute on Drug Abuse, is fifty to 100 times stronger than Morphine from which Heroin is often derived. As far as knowing if it is closer to fifty or closer to 100, isn't known to the one taking it, because this stuff is mixed by illegal drug pushers who care little of the consequence of putting these concoctions into people.

Potter asked, "What in the Hell were you thinking?"

Andy said, "I had it all planned out before I even left California to go back home. I wanted to see if I still even liked it any more. I know that sounds like a load of crap, but it's true."

Potter said, "True or not it is one of dumbest things I have ever heard. Do you think you can take it or leave it now? Are you still using?"

Andy said, "No, I do not think I can take or leave it, I stopped using this morning."

I said, "You more precisely ran out, isn't that correct?"

Andy said, "I ran out, and I stopped."

I said, "Since I don't think you flew with drugs on your person or in your luggage, and you've been back for two days, you have a supplier in California. Did you factor that into your plan tough guy?"

Potter said, "What about the drug test they gave you on arrival, or the one they give us every Wednesday? What about that?"

Andy said, "I have clean pee."

Potter said, "So now what?"

Andy said, "I don't know. This treatment may not be for me. It doesn't seem to work all that well. I expected much more than what I got."

I want to punch him in the worst way. Instead, I say, "That isn't what you thought a month ago when you were in class every day writing and sharing."

Andy said, "Yeah, well things have changed for me. I am going to come clean with my Case Manager in the morning, and most likely be kicked out after that. Not like I can do anything else anyway."

Potter said, "Why would you throw it all away, you were doing fine. The last thing you need is to leave and do more dope. Come clean and beg them to let you stay. Stay another ninety days, whatever it takes."

The return of denial is subtle. It isn't anything that is going to hit you between the eyes; although most wish it would. Andy was kind to me when I needed a friend upon arrival in the Detox House. We sang, *Rocky Top Tennessee,* and it made us smile on a day that had a lot of adversity. We entered the Alternative Track at the same time. He worked as hard as anyone the first month or so.

Andy started missing the first hour by volunteering to clean the bathrooms. Not long after, he began working on computers in hour two looking for a job and a sober living option upon exiting Hope by the Sea. I believe Andy's denial began before he stopped coming to class. He admitted to me many times he wasn't writing anymore, more than a month ago.

Another component of Andy's denial and subsequent relapse was getting romantically involved with the female clients at Hope by the Sea. Despite separate buildings, houses etc., this happens. Tuesday night at *The Effect* is co-ed, and church and yoga classes are too. Those who enjoy the privileges of the El Dorado House can leave the house for three hours unsupervised. The females have a similar house with similar policies. Hope by the Sea prohibits any shenanigans between the sexes.

Most everyone seeks a healthy relationship, or at least one perceived to be a healthy relationship. Beginning a relationship with another client at a treatment center doesn't require an expert to suggest, it could likely be unhealthy. Early recovery is a fragile time that is stressful and emotional. This alone causes many to leave treatment and use again.

On more than one occasion, I have entered a relationship in early recovery. Both ended badly, and, in both instances, I was hurt and emotionally unbalanced by it. I had wanted to be with someone with whom I could find happiness in my life. Instead, I fell deeper into despair and sorrow. Drugs and alcohol numbed this for a time as it has my whole life.

Talking to Frank one day, the subject of relationships came up and I will never forget what he said to me. He told me when it comes to relationships, we tend to attract and project what we are. If you're miserable and have low self-esteem, you will attract the same or similar persons. If you are comfortable in your own skin, are confident and successful, you will project and attract those types. He went on to tell me, each person brings something to the relationship that is a betterment to the other. In this kind of relationship, each are comfortable, even happy before they meet. When this happens, a healthy relationship is born. Relationships built this way rarely fail; instead, they deliver happiness, love and contentment.

Simply put, Andy engaged in risky behaviors that led to relapse. Denial is what made Andy think he could handle a relationship made in treatment, and a planned use of drugs on a visit back to Georgia. Denial is also what made Andy believe it was a good idea to stop processing his feelings on paper, or even come to class. Andy, like myself, is trying to learn how to live with the trauma he experienced as a child.

Hope by the Sea allowed Andy to stay. He started all over at the Detox House and began the process anew. Many don't make it back to try again. Some overdose and die, while others continue to hurt.

CHAPTER 72

My Grandpa was a man who cared more about others than himself, but not in a co-dependency sense. I watched my whole life how he loved, treated and cared for my Grandma; also, my Mom after we lost Dad in 2002. He never raised his voice in anger in my presence even once. I was seven, maybe eight years old, and my brother Joe was bullying and hurting me. Grandpa took hold of him with strong arms, put him over his knee and swatted his behind a few times. It was over in seconds, and he never spoke of it to anyone. Joe had it coming; no doubt about it. In times like that when people would tease me verbally or hurt me physically, it validated my feelings of hopelessness and that I deserved to be treated badly. Grandpa disciplined my brother, but anger was not present. The following is my first letter to my Grandpa.

Letter to Grandpa # 1

December 13, 2016

Dear Grandpa,

When we moved to the Twin Cities from the farming community, it became home for a lifetime for most of the family. It was 1988, and it had been two years since you had sold the farm. When you sold the farm, I was devastated and angry. It was as if the one sanctuary I had in my life was gone forever. When Mom and Dad told me, the devastation I felt was heart breaking. I look back now and realize it was even more devastating for you, tearing your heart out at the core.

In 1989, you and Grandma sold your farm that was a mere two miles away from my home. It is my belief when we pulled up stakes a year prior, it brought sadness to the home where you and Grandma had lived my whole life. You never let any hurt show as was your way.

You were always more concerned for the well-being of those you loved and cared about. You are the most selfless man I have known or likely will ever know. A few lines in a book can never match the man that is my Grandpa. Grandma, as you well know, was also an amazing person and she loved us boys as much as you did.

One thing I loved more than anything was the way you let me be me. I didn't have to explain things that happened in school. The very mention of it made me frightened and scared. Grandpa, you were the person who would not let harm come to me. I slept at your home a lot. I don't think I ever told anyone that noises and normal sounds in our house would frighten me, and sometimes I could not return to sleep.

You sold the farm when I was 13. It shocked me, and I felt the only respite in my life was gone. I felt alone in a world that didn't want me, and I didn't want them either. The world and how I perceived it, was a place that was terrifying, plain and simple. Your world in the fields was the place I felt safe and comfortable to be me without reprisal from others. Thirty-five years later, every time I see tractors or combines in a field, it warms my heart and brings tears of joy of thoughts of better times -- mostly.

In 1988, we moved to the Twin Cities leaving behind my dreams of one day farming the land where I had spent my whole life. It was my source of hope that maybe everyone was wrong, and I was a good person deserving of things that were good. Before leaving Deer Creek forever, I gave my toy tractors to a farmer in the area who was a good friend to all of us; and I knew he would appreciate them. Phil and his wife attended my wedding, and I have fond memories of him. He thought highly of you too, Grandpa, as everyone I have ever known did.

I was happy to leave Deer Creek Valley, and specifically Glenville High School, and everything about it. Any place would be better than that world; it just held too many things that forever changed who I was or would be. You and Grandma left about a year later. You got a big travel trailer and set your sights on Arizona for the winter. After one winter, you moved to the Twin Cities, too. Being sixteen, I could drive and see you often.

In the last summer on the farm, I had gotten a learner's permit, so I could drive. At the ages of four and five, I was sitting on your lap driving tractors and boats. Also driving trucks and cars probably sooner than I should have. After my first driver's education lesson, you picked me up in your motor home. The look on the instructor's face when he saw us driving away with me behind the wheel was rather unique. I learned so many things from you that day. How to trust your side mirrors for being in the proper lane. I would bet a bottle of pop; the driving instructor has never again seen the likes of us that he saw that day.

Moving to a large city I thought would be the answer to my prayers; and I would somehow be rid of the feelings of worthlessness, and that I was an awful person. It only made it easier to keep people at bay. I soon found myself hanging in a crowd of unsavory types, not all that different from Glenville. You were in Arizona, and my safety net that was you ceased. When you were back in Minnesota living close, I was glad to have you close once more. But, I was the one who had been doing the changing.

I began doing drugs regularly and drinking was a problem, and I knew it had me at a very young age. School was important to you, and you had set high expectations and priorities for my Mom, but I didn't measure up to those. I had the brains, but I didn't have the capacity to function; I barely made it out alive. You never made me feel shame for quitting school, showing me only love. Did you have a sense that I was unable to be in school without fear and hopelessness?

As the drug use and alcohol increased, I fell further into darkness. My life was working, and the use of substance was to feel any measure of what I perceived as normal. That isn't true either. I was ashamed and harbored shame my whole life. At the time, I had little to live for in my troubled mind.

The connectiveness I was desperate for my whole life with my parents, my brothers, girlfriends, children and the mother of my children, I could not attain.

Relationships with women were always sabotaged by my social awkwardness and feelings of unworthiness which made these things unlikely. I know conversations of this nature are not normal, but neither am I, so maybe it is the perfect place.

Grandpa, I believe if it were not for you, I would have been forever lost when I was eight years old. You were larger than life and my hero. I felt protected and safe. My Mom and Dad were wonderful, loving parents so this isn't saying anything negative about them. I had a hero and a best friend in you who has made me eventually feel safe. Today, I feel safe, and I feel my life can be fulfilling; and happiness that has been so elusive may now be realized.

> *Today, I feel safe, and I feel my life can be fulfilling; and happiness that has been so elusive may now be realized.*

I wish you were alive today. I want you to be proud of me and approve of how I live going forward. I love you, Grandpa, you are the best.

Love, David

Frank said. "How was it?"

"Writing things about Grandpa are enjoyable when the content is positive. When Grandpa sold the farm, I felt betrayed and hurt. I wished it would have been anyone other than him who sold it. I realize it doesn't make sense, but at the same time I did not like feeling that way about him," I answered.

"What is the *way* of which you are speaking? Is it the negative feelings or guilt? What are you trying to convey?" Frank inquired.

"I feel guilt and regret for having harsh feelings surrounding the dissolution of his farm. It was a real blow to me. I almost never would talk to anyone about my feelings, particularly those connected to guilt or shame. I didn't deserve to be happy. I didn't deserve to farm with the man who loved me so much. Therefore, I buried them, as I bury everything else," I said with emotion.

"Burying or ignoring our feelings and suppressing emotions makes us hurt worse in time. Numbing it with substance or romanticizing events with lies, are coping mechanisms we create to protect us from perceived fear. So, what are you afraid of David?" He questioned.

"I am afraid of a lot in my life. With Grandpa, it would be if he discovered my shame and feelings of worthlessness, I would lose him, and he wouldn't love me anymore. I know now and have zero reservations that my Grandpa loved me and was proud of me. During my teen years and into adulthood when I was filled with shame, I had many doubts he loved me," I said with strong feelings.

"Your Grandpa was a hero figure to you when your trauma happened with the teacher. It is reasonable to put him on a pedestal of sorts. What happens is these expectations we place on ourselves, and the one on the pedestal, become unattainable. The shame inside of you has been hidden and masked most of your life. Now it is coming out, in a way, that is overwhelming for you. You still have a lot of work ahead of you to rid yourself of the negatives. The positives can then overcome the adversity that has been a part of you for so long. Let's write to Grandpa, focusing on the guilt and shame you have kept buried; then we can begin working on other concerns." Frank requested.

"I will begin right away." I told him.

I thought about what guilt and shame were still locked away and little else the rest of the day and evening. Is this why I become emotional at unexplainable times like at that show in Branson so long ago? Is it why when I watch TV, or a movie I may have seen a dozen times, that on the thirteenth time, I fight back tears? Showing tears and deep emotion is extremely hard for me. I fight to hold it all in, but not because I don't trust my surroundings. I feel if the tears begin, they won't stop because so many of them are in me. In the fall of 2013, I went to see Dad and Grandpa at the cemetery. I must have cried on my face for more than an hour. I was in a meltdown that wouldn't stop. I felt even worse when I left the cemetery that day, much worse.

Frank wants me to dig deep, beyond what's behind the eyes, beyond the masks I wear to protect myself. I fear rejection of people and places. I have had little connectivity in my life. Being afraid of being hurt as I have been so many times, makes me think detachment is safer. Wanting something doesn't mean one should pursue it. The negative consequences of the action in almost every case has been to medicate with drugs and alcohol to feel nothing. Only then does any peace live in me. Shame is silenced in nothingness as are the demons feeding it.

> *Being alone in a room of people, even family, has made me feel alone, unwanted and even unloved. I am not saying I am not loved, I just don't know how to receive it or express it.*

Living this way probably sounds lonely or even sad. The reality is exactly that, especially the loneliness which is deafening at times. I am committed to *The Work* here because I believe it will give me the life I choose, not one chosen by others, or by the masks I have worn. Being alone in a room of people, even family, has made me feel alone, unwanted and even unloved. I am not saying I am not loved, I just don't know how to receive it or express it. I will write to Grandpa tonight and be prepared to share it in class.

I believe doing this writing will finally allow the guilt to be released regarding the loss of the farm. I feel I never made that right with him.

CHAPTER 73

Frank was ready for work and asked if I had been able to complete the assignment. My work ethic standard has been high my entire life, and Hope by the Sea, if anything, has increased the standard. It is good to see Andy back in the Alternative Track and writing again. He read his letter right after I read my letter to Grandpa.

Grandpa Letter #2

December 14, 2016

Dear Grandpa,

When we left the farm in southern Minnesota I was hoping, praying in fact, that all my problems would remain there. They did not. I was still broken inside and had no reason I could understand. It didn't take long for things to become troublesome. The friends I made, if you can call them that, only led to further adversities in my life.

It was after getting married that things became real for me, and my work ethic went into overdrive. I had this motivation to show everyone who said I would amount to nothing how wrong they were. I began working insanely long hours that were sustained by assorted drugs and alcohol. These dangerous balances kept me functional in work and life for too much time. I had no idea what it meant to be married other than supporting my family, and that meant working a lot. My Dad was gone a lot to work as was my Mom at various times. Based on this, I felt I was fulfilling my obligation.

When Grandma died, it hit me like a ton of bricks. I was at work that night and chose to stay because I was doing a lot of cocaine and was strung out. I didn't see you until the next day, and I was just as strung out then. At the church at her funeral I was to give the eulogy. To accomplish this, I did a few lines of cocaine in the bathroom. I fell apart and became overcome with emotion. Jeff was the only one who knew this. I was being consumed by the shame I had come to recognize. Grandpa, I dishonored you that day at a time I should have been your proud, loving and grateful Grandson. Instead, you got a selfish, poor excuse of a human being.

Cocaine and alcohol were done pretty much nonstop for the next six months. You lived in the neighborhood I worked, and I often was up for days at a time. I would come see you some mornings, telling you I was there to see how you were doing, and asked if I could do anything to help. I was out of my mind then, and sitting there talking with you, I would be overcome with guilt and shame. The man who was so instrumental in my life, and the most selfless man I knew, I was treating with this lack of respect. I never talked of these things with anyone, the shame just grew inside me as a cancer.

Not long after this time, my wife Peggy's Mother passed. Peggy sank into this awful sea of depression that she has never really returned from. A year after Grandma passed, you moved into Mom and Dad's home to live with them, and many things changed.

Moving back to Minnesota, my wife's depression, and Dad's death, left me a cold, bitter person detached from life. I was tired and content to work and engage in addictive behaviors. Living fifty miles from the office in Lonsdale, driving drunk or impaired by other substances, generated legal and financial problems and says nothing of the condition of my marriage and family.

I rejected and distanced myself from all except those activities involving drugs and alcohol. You lived on my way to work, even were hospitalized a couple of times, and I didn't even have the decency to visit you. You denied me nothing, and there was never even one instance you didn't drop everything to help me. Distance, daytime or nighttime, it mattered not to you. You are all the things that make humanity good.

After Grandma died, we began taking annual fishing trips to Canada to a place you had been visiting for over fifty years. Those trips have conundrum qualities for me. Spending time with you, Dad, my brothers and some of my uncles are times I will always cherish. These trips were also non-stop daily benders for me consuming from morning to pass-out. I filled water bottles with straight Vodka. I began the week with twenty-four 20-ounce bottles that barely lasted half a week. You and I each had boats, so we rarely fished together, each opting to be the skipper of our respective vessels. All I know of boats, motors and farming is a result of your expert tutelage. Despite the drugs and alcohol, I consider my knowledge in these areas above novice thanks to you.

Then one day, Grandpa, you were gone. There would be no more boat shows, no more boating and no more anything ever again. I didn't want to further shame you like I believed I did when Grandma passed. Mom delivered your eulogy. We put you in the ground in the Deer Creek cemetery next to Grandma and Dad. When I think back on the last dozen years of your life, I realize I truly am a terrible person. Why would I do this to the man who because he knew I was troubled, and he loved me, let me disk a field at the age of seven by myself?

I know you wouldn't want me to be upset, or even want me writing this letter. You would want me to have a happy life. This is all you ever wanted for me, all my brothers and those you loved so selflessly. Kind, generous, gentle and compassionate are not mere words people use to remember you; they are true feelings and beliefs you demonstrated to all you loved every day of your life.

Love, David

Frank said, "How was it?"
I said, "It took a lot out of me speaking of things and feelings I never wanted to surface. The feelings of guilt, shame, and self-loathing are more intense than I thought possible."
"How do you feel about your Grandfather right now? What I mean is: are the dark, loathsome feelings of shame different today than yesterday when we discussed the letter to Grandpa?" Frank asked.
This made me irritated initially, but one of the many skills I have learned from Hope by the Sea is to let things sink in before responding with heat. I have not been a quick study in this area.
"I think the letter is clear the feelings were more intensified than yesterday, and I feel a little combative and annoyed with the question. One of the greatest men I have

ever known in my life, I treated in a way that even now makes me deeply emotional," I managed to say through my tears.

"David, I respect and admire the work ethic you show, and I know how hard this kind of work is from personal experience. The gift which may seem out of place, is in describing these adverse parts of your life, you have discovered and uncovered that which has handicapped you most of your life; and now, my friend, it is time to release the negatives surrounding Grandpa. The positives with Grandpa are infinite and should be a part of you, free of shame and guilt." Frank said with kindness.

"I think the letter is clear the feelings were more intensified than yesterday, and I feel a little combative and annoyed with the question.

"I understand the concept of releasing the negatives, and the value in doing so. I fear it can come back and sabotage my life again, how can I make this less likely to happen?" I said with anxiety.

"You need to begin to use the writing tools as life enhancements and not simply as an addiction coping mechanism. Loyalty to the writing processes will enrich your life in ways you cannot imagine right now. The only thing that hinders excellence is you, meaning the writing will identify what requires action and show your successes."

I said, "I realize and believe addiction to be a symptom of my mental diagnoses that I work in concert here at Hope by the Sea. I have already been blessed with evidence that this *Work* is delivering results. Some are baby steps and others are leaps forward that unlock thoughts I hadn't considered before. I am finding value in mental health therapy I rejected my whole life. My Therapist here at Hope by the Sea has been amazing, and a true professional who cares. I believe it all works together, if I allow it to. I find value in everything, some things more than others, of course. Is this a healthy way to be thinking?" I asked.

"I believe it is. The lived experience of everyone is different; and therefore, the needs of people are different. This isn't unique to addiction; it covers all of life's spectrums. Problems, physical and psychological alike, are going to have forever changing perceptions and sensitivity to life's challenges," He answered.

The rest of the session I considered his observations carefully, and it was still on my mind when I left his classroom to go to lunch.

CHAPTER 74

The kitchen didn't have any apples and the horses will snub me if I show up empty handed...what to do? Ringo slipped me some granola bars, so the crisis is averted. I think they like the granola better than the apples. I am on my way back when I spot Harlan and his clipboard sitting at a picnic table, looking like someone is tickling his middle toe.

"How is it every time I see you, this look of serenity like you have now is ever present?" I asked.

He said, "I have bad days just like everyone else does, and I think you already know that, so what's going on?"

"Just one time I would like you to allow me to meander a bit before telling me I am full of *B* as in **BS.**" Would it be too much to ask for after all these talks of ours?" I asked with indignation.

He said, "Still waiting...."

I said, "How can a person right a wrong or make an amend to a loved one who is dead? The guilt and shame eat at my insides."

Harlan said, "That's a tough one son. A lifetime is a long time, but not enough time for the people who loved us, or we loved. Taking for granted life has an infinite supply of tomorrows, can carry a lot of pain."

I uttered, "All this talk of releasing pain, it feels as if doing so will unjustifiably provide more pain I don't deserve. Who the heck am I to decide when I have suffered enough? The core of my soul deserves what my life has been giving it. When I go to sleep at night, I don't feel absolved of the things I have let go, even going so far as to burn it away in a metal can outside the house by the pool.

> *"Just one time I would like you to allow me to meander a bit before telling me I am full of B as in BS." Would it be too much to ask for after all these talks of ours?" I asked with indignation.*

I don't deserve goodness. I am a bad person. I have lived an awful life. Why am I still here on this earth? How is it possible that I haven't hurt or killed others in my actions?"

Harlan said with tears now, "I went to treatment with seventeen other men thirty-five years ago this May, and I am the only one to survive a year. The rest succumbed to the disease, and it cost them their lives. I don't know why David, I ask God this every time another brother passes."

I, too, am emotional now and the words are slow coming. "This world is not forgiving and is often cruel and punitive where addiction is concerned. Why are we here?"

He said, "Why did you go all the way to the top to keep Andy from getting bounced out of here for his behaviors? He is living in the El Dorado House for God's sake."

Irritated, I said, "What in the world does that have to do with anything? I have known him pretty much since arriving here. It angered me they were ready to boot him while countless clients stay because of economic factors."

"What you did is save somebody's life, maybe. Life doesn't have a lot of guarantees that I know of. How about you? Addiction can date you on a Monday, marry and bury you on a Monday night, and you already know that, don't you? Andy is still in the fight. I am still in the fight. What are you going to do?" Harlan asked.

"I have little time left here, and I have felt strong many times in my life. I have achieved successes and suffered failures. I am a father, not a good one, but a father. I am scared I am going to die when I leave here. I am positively stunned it hasn't happened yet. I tremble in fear at the thought of leaving here. I continue to have recurring nightmares I fear will never leave me. What kind of life is that?" I asked.

Addiction can date you on a Monday, marry and bury you on a Monday night, and you already know that, don't you? Andy is still in the fight. I am still in the fight. What are you going to do?

"I know you are Alternative Track, but I also call your Mom every week, and she tells a considerably more optimistic accounting of your life. She also told me you were growing stronger in your Christian faith. My faith is paramount in my life. Until that part of my life was right, I wasn't." He said.

"Playing the Mom card is dirty pool in your work, isn't it?" I sniffed.

Harlan said, "My work has deadly stakes, and you bet I don't hesitate to call anyone I believe can help. You have a Mother who loves you and has incredible amounts of compassion to help you beat this. I am going to retire soon, and you have what it takes to make it. You learned to use the pick and shovel (pen and paper) and used them to uncover, discover, and discard what has fed the addiction you came here to fight. You have what you came for and more, but mostly you have hope. Real hope will always sustain you, if you let it."

I said, "My Mom is amazing, and I am glad you haven't retired yet."

CHAPTER 75

Journal Entry

December 16, 2016

This pneumonia in my chest has taken the wind from my sails and fatigue is becoming a real problem. Three trips to urgent care, nebulizer treatments, and assorted medications have done little to help. I don't have time to be sick. My time here is short, and I require every second of it. On a positive note, I received a package containing some fresh lefsa from my brother. Lefsa being a Norwegian potato delicacy rolled in sugar and butter.

Big Dave, not me, slipped in his sobriety and wrapped his truck around an electric pole totaling his truck. He wasn't hurt physically but was arrested for DWI -- Driving While Impaired. This was his second of 2016. His wife sent me a text message asking me to pray for her husband. Big Dave left Hope by the Sea after thirty days. This is a recurring thing for many families with some ending in death or prison. I hope my friend will be okay.

> *If you grew up in the Foss family you are rarely, if ever called little anything. It took coming to California in 2016 for me to be called little Dave. This is because next to this tall giant of a man, who I am proud to call my friend, I am small.*

If you grew up in the Foss family you are rarely, if ever called *little* anything. It took coming to California in 2016 for me to be called little Dave. This is because next to this tall giant of a man, who I am proud to call my friend, I am small. I also got a kick out of being called little Dave. Big Dave also resided in the Horse Shoe House, and we had many a laugh and sometimes shed tears together.

Having the unique privilege as an adult to work on becoming a better person is quite extraordinary. What I find troubling and heart wrenching is the infinite number of people who never have the chance. I speak of not only those who struggle with addiction, but also of all humanity who need help. Addiction is not the only thing that could use an injection of compassion in life. If it weren't for the compassion shown to me by Mom and Thad, I am certain I wouldn't be here, and this would have never been written.

Addiction, co-dependency, anger, lust, pick your sin or poison, we all have them. Some might be thinking now that squandered chances, and repetitive, predictable self-pity require firm, rigid accountability rather than compassion. After all, everything has a point where the barriers of no return are crossed. Is this not the correct way to feel? Is it as simple as all that? Your son, daughter, spouse, friend or even employee? Case closed. No? Yes?

Big Dave, like many others, decided to leave Hope by the Sea after about a month. This may seem adequate to the twenty-eight-day Hollywood model many believe to be an accurate depiction of addiction, treatment, recovery and resuming life. I am not saying there are not success stories in such models. I am saying most, specifically those with co-occurring diagnoses, need more treatment time. Mrs. Big Dave, who sent me a plea of love to pray for her husband, might have some thoughts on whether a month is sufficient time to stay in treatment.

CHAPTER 76

Depression is ever present in families who have addiction in them, often going back to childhood where trauma and adversity are experienced in ways that can follow you your whole life. It is also common for children in this environment to be subject to this as far back as the womb.

My son, David, who is 16 was exposed to very dark depression before his birth. His Mom was grieving the loss of her mother who died suddenly a couple of years earlier. The depression she fell into at that time, I believe is still there in some ways. David has been depressed much of his life. Some of it is due to the head trauma he suffered and endured at three years old which nearly killed him. Some may have come from having his Mom in deep depression from his infancy. These events established and forever altered the way my son's brain developed and operates today. I am not a clinician, and this is not a text book, so I am not going to be getting overly technical as to how this ties in to addiction, co-occurring disorders etc.

The rift between my kids and me is bad. I have not spoken to either of them for months. Therapy and writing has brought me to a place of accepting there is likely no easy or even visible strategy to mend these fences currently, and it will require some time.

Speaking with Frank last night before meditation, we talked a bit about my kids. Depression most certainly has existed in them at different times in their lives. David seems to have more of it. Add in the head trauma he endured, it is almost certain his brain circuitry and pathways developed in a way different from others. He has many similarities to the way I grew up, so many it scares me. Frank told me to do some letters to David from the prospective of depression. He said we didn't have much time and should have already been working on it.

I stayed up late writing and trying to understand what I should be writing about. My son has shown signs of depression for some time now. My daughter, Chelsey, exhibited signs also but because Chelsey is strong and now twenty-one, I can see why Frank wanted me to begin with David.

First Letter to My Son, David, on Depression

December 15, 2016

Dear David,

Before you were born your Mom suffered from clinical depression resulting from the sudden death of her Mother. This depression lasted the entire pregnancy and, in some ways, continues today. I realize you are depressed and have been for a very long time. I do not know when it began specifically. I do know leaving Cottage Grove in 2012 and moving to Lakeville, was hard for you. I think you began isolating more and more at the ranch in Lakeville. Changing schools wasn't something you wanted to do.

I didn't want to leave Cottage Grove any more than you or your sister. I should have fought for you more instead of just letting it happen. I let your Mom decide, believing it was a bad move because you were perfectly happy where we lived in Cottage Grove. I traveled a lot in 2012, and if I had not, maybe I could have done something to prevent the move. I know you don't make friends easily because I am the same way.

All you really had that you cared about I suppose was your dog, the horses and your Xbox. Things got worse when the company expansions were not producing as projected, and we ended up moving again. This time to Hastings where you were picked on, and you didn't tell anyone except your sister. By the time I heard of this, I had moved to Missouri; your Mom and I had separated; and, the divorce was on tap. When Chelsey told me, I was angry with myself. I blamed myself for moving you to all these different schools.

I understand why you didn't tell me about being picked on. You were upset about the divorce. I was picked on and more, so I know how terrible it feels. You started medicating with food to feel normal, but it only sunk you into further despair. By the time you came to Missouri, you were as big as me, maybe a little bigger even. The despair and complete unhappiness was also hard to miss. I related to the pain, and the crippling depression too.

If I could change just one thing in my life; it would be to have been a better Dad, like mine was to me. As your Father, it is my job to raise you with love and selflessness. I do pray and hope that one day our relationship can be healthy and loving.

Love, Dad

Frank said, "How was it?"

I said, "I found it to be difficult sifting through this time of my life. It has some rather powerful feelings and emotions. It has been a long time since I have talked to David, or to my daughter, Chelsey, making it even more challenging to write about the feelings surrounding them."

He said, "That will not be easy to deal with, not only with the feelings to process, but also the time that will continue to pass. Did your son's Mom, experience depression in her pregnancy?"

I said, "Definitely. She was in a very dark place before and after his birth. It was hard on the whole family."

Frank said, "When your son was hurt at three years old, did that require surgeries for severe head trauma?"

I said, "Yes, that and more. Initially he had several surgical procedures and was in the hospital more than a month. A bookcase he was climbing on gave way and landed on him breaking his skull, crushing his sinuses, and his eyes were swollen shut for thirteen days. My son, who less than two weeks before had turned three years old, was now in a fight for his life."

Frank explained, "So much is going on in the adolescent brain at that age, and coupled with the depression of his parents, makes it a perfect storm for a life of mental anguish and ripe for addictive behaviors. Let's keep writing to your son and depression."

I said, "I will write it today and have it ready to go tomorrow."

CHAPTER 77

My Therapist, Nancy, and I meet several times a week, and the work we have begun together has surprised me in a lot of ways. Nancy has been an American for over thirty years and is originally from Israel. Talking through PTSD, depression, anxiety, fear, kids etc., has complimented the work done in the Alternative Track. Professional Therapists are essential to the treatment process. The individual attention provides the safe environment to talk free of judgment.

Something else happened in those meetings I didn't expect. We were discussing depression when Nancy said, "When depression comes to visit, and it will, it is important to recognize it for what it is." She said depression visits her at least once a year, and if she ignored the symptoms, it would become a serious ailment for her.

I said, "That is the most remarkable attitude toward mental illness I have ever heard. Encouragement and hope are rolled into one thought process with actionable steps. How is it possible to maintain such a level of positivity?"

> *Nancy said, "When depression comes to visit, and it will, it is important to recognize it for what it is."*

Nancy and I had talked about faith in past sessions, and I gave consent weeks ago to bring God into our sessions when she felt it would help me. Therefore, when she told me that God is behind her outlook in all she does, I am not surprised. Faith is something that has been intermittent at best throughout my life. I never would have thought going to California and working with a Jewish Therapist, would bring me closer to Christ. I long for faith in which all my burdens and joys are given freely to Him, and my life is lived for His glory.

I know God is all powerful and can heal me today of all addictive behavior and rid my body of sin forever. I also believe the Lord helps those who help themselves, and even more when we reach out and help others. Nancy taught me to see God all around me. The little actions and inactions of life are where most living takes place. It is at Hope by the Sea where I find God working through others to help and heal one another, staff and client alike day in and day out. It is my choice to incorporate God into our therapy sessions, and it was the right thing for me.

For the bulk of my eighteen years of marriage, there was little priority in my family home for things like God, Jesus, the Church, or even the real meaning of Christmas. I had a good base of information to believe the Bible is true; and that it is God's written message to the world about who He is, among other important things. It took Nancy, a Therapist of the Jewish faith, to bring it all home. It turns out God is always with me, even when I shun or deny Him as Simon Peter did after the arrest of Jesus.

At my session with Nancy, today, after our usual pleasantries and greetings, I asked to share my following feelings about depression and denial with her. "I worry about both of my kids being susceptible to depression and denial. The apple didn't fall far from the tree in many ways. A strong denial can resemble something that brings fear, shame, even guilt and misunderstanding. I recognize these things in them. It is like I am looking in a mirror of my life at times.

What I call the *not me syndrome* is perhaps the earliest example of denial in the life of most families. Questions like, 'Then, who did do it?' usually spark the unison answer of *not me*. It has become as natural as cartoons on a Saturday morning. *Not me* likely has a bed in every home in America. *Not me* has become a cute, even funny way, to look back at our lives, maybe even when talking to our own children and grandchildren. We as adults need to recognize the danger of trivializing the behavior of denial.

Denial and false, idealistic recall that begins with innocently intended learned behaviors, can also lay foundations for negative behavior, too. To our brain the *not me* character is simply a liar, not the humorous, mischievous star of the story.

The more any behavior is practiced, the more it will build on our learned experiences over our lifetimes. For some, repetitive behavior enhances talents like singing, athleticism and academic achievement as well as other gifts and talents. Our brains are like clay. They are moldable and impressionable. Our realities are often determined by these behaviors.

Then, there is substance addiction, and that **absolutely** includes alcohol. It wouldn't be difficult to list a thousand plus behavior and substance abuse disorders. Repetitive behavior in these areas is a recipe for disaster.

I believe in some capacity, words like denial, enable, relapse, even compassion, have come to mean things they didn't before.

Before we experienced it, when someone we love, a friend, a boss, or a co-worker had adversity in an area, it was always somebody else's child or friend. Who wouldn't take solace that it was not our child or friend who was addicted?

Nancy, I have experienced and even lived most of this. Why do people do this? Is it easier to pretend a problem doesn't exist, and if given a little time, things will be fine?"

She said, "Two similar, but very different questions. Wouldn't you agree?" I shook my head yes, so she continued, "I would hope anyone would love me enough to give me a little time, even if only to explain myself. Sweeping it under the rug is something else altogether, isn't it?"

I said, "That's when denial engulfs people often for the first time. It feels like protection, love and compassion depending on the circumstances. Employers, friends and others do the same thing. People in general are good, and they want to help those in need. The closer the relationship, the more they tend to want to know and understand what to do."

Nancy said, "It does to me, but this is my work; I live and breathe it day in day out. What I have learned is this: when people are lied to, hurt again and again, some physical, some not, it gets to them, even changes them. Many books, family programs, even faith-based treatment centers need to have two fundamental components to work. You must have compassion in your heart, and hope in your soul, and you must give these gifts to others to save them --and, to save you, David."

I continued on, "I heard some of the staff say, and I have read in many books that enabling someone is in effect making it possible for them to use substances again. Does it mean we cannot help or show compassion to others? Does it mean I cannot help someone get a job because they might buy substances or gamble their money away? What are the right answers to these very important questions? What separates a support network from an enabling hook-up? Is it the same for everyone? All have different lives, experiences, hurts, abuses, traumas, and unique learned experiences. This cookie cutter method has been tried by many, and perhaps for a few addicts, it will be enough to save their life.

> *You must have compassion in your heart, and hope in your soul, and you must give these gifts to others to save them --and, to save you, David.*

I believe without the support of my Mom and Step Dad I would have had nowhere to go after my time here at Hope by the Sea; and I likely wouldn't have made it here in the first place. The reality is for many who leave treatment, they must live in the street to avoid violent, substance-active residences. A few try to build a new life by getting jobs in Treatment Centers that have housing, interaction with compassionate staff and some accountability. Some go back to the same environment they left, while others go home to atone for legal infractions.

Nancy, why are there no re-entry programs back into society for those coming off substance abuse and coming out of jail?"

Our time is up. "A good question for another day. Thank you, David. Have a good rest of your day." Nancy concluded.

"I will, Nancy, and thank you."

CHAPTER 78

While feeding the horses, we discovered they like the granola better than apples. I have been showing the horse *ropes* to a couple of new arrivals, so the horses continue to get what they like. I don't imagine they will have any problems keeping the apples and granola flowing. Is it possible I have been at this place this long? The time passed in mere moments and in a couple of weeks it will be in the past. I must admit this thought still has much fear for me.

Today, Harlan isn't outside, so I seek and find him in his office. I pour us both a cup and take a seat. I have been thinking about the meeting with my Therapist earlier and am coming to believe things like denial, enabling, compassion, and accountability are all words and actions experienced in a typical, happy family. I guess an atmosphere of love is something many take for granted and others dare not to dream. The topics I talked to Nancy about earlier, I explain to Harlan, and ask him what he thinks of it.

Harlan replied, "Those are some topics that cannot be answered easily or consistently from one individual to another. Answers to them without words like abuse, trauma, torture, abandonment, rape, molestation, substance abuse, behavioral addictions and disorders are challenging. There are many more conditions and addictions I could go on about, but I think you get it."

I said, "When each person selects what applies, plugs it into lived experiences, learned behaviors, and various living environments throughout life, it becomes clear how complex life is in addiction, even life in mental torment. With exception of some of the Track specific things, and one-on-ones with Therapists and Case Managers, this is a one size fits most, is it not?"

He didn't like that, and his face began to change, and his ears were getting red. "David, is that what your experience has been at Hope by the Sea?" I said, "No." And he continued, "I hear you daily yapping to someone as to how they have to find tools they will use with loyalty. Take your program, you are a testament to the Alternative Track, and you work your butt off. Nobody can dispute it. You have gone to Celebrate Recovery on more than one occasion, and it is rumored you even had fun there when your Mom was here. When you went back to CR after family weekend, I started looking at what additional non-Alternative Track stuff was in your file. Guess what I found?"

I said, "You see I attend The Effect and church with some consistency. I also attend an occasional AA meeting on Friday as well as Saturday morning. That's probably about it."

Harlan said, smirking now, "You have helped at least a dozen men here with cover letters, resumes, and interviewing skills. You taught a fifty-minute module on *I relapsed. Now what?* that has the whole place talking."

I said, "What is wrong with any of that? People asked for my help, so I gave it. It's not a big deal. I like helping people, and when watching someone do something completely wrong to the point it is dumb, I feel a need to inject some helpful thoughts."

He said, "Helpful thoughts, you say. I got to write that down. I could sit here for days and do this with you, and I am convinced we would both receive value in doing it. My question is, what does most of what we are talking about here, have to do with your core Alternative Track program? With exception of the stuff you shared about your therapy session with Nancy; that was great stuff by the way."

> *Harlan said, smirking now, "You have helped at least a dozen men here with cover letters, resumes, and interviewing skills. You taught a fifty-minute module on I relapsed. Now what? that has the whole place talking."*

I thought a little about what he was asking, and even though he was setting me up, I answered honestly. "Most of it has nothing to do with the Alternative Track. I don't care for meditation at night; thus, I go to CR and The Effect. Fellowship is something I want in my life; the fellowship of good, decent people. I don't care where they come from, only that they are good."

Harlan said, "Sounds to me, you are taking as much out of the experience as possible. Going to other Tracks and taking things to customize your own recovery is smart. You wonder why there isn't more of that sort of thing, don't you?"

I said, "It isn't any of my business, and these folks don't need me cooking their grits. I believe if it were encouraged, and there was more structure in the afternoon having Track Specific Options, it would be helpful to many of us. It is difficult to do this when all three Tracks meet at the same time every day. I am a pain in the rear end at times, but I try to find ways to get something I believe will help me live my life free of this horrible dependence. I have seen most people won't go beyond the complaint stage."

He said, "There is validity in what you say, yet I don't know if you have noticed the revolving door of personnel? Hard to get the processes in place in that environment."

I said, "I see more I would like to be different. As a Business Development Strategist, I see lots of opportunities for improvement. The part of me who came to California expecting no help, or hopes of living much longer, has done a total turnaround. It says, don't change a thing. On the other hand, I would have benefitted from more mental health specific things. I wish there could have been more time allotted to learning about PTSD, and what makes it tick. I still know little to nothing about it."

He concluded, "We can continue this next time. I need to get my old bones home."

I said, "Drive safe. See you tomorrow."

CHAPTER 79

Writing about depression is depressing. Writing to my son about it is an amplification of emotion. Frank told me he is trying to save me a ton of time by writing about this now. As usual, I have not a clue what that means. It has also been my experience Frank seldom is wrong about much as it pertains to The Work. The following is the second letter on depression to my son, David.

Depression Letter to My Son, David – # Two

December 16, 2016

Dear David,

In 1988, my parents and I moved from the farm to the Twin Cities. The years on the farm in the Glenville school system left me damaged and scarred for life. The fact we were moving, moving anywhere had to be better, didn't it? It did not take long at the new school to discover all my problems were inside of me and followed me. My low self-esteem, dark feelings of not being good enough or worthy of love made the trip intact.

I wonder if you felt this way in your school years? I wonder if you felt like I did at your age and younger in Hastings, Lakeville, Missouri, Champlin, or now. The bag of hurt and despair becomes enormous to drag around each day. This causes a tiredness that will not leave you, no matter how many hours and minutes you spend sleeping. For me, many nights were spent alone in thought, a loneliness that becomes entrenched.

Many parallels between us, David, have become easy for me to see. Looking you in the eye is like a time warp because I see me in you;

and it scares me a little. I don't want you to live your life believing as I have, that pain is hardwired both physical and psychological, and a part of you forever. I don't want you to suffer as I have. I don't want you to numb your life with substances. I did at your age, but thanks to the gift of discovering my *birthplace of addiction* and pain, I now have a shot at a better life free of addictive substances.

At your age, school was in the rear view for me. I went to work, and gradually on and off over the years, I required more substances to medicate myself. I didn't know the source of my pain, the face, or the color, only it was insidious and out to kill me. I don't want this kind of life for you, son. You deserve better. You deserve a Dad you can look up to and respect. I had the kind of Dad you deserve to have too. I am sorry for not fulfilling that role in your life.

Even though I had role models around me most of my life who demonstrated through action what a good person is, it did not help bring light to the darkness beneath the surface and behind the eyes. I trusted nobody with the shame and depression that simply stated, was me. I never allowed help to penetrate the walls I had put up for my protection when I was eight. When people would try and corner me, or I felt trapped, I would shut down and detach from whomever was trying to reach me. It wasn't personal, only a protective mechanism that engaged when I was in danger, at least what I perceived to be danger. I see some of these signs and tendencies in you, and believe me when I say, *"Boy, you don't want to live like I have."* My life unfolded as it did, based on my actions and my inactions, which, put simply, is life my son.

It isn't easy living the life you want. You have a beautiful mind and dreams of what you want for your life; and you are smart enough to realize them. It is no secret what I think of school, so, I get why you don't think much of it either. At your age, I had a work ethic and a burning desire to succeed and be successful. Much of the energy was spite. People said I couldn't, and that upset me in ways that uncovered brains and motivation I didn't know I possessed. I am guessing you don't have these strong motivations now. I am guessing you can't see much past your depression.

> *"Boy, you don't want to live like I have." My life unfolded as it did, based on my actions and my inactions, which, put simply, is life my son.*

If I could shoulder all your pain, I would. I believe I wish a lot of the same things you do. I finally learned here in California to give up hope for a better past. You see, David, our pasts had to happen for us to be who we are; and until radical acceptance of who we are occurs, adversity and depression will be the driving forces in our lives. Nothing is going to undo a broken yesterday, it is simply gone. It took forty-three years for me to learn that and accept it.

Look, what it boils down to is depression, trauma, and hurts that will always be with you. The question is, are they going to control you? The power is inside of you. I love you.

Dad

Frank said, "Okay that was good, how was it?"
"Challenging, because I am uncertain as to where this is going or why I am writing it in the first place. I don't mean to sound negative, I'm just not sure if I am doing it right."
"Discussing the feelings surrounding depression in you, and the parallels at play in your son is not easy. The feelings are raw as you haven't really considered them until recently. There is no right or wrong way to write. It is important that you write freely and honestly and focus on the feelings more than the story," Frank said.
I said, "I feel responsible for a large part of his depression and don't really know what to do about it. I don't want to see him go down a road like mine; yet, I know I likely can do little to influence the path he chooses at this stage of his life."
Frank said, "Understanding how depression works and from where it came, is going to vary from person to person as well as how it impacts our lives. Both you and your son were at high risk for depression, and it sounds like his Mother is also. Treating it is critical to happiness, and any measure of contentment in life. At some point, you will want to try and facilitate a reconciliation with your son and have a relationship. Let's reverse it and see where that takes us. With Christmas coming, we only have a few days to get this done, so let's make sure we put some priority on this."
I said, "I will get started this afternoon."
I haven't seen or talked to my son since July, so writing to him is not only personal, it is quite emotional. Things happened so fast during the separation and ultimately the divorce between his Mom and me, we barely talked about it. Then, I was two states away, and we talked by phone, but it never amounted to much. This was in 2014.
David came to live with me late in 2014 in Missouri. This was somewhat awkward for both of us considering I was gone so much of his childhood especially the past four and a half years. There was a lot of multi-state travel for me when I was working in the businesses I was partnered in at the time. When I reflect on this time, it isn't difficult to see in hindsight why David is troubled now.

CHAPTER 80

I am noticing two things this week. The first is the place is emptying out with residents going home for the Christmas and New Year's holidays. The second is the tension level of those leaving rose as did the visible signs of stress and anxiety. What is it with this time of year anyway? Many families across the country are spending beyond their means, and some are setting expectations no one could meet on their best day.

Those of us who remain are mostly looking forward to some good eats and fellowship. I am excited about Christmas Eve services for the first time, probably ever. Singing the Christmas carols in the way that is somewhat traditional is going to be nice. This year I feel Christmas will be what it is supposed to be, the celebration of the birth of Christ. My parents, when I was growing up and even into adulthood, tried to keep the real message of Christ's birth centric in our celebrations of Christmas. I wasn't receptive to hearing the message then. Most of my life I simply didn't have any hope, and I thought it was a myth.

> *This year should be viewed as a good one, even among the best because of the gifts I am giving myself, and the renewal of my soul before God.*

Frank told us as Christmas gets closer and eventually arrives, to be expecting some dark emotions, guilt and shame. This year is not like all the others when I had regret and sadness. This year should be viewed as a good one, even among the best because of the gifts I am giving myself, and the renewal of my soul before God. I will continue to be mindful in the coming days and write about what happens.

Another fascinating thing about California is when it rains here it is reminiscent of four or five inches of new snow right before afternoon rush hour in Minneapolis. Fender benders, evening events called off for safety reasons and the like are the news of the day. It meant there would be no evening activities at Hope by the Sea tonight, and it also happened to be Friday. Due to some House Manager shortages, Nick from the Horse Shoe House was working at El Dorado. My two housemates were out on passes, so it was quiet until Pong and Eric, drivers for Hope, showed up and said, "Where are we eating tonight?" It wasn't long before the four of us were headed to the Outback for dinner.

It wasn't far to the restaurant, but with the rain, it could have been trouble. It turned out with all the cancelled events across the valley, the freeway was different from other Fridays. There were vehicles speeding along upwards of eighty miles per hour uninhibited by other traffic. The store and restaurant parking lots were all full, probably waiting out the rain.

I couldn't tell you the last time I ever went out with a few friends, and it did not have an alcohol, or drug component. I have known these men for only a couple of months, yet it feels like years. The laughs are endless, and the stories never ending. On this evening at dinner I feel at peace with my life for the first time in years. My body is completely detoxified, and I am developing more confidence each day -- confidence in me, in my program and in the future.

CHAPTER 81

I didn't work on the reversal letter until last night because I knew it was going to be tough to write emotionally, and I wanted to read it as soon as possible once written. I haven't talked to or seen David for almost six months. I don't even know what to think about that right now; I just know it isn't good. Would I ever have the relationship of old? Probably not. Whether there will be any kind of future relationship is anybody's guess right now.

The following is the reversal letter on depression from my son, David.

Depression Reversal Letter from Son, David, to Me.

December 19, 2016

Dear Dad,

I am upset and angry you constantly lie, use drugs, and drink all the time. For three straight years you have said through action I am not as important as your precious drugs. This Christmas is going to once again suck, and you wonder about my depression? Is that a joke?

I have been depressed for a very long time now. I have been picked on for years and don't know what to do, or even care anymore about anything. Ever since we left Cottage Grove, I have had terrible school trouble; and, what few friends I had in 2012, were forty miles away. We lived in the country and I felt stuck. I made no new friends, and I was often home alone with Ladie, my video games and a bunch of horses.

I resented living away from my friends. I had no say in my life at all! I was hurt, and you didn't care. You told me we could take a four-wheeler course, but that was just another lie. Chelsey got to go everywhere because she could drive. I was left out of absolutely everything and still am. You were never home, and even when you were, there was tension in the air between Mom and you.

> *Chelsey got to go everywhere because she could drive. I was left out of absolutely everything and still am.*

I feel alone and empty most days and don't even want to get out of bed. I **hate** school; it seems like a major waste of time. It shouldn't be a surprise to you though, Mr. Drop-out, right? You quit and always said you never looked back or had regrets. Why is it different for me? Why can't I quit and never look back like you did? If you would have let me get my Driver's License like Chelsey, I would have been set. You blew it off like Birthdays and Christmases. How do you live with yourself?

People are mean to me. Chelsey is mean to me, and Mom yells at me all the time. I don't want to wake up most days. I still stay up all night and sleep all day. You don't care; you have demonstrated that. You don't love me; maybe you never did.

David

Frank said, "How was it?"

I said sadly, "I am having a lot of trouble with this series of letters. It is shameful to be the man on this paper I read from right here."

"It is always going to be considerably harder the closer the person is, and kids are about as close as you're ever going to get. A lot of feeling here. You are getting better at writing, and it will serve you well in life if you keep writing." Frank consoled.

I said, "I know it is like a cancer, all this pent-up guilt, shame and unprocessed grief in my life. How will I know when I have written enough, and realize I can move on and burn the letters?"

"How do you believe you should proceed with your son here and now?" Frank asked.

"I think I should respond to this letter, burn them all and release all the negative emotions?" I responded.

"That is what I recommend as well. It is time to rid yourself of these feelings, or you may never be able to attempt to have a relationship with your son. It is okay to let go of this, do you believe that?" He inquired.

"I am sure trying to." I said as positively as I could.

"That's an honest response. Okay, answer it and release it by burning the letters," Frank concluded.

I said, "I will answer it today."

CHAPTER 82

I arrived early today to meet Harlan in his office and to ensure adequate coffee was available for us; a required step for meetings directly following lunch. I haven't been able to stop thinking about the letter this morning involving David. It must have been written all over my face because Harlan got right to it.

He said, "All right, let's have it. We got a lot to accomplish today so we don't have time to mess around."

"With tact like that, it's not hard to see why you are so loved by everyone here," I muttered, and continued, "I am having a hard time with some writing I did last night and this morning. I am also experiencing some fear about leaving here at the end of the month."

He said, "Tell me about the writing."

I said, "I have been writing to my son about depression both his and mine. It also showed me a great many things about me as a father that are outright deplorable. I haven't seen or talked to him in months, and now that I will be leaving and re-entering my life, I am feeling overwhelmed."

Harlan said with a somber look now, "The hardest thing in the life of an addict is having the wisdom to come to treatment. A close second is having the courage to leave and resume life. I have been where you are, and I am not going to blow smoke up your butt. *The Work* in many ways is going to begin when you leave. I am not diminishing *The Work* you have done here. Without it, you wouldn't have the sense to be scared to death about what lies ahead."

> *The hardest thing in the life of an addict is having the wisdom to come to treatment. A close second is having the courage to leave and resume life*

I said, "Sounds like the light at the tunnel's end is about half way to the North pole. Am I missing something here?"

"Yes, you are, you're forgetting life is what you make it as a testament to what you are willing to put into it. Nowhere is it written it will be easy or free of adversity."

I said, "All right, I think I get what you are saying. I have to live, and it means processing at the speed of life, not the speed of David."

Harlan said, "Look son, a lot of people have come across my way here, and I have seen many good people and bad ones alike. My experiences and instincts tell me you are going to make it. I don't say this lightly, but rather on a belief that you are willing to work as hard on your recovery as I do on my own. I tell you that is what it takes if you want to live, versus mere survival."

"Did you have to put things together again with your kids after you got sober for the last time?" I inquired.

He said, "I had two ex-wives and countless broken promises and shattered trust of my kids, family, and every friend I ever had, all gone. That was my foundation when I left the treatment center thirty some odd years ago. Sound familiar at all? You are not going to die from terminal uniqueness my boy."

I said, "I will have to be patient."

"You'll have to be patient." He agreed.

I said, "Well, I suppose that is to be expected considering the erosion of trust. I can't fault anyone for being hesitant to believe in me again."

"Let's meet again on Wednesday so we can do what we were going to do today." He offered.

I said, "Okay, I will be here."

If there were more folks in the world like Harlan, it would be a better world; that is for sure. Harlan was a successful contractor prior to working in this field. Not needing the money, and free to retire at any moment, makes me respect him even more. Giving of his wisdom and knowledge as freely as he does, is invaluable to me and to countless others who have come through Hope by the Sea.

CHAPTER 83

I am anxious to read the response and final letter to my son on depression. Sleep really isn't an option; my mind is way too busy inside my head, and I can't slow my thoughts, so I am glad to be at class.

My Response to Reversal From my Son, David, on Depression.

December 20, 2016.

Dear David,

I am sorry you have all this anger in your heart, and you feel so alone in the world. It saddens me to hear you are hurting so much. It isn't your fault son. It is my failure as a Dad that has caused you such heartache and despair.

I remember going to Des Moines with you some years back to attend *Friday Night Smackdown*. That was the first time we ever went anywhere just for fun without your sister or your Mom. You were impressed with the niceness of the Hotel and dug the fancy restaurant also. I think what trumped it all though was the room service around midnight after the wrestling event.

I wish I could tell you life is a piece of cake, but it isn't, and that is the truth. I tried to instill in you and your sister that life is going to be what you make it to be, not anyone else. You, you alone, are responsible for the happiness or lack of it in your life. Others will encourage, discourage and no doubt even influence you; but in the end, it boils down to, do you want to be happy or sad, David? Do you want to be successful, or do you always play it safe, insulated from failure and success?

I am your Father, and I do love you. I would change the past if I could. Everything you said about me is true, all of it. I have been a terrible role model, and I have lied, God knows how many times. David, I lived forty-three years on this earth before I learned this simple, powerful fact. The way you move on from adversity, the way you forgive people and things said or done to you by them, is by *Giving up hope for a better past*. It is relevant to mention that forgiveness is about you and Jesus, not who or what you are forgiving. Don't worry about anything else, leave the rest in the capable hands of God. I pray you find a way to unburden the considerable amount of anger, and other dark emotions bottled up within you.

> *It is relevant to mention that forgiveness is about you and Jesus, not who or what you are forgiving. Don't worry about anything else, leave the rest in the capable hands of God.*

When I was about your age, I often felt nobody cared or even loved me. I quit school as you know. What you probably didn't know was the disappointment, and in some cases anger, that existed in my Mom and Dad and my Grandparents. Most everyone else thought I was a failure and would remain one my entire life. Much of this was in my head, literally due to the traumas I endured at a young age. You experienced a severe trauma when you were barely three, when the bookcase landed on you and thumped your skull, fracturing it and nearly killing you. My trauma was at the hands of the cruel Mrs. F, and despite the differences in the incidents that caused our traumas, the commonality was pain. The physical and emotional pain has altered the circuitry of our brains.

I thought about the trips you and I would take each year to Michigan to spend Thanksgiving with Grandma and Thad. I cherish the time we spent, laughing about almost anything. We never did let your sister or your Mom horn in on that tradition of ours. Eating good food at Grandma's and watching *It's a Wonderful Life* is a tradition I will always enjoy. And, of course, no Michigan trip would be complete without a visit to *Micky-Lu's* burger joint.

> *Eating good food at Grandma's and watching It's a Wonderful Life is a tradition I will always enjoy. And, of course, no Michigan trip would be complete without a visit to Micky-Lu's burger joint.*

I am learning to process and purge the negative's that have been stuffed inside me for decades, allowing room for the positives. The negative clouds out the positive, and I am stunned at how much I simply couldn't see before coming here to Hope by the Sea. That sounds like a load of horse hockey to you, and would to me too, if I had been you seeing me doing drugs and drinking for the months preceding my arrival here. I have positives all around me, and David, those include you. I am so proud of you. Even the darkest chasms of addiction couldn't change it, and it never will.

I want you to have the life you deserve and want. I am here if you ever want to talk when the time is right. I realize that is probably not today or any day on the immediate horizon.

Love, Dad

Five positives about me as a Dad.

1. I have never inflicted violence on my kids.
2. Took my family on a great houseboat vacation.
3. I brought home our Golden Retriever Pup, Ladie, as a surprise.
4. As long as I have air in my lungs, I will never give up on either of my kids.
5. Got David a PS2 with all the trimmings when he got home from the hospital the first time.

Frank said, "How was it?"

"It was hard. I think writing about the kids will bring a lot of uncontrollable, maybe even unforeseeable adversity. I have more to do writing wise to both, but David is priority because of his age. Chelsey is twenty-one years old and is full of piss and vinegar currently. I said with emotion.

Frank stated, "I hope everyone in the room is paying attention because it was just laid out what will be necessary for all of you throughout your lives.

"Why did you write the positives at the end of the letter?" Frank asked.

I said, "I was feeling pretty low after writing, and you asked me to pull positives out of other Work when it was finished. I felt better in those times after writing them and figured it could work here. I was positive it wouldn't make me feel worse."

Speaking out a little louder, Frank stated, "I hope everyone in the room is paying attention because it was just laid out what will be necessary for all of you throughout your lives. Writing positives after the negatives is why we go through the unpleasantness to begin with. The absolute best time to write positive things is always going to be after writing about negative things.

Good job! I will not be back until the third of January, so keep working, but now you are free to choose what, when, and how. I rarely tell someone they are ready, and I don't see a need to do so now. I am just going to say keep writing."

I said. "All right and thank you."

He said. "You're welcome." "Let's take a short break, and then we will do a future projection to end the day on."

CHAPTER 84

Frank wants us to get to work so everyone will have a chance to complete their projections.

Future Ten Year Projection

December 21, 2026

Dear David,

The last ten years went by in a New York minute.

I am now ten years and eighty-two days into my new life free of addictive behaviors, and I have attained happiness and contentment I thought unattainable. I am experiencing the tip of the possibilities that still lie ahead. I am learning the tools I used daily there at Hope are still useful a decade later; frankly, I would be lost without the writing.

The success of *Birthplace of Addiction* that was published in 2018 has been enormous. It was forty-one weeks on the New York Times bestseller list; twenty-seven weeks as number one. This opened doors to write a whole series of addiction books God is using to transform the lives of millions of people. With the help of scores of hard-working people, the program and processes are being taught in both outpatient and inpatient healing centers in nineteen states.

Working together with other professionals at Hope by the Sea, has provided the humility my life has always lacked. Working as a Clinical Case Manager and Program Director redirected my life in ways that allowed me to become the person I always thought I should be. Compassionate leadership has proven to be infectious to all staff and clients alike. All those years of running companies and teaching success modules have been put to good use in the treatment field. Working alongside Frank, taught me the intimate details of the Alternative program; and the three years we were working together brought out the best of both of us forging a friendship that has stuck beyond those years at Hope by the Sea.

In 2022, I branched out on my own from Hope by the Sea. Here I fulfilled my goal of owning my own company doing top notch work in the service of others. Investing in sober living housing to help recovering addicts transition back to being productive, happy citizens. This part of the business is run by our daughter, Chelsey, while David is in school to become a Clinical Therapist.

Hold on to your hat for this! In June of next year, I will have been married for six years. Who would have thought? She came along on a lot of the book tours and runs the foundation we started called the Golden Gates that rescues Golden Retrievers exclusively. We also breed and train Golden Retriever Service dogs for military families.

My brothers and I see each other a few times a year, and we get along wonderfully. Jeff runs the Minnesota Treatment Center; it is the largest one we own. It has a capacity of 600 residents and has 3,000 beds in the Sober Living side. Mom and Thad are in Michigan and fly out to California a few times a year on the company jet. There is a facility in Menominee that is near and dear to me, so I spend a lot of time there. Life is awesome, family even better than that. God continues to bless and enrich my life, and I am grateful and humbled by this.

David

It will be tough not to find excitement from writing a positive projection about tomorrow and beyond. Future projections have been among my favorite activities here at Hope by the Sea. Of course, it is a process like anything else, and if it isn't done correctly, it can significantly diminish the benefits of the projection.

Future projections should always be done with complete positivity; negative energy doesn't belong here. The positive words and thoughts about the future you are dreaming of is what should go on paper. Goals of attainment go in another writing all together. The subconscious part of my brain eats up the positives in future projections like candy or my favorite pizza. It then projects out into your life what is in this part of your brain. **Garbage in garbage out** is absolutely true. We are responsible for what goes in our minds. We are conscious about little.

Remember, neuro paths have been created and strengthened because of *The Work* here. Some of mine are stronger now than those controlling my addictive behaviors before my arrival at Hope. Staying ninety days was the only choice for me, and if I could have stayed ninety more, I would have; but my insurance has been cancelled so I must leave on New Year's Eve on day 92.

My projections are often a culmination of my prayer journal, and I always say a prayer before writing them. I know positive things will happen for me; and addiction and the hurt that fueled it, will remain behind me existing only as a record of my past that had to happen.

CHAPTER 85

With Frank gone for the rest of my time at Hope by the Sea, it makes for a different atmosphere here. Kathy is the Clinical Manager and supervises all the Therapists here. She is filling in for Frank, and I like her. She is very caring and kind, and I am thinking a competent Therapist. She has a different approach from Frank. Kathy plays soft music and asks a lot of questions, while Frank had us write, share, write, share, and write some more. Most of my writing will now be done in my journal going forward via the daily check-ins.

Kathy asked us to write something to share with the group which is now down to three people. I enjoy writing, and it is a huge part of me now. I didn't, therefore, require any more direction than that. The others shouldn't have either, but with Frank gone, they thought they didn't have to work and could just cross talk and be disruptive. I was about to let them have it when Kathy took care of it. Everyone was writing in less than thirty seconds, and it was silent except, of course, for the elevator music.

I decided to share the following entry from my journal.

Journal Entry

December 22, 2016

I don't want to be held hostage because of my inability to express my feelings in a healthy way. It is what life for me is boiling down to. My self-esteem has been in the toilet most if not all my life, and it scares me to the core to be any other way. I need Jesus to be in my life, and perhaps there is no better time to confirm my walk with Him than on the day of His birth which we are celebrating this Christmas. It is no coincidence that I am here right now in this place. God always has a purpose. I pray for compassion and wisdom because my confidence is shaky at best. I don't have confidence in myself, or trust even for that matter. Maybe that isn't quite true in every respect. I am confident in my ability to publicly speak about a great many things. I have confidence to help others in recovery. I am excited about the prospect of writing a book, and the procurement of a publisher to promote it. Knowing what to do and when to do it, are really the million-dollar questions for me. I am going to pen the first draft as I have penned everything here. Simply put, I am going to write the book to the best of my ability and let the chips fall as they should.

There is a way out of darkness and into light. This I write because I believe it is required for my own healing; and my greatest wish is that it will provide some relief and resources not only for me, but to all of those who I have and will interact with discussing topics of trauma and addiction.

> *This provides a road map to be free of the chains of all of it. Yes, I said all of it.*

The substance abuse by me and many is so often a symptom of something much, much greater. At Hope by the Sea, it is believed and demonstrated daily that mental health is intertwined with all aspects of addiction; and once it is realized, the discovery of the **birthplace of addiction** is born. *This provides a road map to be free of the chains of all of it.* **Yes, I said all of it.** As I write this, I know full well I will never say this is, was or will be easy to be free of the Hell that is life for someone like me; someone who has carried this 800 lb. stove around with me my entire life.

I was talking to one of the counselors in the park named, Donald, a day or two ago, about the differences in the tracks offered by Hope by the Sea. Donald being an avid twelve stepper felt the programs were virtually interchangeable, and therefore, the Alternative is unnecessary. Quite naturally, this got my dander up in a physical, emotional way, and my skin pigmentation was turning crimson. I knew we were about to have a heated discussion about this matter. I explained to him that I was a Christian in the Alternative Track who has nothing against the twelve steps. I told him it was unfortunate for him that his ignorance and insecurity would not all0w him to see past his precious Big Book. Donald stormed off and was terminated the next day. It was not because of what I said to him, or what he said to me, because that is not the way I dance.

I consider myself an Alternative core disciple who believes in God and Jesus Christ as my personal Savior, who also likes to cultivate the relationship of good people from all walks of life. What is important to me is that I will be able to embrace and execute my program for a happy and fulfilling life spent in the service of others. I have been all over the board in this check-in tonight, because I guess I had a lot of things to sort out.

My mind is working overtime lately, and for once, I believe it is a beautiful thing to bestow. Thy will be done in Jesus' name. Amen

Kathy paused for a minute and said, "That was incredible writing David, and thank you for sharing that. You are leaving soon, how do you feel about that?"

I said, "My nerves are churning like butterflies in my stomach. Anxiety and fear are at play. I did a lot of work, and I suppose I am ready to leave. At the same time, I am fragile and weak even about my confidence to do the right things."

She said, "What specifically gives you these feelings?"

I said, "Specificity of what gives me feelings, good or negative, would likely give me an actionable road map that would allow me to see what I should do. In the case of the negative feelings, it is vital to be vigilant in identifying them before they fester and take hold. To answer your question, I am leaving Hope by the Sea in a few days, and it has been a long time since I have seen anyone in my family. Thoughts of failure are also not far removed at this point."

Kathy said, "What can we do to help you better prepare for your transition?"

I said, "You are doing it right now with your questions, genuine empathy, and concern I have experienced in bushels since arrival. I am going to always have a certain level of fear and anxiety. The writing tool sustains me and shows me how to transform negative to positive daily."

She said, "Thank you for sharing that, you do nice work."

I said, "Likewise."

CHAPTER 86

I wanted to make my housemates a nice breakfast on Christmas morning at the El Dorado House. Matt helps in the kitchen and said he would get me the necessary ingredients. Since he is getting things, I had him get me some baking supplies to make some homemade cookies. The Christmas blues are alive and well around the house, and I am hoping some treats and watching the movie *It's a Wonderful Life* will lift our spirits.

The first thing is to get the cookies going. When I was a little boy, baking cookies was one of my favorite things about the Christmas season. My Mom, being an excellent baker, would prepare sometimes up to a dozen different kinds of cookies to be enjoyed at Christmas and through the New Year's celebrations. Whether it was frosting sugar cookies or putting sparkle on others, it all felt right. Those early Christmases, the first six or seven years, were the best of my life. At this age, I believed everyone was good and posed no threat. I believed I was a typical, happy kid who loved baking and Christmas as much as my Mom did. I would give anything to go back to then, even for a few moments.

> *The Christmas blues are alive and well around the house, and I am hoping some treats and watching the movie It's a Wonderful Life will lift our spirits.*

The other Men in the El Dorado House were in their early to mid-twenties, and we all got along surprisingly well, considering they were of similar age to my own kids. The fact we were all in the Alternative Track didn't hurt either. Happily, on this Friday night we sat, ate freshly baked cookies, and watched the ***It's A Wonderful Life*** movie. Three questions gave me pause, and I don't think I will soon forget them. The first was, how did they get the color out of the movie? The second, is there a setting on the TV that turns off the color? The last was, who is Jimmy Stewart? That last one made me realize how sad this Millennial bunch is. As far as the black and white business -- I got nothing for that.

The following is a check-in from my Journal.

Journal Entry.

December 23, 2016

I do believe some progress has been made here, especially with yesterday's lengthy check-in. I find myself excited to see the journey of discovery this writing will take me to. With Frank gone, I have been spending more time in the computer lab these past couple of days researching the certification requirements to work in the field of recovery in southern California. The prospect of joining the lecture circuit would be an amazing thing also. I would enjoy promoting a book this way to a wide array of people. I could speak to clinicians, counselors and victims alike, gaining valuable insight along the way. I am hoping and praying that God will enrich and bless me to be an instrument in service of others going forward in life.

David and Chelsey are on my mind more and more, and I don't really know how I should be feeling. I find myself feeling nothing, and I don't understand why that is. They are my children, and we have been hurt by each other. Why do I not feel remorse? I feel that I have been a bad dad. I believe I have fallen short in so many ways throughout their lives. My mom radiates love at an infectious level rarely seen in another. I tend to be passive and private not wanting anyone to see me in a vulnerable state. This has been my way for so very long.

Even as I attempt to modify my neural pathways, the hardwiring is very strong and draws me in as a tractor beam would a vessel in space. Knowing what is right doesn't always match your feelings at any given moment. Thinking I should feel sad or troubled and feeling nothing, produces guilt and shame for not feeling. How then do I deal with that? Perhaps I need to give it to God and let Jesus tend to it. My wisdom is of this earth, but the Lord is all knowing and all seeing. Jesus knows me better than I know me, and I must learn to trust Him for me to be complete.

Positive things I admire in me.

1. My communication skills, written and oral, because they allow me to look at all sides of all things.
2. My temperament is usually even keeled, and I am appreciative because I can learn more and be of more service in that mode.

Birthplace of Addiction

3. My work ethic is something instilled in me by my father, and it has always served me well, except when I am in workaholic mode and then, it doesn't.

CHAPTER 87

Today is Christmas Eve and the schedule at Hope by the Sea is more festive to say the least. Cyndie is one of the co-owners who pretty much ran Family Weekend, and some say runs the whole shebang. One thing that is undisputed is her consistent, rigid style of management which I appreciated about her. I never talked too much because I followed the simple expectations for behavior in the Treatment Center. Today, Cyndie is all smiles making sure personally everyone receives a Christmas present along with a contagious, cheerful Merry Christmas. The Hope by the Sea hoodie is a nice gift and souvenir to boot. Cyndie has a completely different aura when she is smiling; I think she should wear it more often, especially on Family Weekend.

Tonight, after the Christmas Service, the residents of El Dorado head over to the Redding House which houses all the twenty-something-year-old clients at Hope by the Sea. A shortage of staff in the House Manager ranks is why we are spending a few hours there tonight, and the better part of the day tomorrow. James, who got to Hope the same time as I did, has been working a job while also doing half days of treatment. James is staying in California after discharge and has a topnotch work ethic. He is working both Christmas Eve and Christmas Day. He walks to and from work to the El Dorado House.

I told the powers that be that the residents of the El Dorado House would be home both evenings and afternoons, so that James did not come home to an empty house on Christmas. Nobody, and I mean nobody, should work on Christmas far from loved ones, and needlessly come home to an empty, lonely house. It's not going to happen on my watch.

> Today, Cyndie is all smiles making sure personally everyone receives a Christmas present along with a contagious, cheerful Merry Christmas. The Hope by the Sea hoodie is a nice gift and souvenir to boot.

The Christmas Eve Service is excellent! Singing Christmas Carols with these wonderful people is special. I feel the presence of the Holy Spirit. Maybe that's why I seem to be able to sing so well. The service is about an hour and a half long, and we even sang on the way back home in the vans.

The Redding House is sprawled over several acres and has basketball courts, tennis courts, an outdoor kitchen, mini golf and a huge pool with waterfalls and a lazy river.

The House itself is beautiful. The fifteen or so residents have adequate space, and entertainment areas to settle these Millennials down to only moderate racket and chaos. I could quickly see this could be a long, couple of days if something didn't give. I decided to find a quiet corner to do some writing; it is, after all, what I do.

Journal entry

December 24, 2016

This is the first Christmas of my life I have no family in the mix at all. I don't have a lot of feelings on that. Last night, watching, ***It's a Wonderful Life***, I was reminded of some things. We all have an impact on one another's lives; sometimes a lot of impact, sometimes not so much. Then, there is the ripple effect of influence we seldom even know exists, but it all matters.

I hope David and Chelsey have a good Christmas. I thought I would have more feelings about this as the holiday approached, but I remain stuck. The guilt and shame I have as more of a broad, all-encompassing blanket over my entire being, has been lightened; and I believe I now know how to eradicate it over time.

I received a package from Mom; and I am going to begin ***The Prayer of Jabez*** Bible Study and prayer book she sent me immediately and see where God's blessings take me. I will call Mom after Christmas; my brothers and my son are going to be there for Christmas, so the twenty-sixth should be fine.

I wonder a lot, especially in prayer meditation and writing, what happened to forty-four years and the life I now reflect upon. I wonder how so few friends exist from all that life. Will I spend the rest of my life alone with few friends and just survive, not live? Hard not to think of these things; hard not to wonder what is the purpose of my life? What is it supposed to look like?

I believe my restored memories are a gift from God; it has allowed me to trace my defects and shortcomings to their source. It wouldn't be natural not to ask, why? What do I do now that I have memories? I don't wish to live in the past when the future holds the happiness I seek. The life I live in service to others is what I believe to be God's will for me.

Perhaps, when the book is complete, my brothers will better understand who their brother is, and who he has become. I suppose it doesn't matter all that much to them. They have lives and responsibilities; and I have my life to live. Emotionally, I feel empty; I have been who I thought people needed to see me be my whole life. I don't really know who David Charles is, maybe I never did. That is a beginning I suppose. What interests me beyond writing and helping others is vastly unknown right now. I hope I don't become a jerk that people loathe. I like people. I think I do anyway. Not liking people was nothing more than a well fit mask to hide the real me.

James was going to be back at El Dorado in about an hour, so it was time to bolt out of the Redding House. I asked Tripp, one of the residents of the house, to round up the troops so we could get going. Normally, Tripp would have immediately begun lipping off and telling me how he isn't my peep, etc. That didn't happen this time, and he had a serious look on his face; I could tell he had a heavy heart this night, so I asked him to come out to the pool for a minute.

> *I like people. I think I do anyway. Not liking people was nothing more than a well fit mask to hide the real me.*

Tripp was from the Carolinas, and this was his second time here at Hope by the Sea in the past half year. We always razzed one another, and I would get agitated in groups at times due to all the horseplay Tripp loved so much. But when we get to the rat killing of addiction, I will give the shirt off my back to any of these men if in need. Tripp was carrying around a lot of guilt and shame for his behaviors. Tripp didn't want to disappoint his family, especially his Dad. He was also having a tough time not being home for the Holidays. Tripp's Dad had terminal cancer. I briefly shared a little about my Dad, and how we lost him to cancer in 2002. I told him it is enormously stressful for a family, especially this time of year. He was fiddling with a watch he got for Christmas but couldn't get it right. I told him I knew a little about them and would be happy to help him tomorrow. I said, if he wanted to talk tomorrow, I was available. I gave him a hug and told him I would pray for him and his family. He thanked me, and by that time people were ready to get back to El Dorado, and we should be there fifteen minutes before James got home.

It was nice to be back to the quiet, peaceful house. I quickly prepped an egg bake and some other stuff for breakfast and kicked back to enjoy a movie with James as the others took off, probably to the girl houses, where they don't belong. James and I popped in *Lethal Weapon,* and both loved seeing it again. I wished him a Merry Christmas, and said I was going to bed.

He said as I was walking away, "Thanks for making the effort to be here when I got home; I have been alone on many Christmases, so thank you."

I said, "I'm glad we had this time, and you got something good to eat, too. Same drill tomorrow, only we will be back by four o'clock with a Prime rib feast that Ringo is bringing by so be ready to enjoy a fantastic meal. Good night, now."

"Good night." He echoed.

CHAPTER 88

Christmas Day of 2016 will always be remembered. My housemates enjoy the breakfast I prepared for them, and we have some great fellowship as well. James is working ten to three o'clock today. If possible the rest of us will leave the Redding House around two o'clock, and James will not be coming home to an empty house on Christmas Day.

We arrive at the Redding House around ten-thirty o'clock on Christmas morning, and the house surely is quieter than it was yesterday.

Most everyone is huddled around the TV watching a movie, so I took a seat in the Lazy Boy recliner the second someone got up. Tripp hands me the watch he told me about yesterday, and it is a nice one. I know little about anything mechanical, but I excel at fiddling and pushing buttons and looking very busy doing it. Soon enough, it is working; and as I suspected, it is a very nice timepiece indeed.

I am about to get up and find a quiet spot outside to write when Tripp asks me what my thoughts are of regaining full use of his arm and losing the sling. What is going on here? We usually annoy one another something fierce. This isn't just the Christmas blues, this is a serious adult conversation. Well, what do you know about this, I think to myself?

> *I am about to get up and find a quiet spot outside to write when Tripp asks me what my thoughts are of regaining full use of his arm and losing the sling.*

I sit back reclining the chair and think about it a few moments and then answer, "I am no expert, but I dislocated my hip and chipped my pelvis getting hit on my Moped by a Ford Bronco." Laughs erupted all around at the thought of me on a Moped, or maybe it is a Moped versus a Bronco; I don't know, but they surely are tickled. I continued, "Doctors, even specialists, said I would never walk again without a cane or walker. The pain was excruciating and for several weeks I did not get any better. I couldn't walk, or even get around the house without pain."

Tripp asked, "What ended up happening because clearly you walk great now? How long ago did it happen?"

"I was fifteen, and I was angry and feeling sorry for myself. I went to physical therapy and despite the pain, I did what they said. Thing was I wasn't getting any better; I was depressed and wanted to give up and die. This was no way to live. My Mom and Dad and many more had been praying for me, yet my condition remained unchanged.

One night, Mom and Dad asked the Elders of the church to come to our home. They joined Mom, Dad, and me in prayer, and the Elders anointed my head with oil as the Bible says: "Is anyone among you sick? Let him call for the elders of the church, and let them pray over him, anointing him with oil in the name of the Lord" James 5:14.

I got better after that night. In less than a month I was walking uninhibited. In two months, I could run like I could before the accident. So, Tripp, the answer is: Yes, you can regain the full use of your hand, if it is something God wills to happen. And Tripp, I can almost guarantee it won't be easy."

He said emotionally, "Thank you, David, that means a lot coming from you."

I said, "Merry Christmas Tripp, and I hope you persevere."

> *They joined Mom, Dad, and me in prayer, and the Elders anointed my head with oil as the Bible says*

Ringo brought a ton of Prime Rib for El Dorado and Redding Houses to the Redding House for distribution. It is time to get back to El Dorado before James gets back from work. For four people, we have sixteen pounds of Prime Rib with sides and desserts equally proportionate to the Prime Rib. What a meal we had! I also know what we are eating all next week! Ringo sent a quart of strong horseradish to compliment the meat beautifully.

CHAPTER 89

Another Journal Entry

December 26, 2016

The last several Christmases have been tough, but this one is a rebirth of sorts, not only was Jesus born yesterday, but it was also the day I gave my life to Him and from this day forward I pray for wisdom and understanding to carry out the will of God. I want to feel things in life; I want to love; I want to feel being loved.

The more I face the fear in me, the closer I will become to understanding my life. I want so much to not live on potential. I have been told my entire life I have so much potential. I want to realize my potential and bask in God's glory of the realization of it.

I get excited at the possibilities existing in this life, overcoming bad will and the lack of trust in myself. A harsh reality that will continue to exist for a while is the cynicism of others when mistakes are made in early recovery. So many claim empathy and compassion to those who suffer from mental health and addictive behaviors. What I don't understand then, is why it is nearly impossible to escape addiction or mental health illness.

If not for Mom and Thad, I would either be in jail or dead. Insurance premiums and deductibles, transportation costs, prescription costs, the hundreds of dollars sent to me in California for miscellaneous expenses are cost prohibitive and not realistic for most families. This forces people to continue in active addiction, often breaking laws, and as a society we punish addicts by locking them away, calling it ***in the best interest of all***, or to do so ***for the greater good***. After all, it is always somebody else's child, somebody else's spouse, somebody else's sibling, somebody else's employee or somebody else's friend.

Billions of dollars are spent every year locking up drug offenders and keeping them off the street with no success. It's time to redirect these dollars to a more compassionate posture by having more resources like Hope by the Sea. We need reintegration efforts for the first year that people are coming out of treatment. I'm not talking about more of the same, either.

> *Billions of dollars are spent every year locking up drug offenders and keeping them off the street with no success. It's time to redirect these dollars to a more compassionate posture*

Clean and sober cannot be legislated as a one size fits all approach. A classic example of this will be the current DUI laws in the United States. Yes, some people need to go to prison. Murder, violence, mayhem, intimidation and the corruption of our youths and neighborhoods, can never be tolerated. Oh, by the way, I'm not talking about the people who have a gram of Meth or a gram of Heroin, or an eight ball of Cocaine. These people are not traffickers or dealers; they are customers in a never-ending cycle of pain and misery.

In other words, we need to better treat the individual. The one size fits all treatment programs are not getting the job done; and as a society, it is not difficult to see.

Perhaps, I should become a lobbyist for the afflicted; that could be worth exploring. Navigating the political spectrum and perhaps waking America up and putting faces on this pandemic would be a noble endeavor, indeed. Kids, Moms, Dads and Grandparents are all among the faces of addiction today.

> *Waking America up and putting faces on this pandemic would be a noble endeavor, indeed. Kids, Moms, Dads and Grandparents are all among the faces of addiction today.*

I can't help but wonder what is going on at Mom's house. I wonder if David is there. I wonder what is being talked about. I do hope everyone has a good day and all are happy.

It's strange my best friend is my journal these days. I don't really have anyone else who truly gets me, and what it's like to question everything that has ever happened in my life. The sheer amount of people affected by actions, behaviors and thoughts is mind boggling to me.

People fade in and out of your life; but mostly, I am alone and am living the reality I created for myself. I am unable to undo the past; it is done, and it happened.

Today and tomorrow are a ball of clay for God and me to form. Is it really that simple? Can it truly be that with God the day shall become something beautiful?

I love to write about things, even poetry makes me happy at times. Will anyone else like to read these things? Will they benefit from my words? I very much want to help others succeed and find some contentment in their lives.

CHAPTER 90

I don't know if it is the Christmas feelings coming out in me lately, but my check-ins have found a little more edge to say the least. I believe compassion is something everyone has within them, and in most cases, it is completely free to give. I have been at Hope by the Sea for three months, and I can tell you if it is good citizens and neighbors we want to be, we need to do some things differently.

Locking people up for being addicted to drugs is wrong when the person in question has committed no crime other than buying small amounts of drugs for personal use to feed the addiction from which they suffer. Many come out of jail with no job, no home or family for support, and their only friends are likely ones they met in jail. It doesn't take a lot of speculating to know what happens next.

I don't have all the answers, nobody does; but we better start communicating about what is killing our population. Wasted, unrealized potential dies daily in America on our streets, in prisons and emergency rooms. Every day of the year! Enough is enough!

I wrote this book not to politicize or even criticize, although a little of both seeps through when discussing something I am so passionate about. My greatest wish is this book gets people talking on TV and radio programs; in churches and schools; in clinician circles and medical professional groups; and by teenagers and their families at their kitchen tables.

Not many in this country or world really are unaffected by addiction any more. In fact, as a society we have become numb to much of it due to there being so much death and pain splashed all over our movie screens, newspapers, and television news programs.

So, death marches on for those who are victims of addiction who are truly the forgotten people in our society who come from all walks of life at all ages in life who become just another obituary in our evening newspaper. *But, they are our neighbors, friends and sometimes our enemies who are crying out for help and are not heard from their self-made prisons or more often from the prisons society has cast them into.*

Instead of extending our arms of compassion to help them receive chemical abuse treatment, and many times the mental health treatment they desperately need, we send them to jail, to prison, or toss them out on the street. **Where are the Good Samaritans of today who will minister to those who are suffering and dying among us from alcohol and drug addiction?**

... he said to Jesus, "And who is my neighbor? Jesus replied and said, "A certain man was going down from Jerusalem to Jericho, and he fell among robbers, and they stripped him half dead. And by chance a certain priest was going down on that road, and when he saw him, he passed by on the other side. And likewise a Levite also, when he came to the place and saw him, passed by on the other side. But a certain Samaritan, who was on a journey, came upon him, and bandaged up his wounds, pouring oil and wine on them; and he put him on his own beast, and brought him to an inn, and took care of him. And on the next day he took out two denarii and gave them to the innkeeper and said, 'Take care of him; and whatever more you spend, when I return, I will repay you.' Which of these three do you think proved to be a neighbor to the man who fell into the robbers' hands? And he said, "The one who showed mercy toward him." And Jesus said to him, **"Go and do the same"** Luke 10: 29-37.

> *We send them to jail, to prison, or toss them out on the street. Where are the Good Samaritans of today who will minister to those who are suffering and dying among us from alcohol and drug addiction?*

The following is a letter to Jesus I wrote to read for Harlan.

Letter to Jesus

December 28, 2016

Dear Jesus,

Three days ago, I made a proclamation to myself that I was affirming my life going forth to do thy will. I chose your birthday to do this because it is a day of new beginnings. A time to wash away the dirt and grime from the inside out. Spending upwards of ninety days in California, allowed me to reinvent myself in any manner I chose to. Revitalization is what this is.

Not long ago, I felt spiritually dead and morally bankrupt with no goodness in my life. I believed this to be true and didn't want to live any more. I just wanted to fade into nothingness in a forever sleep. I saw no good in me, and I believed I had failed everyone and possessed nothing I could contribute to anyone.

I believed I was a terrible father and role model to my kids. My brothers were not talking to me, and I was facing eviction and jail. Financial stresses were abundant, and my mind was altered by powerful drugs, alcohol and mental health problems including nightmares and night terrors.

I have been busy not embracing you for many years, and even in the state I was in, believed you could not or would not help me or heal me. I was irrevocably going to live this awful misery that defined every fiber of me.

Then came the time I went to stay at Mom's house. She was and still is the one I am in touch with. Mom did not stop believing in me when I had and saw no hope or desire to live. In the weeks that continued, I began clearing away the drugs from my mind, and thought I should go to treatment, but not because I thought it would help me. I had little optimism it would be any different than before. I didn't want Mom to see me sink lower or even kill myself. She did not need to see that.

I arrived at Hope by the Sea on October 1, 2016, a broken man, inwardly, outwardly and spiritually. I kept my head low and kept to myself as much as possible. I discovered early on the Alternative Track could save me from my addiction.

I arrived at Hope by the Sea on October 1, 2016, a broken man, inwardly, outwardly and spiritually. I kept my head low and kept to myself as much as possible.

My PTSD, depression and anxiety were overwhelming and all encompassing. Through writing and sharing, I began a journey in which initially I had no clue as to where it would be going. Slowly the layers began to peel away; and I saw through discovery and digging, that it was allowing me to release things defining me my entire life.

The other groups and therapies also provided me with a fire I thought was forever devoid in me. I feared it because I didn't think it was real. I felt it was *shock and awe* at work.

Weeks went by and then months of watching people come and go, but what remained a part of me is this fire that is hard to describe or illustrate.

The trauma I experienced at the age of eight, lasted two years. It was the topic of my first month and a half of writing, except for gratitude and journal work. Then, I started working on relationships, guilt and shame. This work left a void in me I didn't expect. I missed my pain; I missed my despair. I was familiar with these things and knew precisely what to expect in these areas. Better the devil you know, was the feeling. How do or did I know if something new was going to be any better than something I had discarded?

This is where you, Jesus, entered the picture for me. I have thought and thought about this in some ways for many years, but a lot more in the past three or four weeks. As I learn to trust and have faith in the fact you are God and can best provide for me, you will make me into an instrument for doing thy will. Essentially, I want to have faith and trust in you to guide me, so I may live a life of service to others and be happy.

Harlan said, "That was wonderful; I have never heard anything like it, in that style of writing. Where did you learn to write that way?"

Life is a daunting feat and I need help making the right decisions in line with what is good and honest. My Mom tells me all things through you are possible. She gave me a bookmark with footprints on it, and there were spots where only one set existed when you were carrying me, Jesus. I need you to carry me now, Jesus. This is what I need now more than ever as I get ready to leave the place that has been so good for me.

I want to continue what has begun. I ask for direction, wisdom and understanding to execute your will in my life.

I want to be a good, compassionate person who helps people rather than hurts them. I want to be a role model for my kids and repair our damaged relationship that now is in darkness.

The life I seek cannot be realized without faith, patience and the willingness to let you be in control, Lord. I have not established the best track record in this area of my life. When I am in control, I often become grandiose, and think it is the great *I* who produces good things. I need humility and gratitude to be centric in my life going forward. I know you will provide this for me.

David

Harlan said, "That was wonderful; I have never heard anything like it, in that style of writing. Where did you learn to write that way?"

I said, "Expression has come easy to me in writing most of my life. Verbal is a different ball game all together. A friend suggested I write this when I first got here. I finally got to it, and I am glad I did it."

He said, "I didn't realize you had this kind of spiritual life. Until recently, you said almost nothing about these things. What gives?"

I said, "Throughout my time here, it has gotten a little stronger each week, my walk with God that is. Then, I started working on it more with my Therapist, and now here I am from where I was. God was always here with me; I spent a lot of years pushing Him away, or flat out flaunting my sins in His face because I absolutely knew the things I engaged in were mostly wrong."

Harlan said, "Staying humble is one of my biggest challenges I face daily in my recovery. It is only for the grace of God that I am here today, and only because of my personal relationship with same that I am humble enough to be worthy of the gifts I receive daily."

I said, "Thanks for listening my friend, I do appreciate all you have done for me."

CHAPTER 91

Tomorrow I will leave Hope by the Sea and resume the life God has in store for me. I take comfort knowing my life prior to coming here does not ever have to continue, it is not me any longer. Kathy has done a wonderful job filling in for Frank this past week, and today she asked us to write about something important to us personally. The following is what I wrote.

December 30, 2016

The Hope I Now See

Dear Hope by the Sea:

When I arrived here on October 1, 2016, I was broken; a mere shell of a human being. Drowning in a sea of despair, I felt hopeless and in a dark, dark place. I simply found no way out of this quicksand I was drowning in.

For the first week or so, I didn't talk much, just tried to listen and do what was asked of me by Frank and other clinicians. As days became weeks, I began to feel things within me that made it seem possible that light may exist after all. Could this swamp of despair really be drained?

One day, I can't say exactly when, probably about half way through, I realized I no longer had cravings for drugs or alcohol. Instead, I had feelings to process and emotions to work through not unlike anyone else. What I was learning to do is face and purge the negative, so the pain and hurts I had believed to be a permanent part of me, could now be released. This work has been a labor of love, a love of myself that I never had much use for in the past because shame was what I knew.

> *One day, I can't say exactly when, probably about half way through, I realized I no longer had cravings for drugs or alcohol.*

These emotions were powerful; riddled with raw feelings that made me depressed writing about them. I pushed on, I pushed through everything, and learned to accept my past as something that had to happen. If my past was not my past, I would not be David today, and my life would not be what it is. This gift of acceptance has allowed me to dream again, have goals, and express gratitude for the abundance of gifts I do have in life.

I have a renewed spirit, and God's presence in my life; a real God's presence in life today I was blind to a few months ago. Hope by the Sea is correctly named because hope is precisely what is in my life today. My transformation is a testament to this place, and the wonderful folks who work here.

The Work is real and only beginning. Building a life worth living is what *The Work* produces every day for David Foss. The reason this place works is the caring professionalism of the staff who make up Hope by the Sea. I don't know of one instance when I felt the staff was less than exemplary.

The Horse Shoe House was a wonderful place to live, and the live-in manager model allowed a therapeutic quality that would be greatly missed, had we not lived on sight. My last couple weeks at El Dorado, which definitely isn't Horse Shoe, still was a wonderful experience I wouldn't change for anything. These last ninety days will occupy a special place in my heart for all time. My cup runneth over with gratitude; and may God always be found at Hope by the Sea.

Sincerely,

David C. Foss

Epilogue

It has been almost a year at the time of this writing, and I am pleased to say I am clean and sober. The journey this last year had its up and downs as I have been learning how to live life. I am learning how to process life on paper as it happens instead of looking for solace with drugs and alcohol. I write every day in my journal and continue to express gratitude daily.

God has been good to me in giving me the necessary fortitude to write this book. I thought it would be a quick project, it has been a ten-month process and counting. It is challenging to find meaning in life without substance. It was a part of my life for so long, but now everything is brand new. I am getting to know who David Foss is more and more every day.

All is not well, however. Tripp Miller, who I discussed in the book, passed away on August 21st, 2017, of an accidental Heroin overdose at the young age of twenty-two. I spoke to Tripp's Father about including him in the book, and he said to do it. I have a twenty-two-year-old daughter; and if she died, I would be devastated. Tripp's Father, Mr. Miller, has terminal cancer; and he had to bury his son. I wrote this letter to Mr. Miller, and I am also including a poem at the end that I wrote when my own Father died of cancer in 2002.

Letter to Mr. Miller

August 23rd, 2017 9:38am

"Tripp od'd and died."

Dear Mr. Miller,

The above text is what I saw when I awoke and reached for my phone; my heart sank, and tears filled my eyes. Each day in the United States around a hundred people die from opiate drugs. Factor in all the other drugs, and of course, alcohol--just another number. These faceless, cold statistics should matter. They all have a story, and are someone's son, daughter, spouse, mother, father, brother, sister, aunt, uncle, or friend who isn't coming home again, not ever.

Tripp Miller was somebody's son, and he will not be home for Father's Day, Holidays, or Birthdays, and his Father will not be able to talk to his son. I have been a drug and alcohol addict for more than twenty-five years of my life, and Tripp is only the second person who lost their life I knew and respected. When the first person died, I never did a thing to remember him or express condolences to the family. I shed tears in private and moved on about my self-centered existence.

Tripp was a kind, young man, and he deserves to be honored and remembered. His family needs to know how he touched people in his short time in this world.

When I first met Tripp, I was unimpressed and found him unremarkable. It was my first and totally wrong impression of him. Trip had sustained an injury from a heroin overdose that left him in a near death state for long enough to damage his arm which was wedged under his body. He had almost no use of it when I met him. I soon learned Tripp had been to Hope by the Sea earlier in the year where he stayed for sixty days. Tripp was only out of there a short time, and then, he came back. This must have been a very difficult decision to come back to the same place again. I know he was carrying around a lot of guilt and shame for being back again, and he felt like a failure. It was my second treatment of 2016 also; and I understand fully the despair and worthlessness associated with being in the same spot of defeat again.

Tripp was a natural leader and would help others at the expense of his own needs. I have the same tendencies; we had similar characteristics, no doubt about it. I was twenty years his senior and saw myself in so many things he did. It was probably why we butted heads in the group sessions on a regular basis. Usually, I was smiling before I could even finish giving him a what for. Intelligent beyond his years, would be putting it mildly, because he truly had a beautiful mind and a magnetic aura that people were quickly drawn to.

On Christmas Eve and Christmas Day, the House I lived in went to the House where Tripp and all the other twenty-somethings lived.

It was apparent it was tough for a lot of us being away from our families on these days. Despite that though, Tripp was all smiles, and it was infectious to those near him; and before we knew it, the entire house was smiling and laughing. It was without a doubt one of the most uniquely pleasant Christmases of my life, and I will never forget it.

One of the things that happens right before discharge is something called a coin-out. This is where a Gold coin with a Hope by the Sea emblem is given to the departing client. Before that though, the coin is passed around to each one there where encouragement, and occasionally insults, are exchanged.

Recording the coin out is prohibited, but I couldn't resist. I wanted to preserve the moment, and perhaps listen to it someday I needed reminding of how precious a gift it is to be alive and clean. Tripp said to me at the coin out that I gave him pause and made him rethink goofing off in groups all the time, and to question his reasons for being at Hope by the Sea. A couple of sentences that at the time didn't even resonate with me then, are very relevant today when I think of my own commitments.

Tripp's compassion for others led him to help others who had the same dark demons he struggled with. In the end, the warm dark blanket extinguished his light and consumed him. God called Tripp home and today Heaven is a whole lot brighter and here on earth a void exists where Tripp lived. I express my sincerest condolences to you and your family. I know already you are a good man, for a son is a mirror of his family values and his were on point.

Affectionately,

David C. Foss

Dad's Poem

By David C. Foss

Like the rainbow of Noah is the promise of a Father's love
Through triumphs and adversity,
The face you see is that of Dad
In a world that is forever changing
A father's love remains constant
Problems great or small; Dad listens
A constant inspiration in the sometimes grim world
Like the light towers of ships saw ships of yesterday
A father sees the good in you when the world does not
A father is always hoping and trying to build you up for tomorrow
A father's love is not bought, it is guaranteed
No relationship is more precious than that of a father and son
A son can fall into no hole too deep for his father to reach
There is no greater love than that of a father for his son
That is, except perhaps that of a loving son for his wonderful father
I love you Dad! David

The Final Epilogue

Dear Readers:

It is with a heavy heart that I must write this final message on behalf of my son, David C. Foss, who spent the last days of his life polishing his work, this book, ***Birthplace of Addiction.*** He was looking forward to promoting it at book fairs and in bookstore signings. He had very high hopes for helping others and prayed much over how he could present his story of trauma, pain and addiction. He wanted to help others who are suffering from some of the same nightmares, shame and guilt he had endured that come with a life of addiction.

He was excited about discovering and sharing what he believed to be the answer to overcoming his addictions once and for all. He wanted the authorities to stop punishing addicts and to begin compassionately treating them and their pain and mental illnesses that very often accompany addictive behaviors.

He wanted to put faces to addiction--those of teenagers, brothers, sisters, mothers, fathers, grandparents, friends, neighbors, co-workers, employees and other family--and tell the world they are victims of addiction who desperately need compassionate mental health and medical care to overcome their addictions.

The billions of dollars spent to incarcerate the victims of legal and illegal substance abuse can be better spent. Those dollars can be used to rescue those victims from their addictions by placing addicts in treatment and recovery centers where they can be helped to overcome their addictions, and eventually learn to become sober, productive citizens again. They desperately need medical and mental professional help, not prison time.

After you have read this book, please tell David's and other's stories to those who can and will change laws to provide help instead of harm for those who are addicts.

David had plans to develop sober, safe houses for those coming out of treatment who have no support at home or anywhere else. Those plans included helping recovering clients to find productive work, and possibly help for training or schooling for those who need it. Providing low-cost housing rentals for recovering addicts who need safe, sober places to live while getting further education or training, or just while they are getting adjusted to living sober and free again and becoming productive people in society.

David and I discussed the parts of his book he was writing based on his journals of his healing time at Hope by the Sea. He would write it out on notebook paper, and I would type it up, trying my best to be sure proper English grammar, spelling and punctuation were being used. It was a joy for me to work closely with him over this past year in this way. We were both delighted when the book was getting very close to being ready for publication. I have continued to get the book ready for publication since his death.

David passed into the arms of Jesus in his sleep on Sunday morning, October 15, 2017, at our home. David had a heart attack that took him instantly at the age of 44 years.

I am so thankful I had these past months with him before he went to be with Jesus. It has been so good to see him at peace with his life. I know he would want his book to be helpful to you and yours.

Finally, after everything has been written and edited, I found a couple of entries from David's Journal he wrote at Christmas 2015, and they will close out this book. I believe you will find it worth reading.

Sincerely in Christ,
Crystal J. Eack
Proud Mom of David C. Foss

An Addict's Plea

By David C. Foss

To begin, I must touch on the Hell of being held in chains by a substance that does not have a name. This nameless entity claims more than thirty percent of the population of the country we all call home. A home that is generous and often expects nothing in return. My parents raised me to be charitable and to always know right from wrong was as simple as what hurts people and what does not.

I have frequently been asking myself why heart disease, cancer, or even depression are conditions that often rally and unite families and tend to make them stronger; yet, addiction in all forms yields a shameful picture to all. I believe addiction is a disease that affects countless people every day; and there is no mechanism to accurately track it, because it is swept under the rug due to shame on the part of the addict, and the families who love the addict. This is the heart of the problem and the tip of the iceberg, for legislators who try to help these very desperate, hopeless people.

Currently, most treatment is forced and part of a sentence in the criminal system. It strains the resources of the rehabilitation community. This formula is grossly ineffective at best because, after all, one can only lead a horse to water. I am not going to offer opinion of that process because I want to discuss the folks who want help overcoming addiction who have not been in the legal system, but do not have means to pay for the services necessary to change their lives.

Folks need to understand that when the time comes to hang up one's glass forever, we are not the successful and articulate people in communication we once were. We look up to see whale dung on the ocean floor. We are unemployed and often alienated by everyone we once considered our inner circle. Our mental capacity is gone, reduced to mere nothingness. The steps required for Rule 25 would be difficult for someone with their faculties in place. In the condition I am now, it is insurmountable and generally leads to arrest and into the forced system that statistically does not work.

Addiction is a disease just as cancer or high blood pressure, and all are deadly diseases. The anguish, self-loathing and Hell of addiction are unbearable and often lead to suicide or the hurting of others. This country invests billions to combat this. Maybe it's time to allocate some of those funds to where it can relieve some of the suffering the disease of addiction fosters.

The biggest problem with the current system is waiting for help -- help you hope will someday come. My Rule 25 Assessment was done several days ago now, and here I am left to my devices, the same ones that will kill me I fear. The one thing keeping me a little above ground is my amazing family. Many people do not have this. My experience has shown me most people in my situation are often lost forever to death or prison. I really couldn't say that one is worse than the other, but for me I would choose death. Why? oh why! does it take mere hours to be treated for diseases of the heart and liver or diabetes and cancer by simply going to the emergency room while an addict is treated like a perpetrator of a crime?

I seek help for a real disease that has empirical data to rival those of Ivy League Schools across this great nation we call home. This is a topic that families, politicians and even the addicts themselves often avoid due to the sensitivity of the issues in question. Perhaps, it would benefit some to hear another perspective.

My name is David Foss, and I have struggled with this affliction for my entire adult life; and now, at the age of 43, I feel my rock bottom has been reached. I am simply out of options short of suicide, and that is something my strong family upbringing and parental obligations simply will not allow. I am grateful to my entire family for these convictions. But, there are a great many people in our society who are in desperate need of the help that can only be found in structured treatment. These folks are not court ordered and may not have the financial means or family resources required. These are people like your brother, cousin, co-worker or neighbor who need a little help. They need to preserve their dignity and pride by receiving compassionate treatment which is given to people with the other diseases I have mentioned. We need less bureaucracy and more resolve to combat this affliction that has plagued our communities and families. Sometimes, very good people do some terrible things. Where I come from, forgiveness and help goes much further than shame and shunning of people, some folks just need a little help to bring them back to the person they were.

The hardest thing for me as I wait for admission to a treatment center is the look on the faces of my children as I continue to use. The pause of life is impossible for me, and drinking is the only thing that seems right -- but it is not, it brings further sorrow and regret amplifying the mistakes of a life that had great promise. I cannot stress enough how this feeling guides addicts like me, we are losers and black sheep to society. Some of us like me rose to the pinnacle of success, and others never got out of the infancy of theirs. I achieved my dream only to see it destroyed by myself through the perils of the disease that nobody recognizes as anything but a blemish on society, only to be fixed by the sentence from a judge. What are we doing? We as a country are capable of so much more than burying this in an overworked court system. This is a physical and psychological disease that demands the attention of this great nation, the United States of America.

If what I have said is not enough, consider the collateral damage this disease leaves in its wake. Divorce, domestic violence, sexual abuse, verbal abuse, and most importantly broken families that are the true victims of addiction. I understand better than most that not everyone is ready to stop or even ready for help. However, to wait for criminality to force it, only vacates resources of those who voluntarily want it. I hate myself these days, and I do not want to. I prefer to stop and do so without hurting others. I am not a man of means or privilege and lack the resources to get the help my children and I so desperately require if we are to survive as a family.

David's Journal Entries, Dated: December 24–25, 2015

The End